A Better Life for Half the Price

How to Prosper on Less Money in the Cheapest Places to Live

by Tim Leffel

Tim Leffel

A Better Life for Half the Price

Published by Al Centro Media, Tampa, Florida.

Disclaimer:
The author is not a lawyer, CPA, tax advisor, financial advisor, or doctor. The information presented in this book is a collection of advice and opinions from a person who has lived abroad and talked to many others doing the same, but none of it is guaranteed to be absolutely current and without fault. Nothing in this book should be construed as legal, financial, or medical advice that should be taken without secondary verification.

Prices, tax laws, visa requirements, and exchange rates are in a constant state of flux. Anything written in these pages is subject to change, so always verify key items before basing a decision on them, especially something so important as where you are going to live. All attempts have been made to ensure visa/residency information was correct at the time of writing, but it's especially important to verify this information with your local consulate or embassy—or the people living where you want to live—before proceeding.

Dedicated to the million+ expatriates who made the leap and are already living large for less money.

A BETTER LIFE FOR HALF THE PRICE

Table of Contents

Introduction

Chapter 1: Open Your Eyes to a Better Way 1

Chapter 2: How Your Bills Get Drastically Lower in Some Countries 6

Chapter 3: Why Move to Another Country? 15

Chapter 4: Are You Cut Out for This Life? 25

Chapter 5: The Importance of a Trial Run 31

Chapter 6: Choosing Your Destination: Head, Wallet, and Heart 37

Chapter 7: What's Cheaper and What's Not When You Move Abroad 42

Chapter 8: Family Life and Pets Abroad 46

Chapter 9: How to Make Sure Your Living Expenses Plummet 50

Chapter 10: Making a Living and Getting a Visa 54

Chapter 11: Where Should I Move To? 67

Chapter 12: Mexico 72

Chapter 13: Ecuador 90

Chapter 14: Panama 103

Chapter 15: Thailand 114

Chapter 16: Cambodia 126

Chapter 17: Colombia 136

Chapter 18: Vietnam 147

Chapter 19: Argentina 156

Chapter 20: Nicaragua 166

Chapter 21: Honduras 175

Chapter 22: Hungary 185

Chapter 23: Guatemala 194

Chapter 24: India 204

Chapter 25: Bulgaria 218

Chapter 26: Portugal 229

Chapter 27: Malaysia 242

Chapter 28: Nepal 250

Chapter 29: Peru 259

Chapter 30: Other Places to Consider 269

Chapter 31: Safety in Perspective 282

Chapter 32: Working Abroad and Making a Living 289

Chapter 33: Taking Care of Details 295

Chapter 34: The Resistance You Will Face 298

Chapter 35: Family Considerations 303

Chapter 36: Caveats and Legalese 308

Chapter 37: Resources for Living Abroad 309

A BETTER LIFE FOR HALF THE PRICE

Introduction

When we moved back to the USA after spending a year in central Mexico, we started blowing through money again like it was water flowing through our fingers. Our rent for a not-very-large house in a good school district was $2,000 a month. We had one car payment and laid out a bunch of money to buy a second five-year-old one used. Most of our bills had three digits, from the internet/phone/cable bundle to cell phones for the family to electricity. Since I was self-employed, we were paying around $420 a month for substandard health insurance that came with a $7,000 deductible that was never met—so total medical costs averaged out to more like $1,000. Add in food, insurance, and all the various expenses that pop up for a family, and we were spending close to $5,000 per month before even counting my business expenses. This for a family that lives a relatively frugal life and isn't very materialistic.

Since the incoming cash flow didn't always match the month's outgoing expenses while running an online business that pays a lot of freelancer invoices and hosting bills, we racked up some debt again in just two years. Despite all the outward signs of my success other people saw, we were struggling to live a rather simple middle class life in a mid-sized city, even though we were earning a fair bit more than the mean U.S. salary of $52,000 a year. If we had been in San Francisco or New York City, we might have been bankrupt.

There were some fights between my wife and I, some painful decisions on what we couldn't afford to do, and some strains on our marriage that we hadn't dealt with before. I look back on those two years now with a mix of anger and relief. Anger that it's so damn expensive just to get by in the country of my birth, relief that I'm not there now.

We moved back to Mexico in the nick of time. It took us a good while to get our empty house furnished and decorated, but meanwhile we were spending less each month than we had been just on rent and utilities in Florida, even after factoring in furniture purchases and renovations.

Instead of struggling to scrape up enough money to go out to eat—or putting it on a credit card—we are now paying cash to go out multiple times a week and we don't sweat it.

Our expenses have dropped by more than half, so we can stress less about money and spend time enjoying life instead. The credit card debt is getting wiped out again and we're putting money into savings instead of just hoping to cover the bills. Our income is roughly the same, but our quality of life is drastically better. What we earned before seemed to never be enough. What we earn now buys a life of abundance.

The interesting thing is, it's the same amount.

The New Reality in the Developed World

As you've probably noticed, getting ahead where you live now is getting tougher all the time. Things are not so hunky-dory for the non-rich in the rich countries of the world these days. You still have boat loads and train loads of immigrants trying to get into the USA, Canada, Europe, and Australia each week, but for those of us living in these countries, the future does not look as bright as it did for our grandparents. Costs keep rising, wages do not, and only the richest of the rich seem to be seeing their conditions steadily improve.

You basically have two choices if you want to increase your disposable income: you can find a way to earn far more money, or you can dramatically cut your expenses. You know better than me how feasible the first option is for you. For most people, if it were easy to double their income, they would have done it already.

If you stay where you are now, the latter option usually involves a series of painful sacrifices. You have to cut back on groceries, eat out less, downsize your living quarters, sell your car, forgo vacations, forget about enhancing your wardrobe, and basically stop doing any fun activities that aren't free.

There's a better solution though that a million+ others have discovered already. You can just move.

Time for a Change of Scenery

If you move from a rich country to a poorer one, you can

cut your expenses in half without all those sacrifices. You can live a better life while spending far less for your basic expenses. You end up with more money to spend or save without cutting back on what you enjoy or living more frugally. It's the equivalent of going on a diet without giving up ice cream or cheeseburgers.

This book is your guide to getting from where you are now to the point where you can live a better life for half the price. It shows you which countries are viable in terms of costs and visa requirements for long-term residency, and gives you the pros and cons of each. More than 50 expatriates tell their stories here, showing you how much they spend in an average month and outlining some of the challenges they have overcome.

I also share some of my own experiences. I'm not some desk reporter who hasn't ventured out on my own. I wrote this book from my home office in central Mexico, and in the past I've lived in Turkey and Korea. I've also lived in the New York City area, Virginia, Tennessee, and Florida. I've been through multiple residency visa applications and renewals abroad and I talk monthly with others doing the same. You can be confident I know more about this subject than most, and have reached out to people who are living the dream in other countries around the world. You'll hear from young digital nomads, couples running a virtual business, families with kids in schools abroad, and retirees taking it easy in a warmer, calmer climate.

I've spent time in every country profiled in detail, plus I've covered many of them in my *World's Cheapest Destinations* book, which is now in its fourth edition. This book should serve you well as an idea generator, move motivator, and guide to how to turn your dreams and desires into reality. I won't be able to answer every question you possibly have in these pages of course, and there are entire books out there on moving to just one country. If you want to explore your options in more depth before making the leap after finishing this book, see the packages at CheapLivingAbroad.com. Meanwhile, let's see what it feels like to have twice as much money on hand without having to double your income.

.

Chapter 1: Open Your Eyes to a Better Way

Christa Roberts lived in New York City before moving abroad. She loved her apartment on 6th Avenue on the edge of the West Village and right near Washington Square Park, but she spent a whopping $1,300 a month on rent and utilities for her share. "I lived with two friends in a two-bedroom apartment, which we converted into a three-bedroom one by hiring a contractor to come in and build a wall half way through the living room," she says. "We had a small table that fit two stools and a small L-shaped couch that was in the same room as the railroad kitchen. That was it for furniture. If you can imagine that, you can see that we could provide actual seats for five people, so when we would have parties people would end up standing or sitting on the kitchen counter. All three of the 'bedrooms' fit a double bed (touching three walls) and just enough space to put a yoga mat next to it. My window faced a brick wall."

Now that she lives in Thailand's largest city, it's a very different story.

"Today, I make about half of what I made in NYC. My new 2-bedroom apartment, however, which has a big living room, a small but separate kitchen, two balconies, and bedrooms big enough for king sized beds, costs me a little over $300 total. (9,000 Baht on rent and then about 1,500 Baht on utilities including electricity, water and internet). This means that instead of spending half of my salary on regular expenses, I'm spending a fifth. Now I can not only have a travel fund but an actual savings account. Despite making a lot less, I can easily save at least twice as much."

Before, I was always watching my money, especially when going out to dinner. It's nice not having to look at each price on the menu before I order and to not feel stressed out if someone at the table suggests another round of cocktails.

The best part though, is that I can travel a lot more. This past weekend I stayed in a huge share-house with about 20 friends located in a prestigious beach town a few hours outside of Bangkok. It was essentially the same experience I had while going to the Hamptons with friends, but this time I didn't have to sleep on the floor and got to enjoy food from our hired chef who was around all weekend. This trip cost me $100 as opposed to the $500 I used to spend on one weekend in the Hamptons.

In New York, I would save all year to go on a few long weekend trips and then one big trip out of the country per year. Now I can go away every month if I want, and am also saving to visit my family this year. Being in a foreign country automatically puts you in a better position to travel and see new places, but financially it's much easier as well."

Right now while you're reading this, there are close to a million Americans and Canadians enjoying a better and cheaper life in Mexico. Around 20,000 at least are in Thailand, 5,000 more are in Nicaragua, 7,000 or so are in Ecuador, another few thousand each in many places around the globe. These are all estimates at best because most countries—including the U.S. —don't actively track who has moved abroad and don't require them to register with an embassy.

I'll throw out some other statistics here and there, but this book is about you and your options. It's about finding a better life for half the price. The stories and experiences you will read in this book are from real people who are different from you in one way: they took the leap already. They're just a little further along on the continuum than you are, that's all. They're retirees and 20-somethings, teachers and doctors, entrepreneurs and former cubicle dwellers, restaurant owners and bartenders. In other words, what makes them different is they picked up and moved.

Moving to another country to enjoy a better life for half the price is not odd, radical, crazy, or dumb. The people around you might say that, or at least think it, but very few who have actually done it will. Often when I asked people what regrets they had or what mistakes they had made, they replied, "I just wish I had done it sooner."

It's Not Your Imagination: Things Are Getting Worse

No matter how you look at it, living in one of the world's

economic super powers is not the easy ride it used to be. The top one percent keep getting richer, while everyone else is having a tougher time finding a good job and holding onto it. That's not just my opinion: it's borne out by statistics, polls, and an open-eyed look around beyond the affluent suburbs. In a Gallup poll taken in 2014, two-thirds of Americans said they were dissatisfied with "the way income and wealth are currently distributed in the U.S." The Council of Economic Advisors in Washington D.C. created "The Gatsby Curve" to plot how well countries are doing with income inequality and the ability of people to move up the ladder to a better life. The USA and UK scored among the worst in the world on both counts. The top one percent own around 20 percent of the wealth and it's getting harder and harder for "the American Dream" to become reality for the poor.

After the latest recession, which we're still trying to pull out of, 15 percent of Americans are living below the poverty line and a staggering one in seven is getting some kind of food assistance from the government. A *New York Times* article in May of 2014 said, "Although economic growth in the United States continues to be as strong as it is in many other countries, a small percentage of American households is fully benefiting from it."

If you feel like prices keep going up where you live but your wages are not keeping up, you're probably right. The *Wall Street Journal* said in mid-2014 that, "Since 1986, average hourly wages have increased by just 1 percent overall."

Many students are graduating from a good university and finding that all they have to show for it years later is a piece of paper and lots of debt. While the official unemployment rate continues to slowly decline from its peak, the number of "under-employed" college graduates in jobs that don't require that education is far higher—in nearly every developed country. In the U.S., the Federal Reserve says "outstanding student debt again topped $1 trillion in the fourth quarter of 2013, making it the second-largest pool of debt in the nation behind mortgages." The *New York Times* reported in March of 2014 that low-wage workers are getting older and more educated, with 41 percent of workers earning $9 or less per hour having at least some college education. More than half of these sub-$9 workers are 25 or older.

Canada fared better during the recession, but unemployment is still just barely below seven percent, wages haven't come close to keeping up with rising prices (especially housing), and nearly all of the job growth is coming in low-paid service sector jobs. The number of "under-employed" is double the number of unemployed. A newswire story I saw as this book was finishing up said that "12 percent of Canadians face serious hunger or fear of starvation."

In the UK, unemployment is also stuck at around seven percent and underemployment hit a new record at the end of 2013, with 18.5 percent of Brits working a part-time job "because they were not able to get a full-time job." Prices had risen faster than wages in 40 of the 41 months tracked prior to the report. Meanwhile, the average cost of an apartment in London continues to tick up unabated.

Housing has continued to eat up a larger and larger share of income as rental or purchase prices rise faster than stagnant wages, in all three of these countries. On top of that, health care and university tuition costs keep rising far faster than the rate of inflation for Americans, and education that was once completely tax-supported is becoming less so elsewhere. Almost a third of Americans aren't saving any money, and are in fact spending more than they're earning every year.

In other words, those of us in "rich" countries are falling further and further behind. Not for the super-rich of course, who keep doing better and better each year. The 111 billionaires in California alone personally hold assets worth $485 billion. According to Oxfam, the combined $1.7 trillion wealth of the world's 86 richest people is now equivalent to the entire bottom half of the world's population—3.5 billion people. You're probably not in that lowest half, but for most of us costs keep going up, wages do not, so we continue to feel poorer and poorer. We keep running faster on the treadmill, and not getting any further ahead.

How would things change if you could snap your fingers and cut expenses in half? It might take a wee bit longer than snapping your fingers, but you do have the power to cut those expenses in half just by moving.

It's time for a reboot. Let's reset the equation.

Chapter 2: How Your Bills Get Drastically Lower in Some Countries

After getting his MBA, American Michael Gans had no luck finding the kind of job he wanted in the USA. After getting no response from 100 job applications, he applied for and got a graduate internship in London, in a division of one of the world's biggest investment firms. After having to pay for a full year of housing up front, he had to live on a stipend of 600 pounds sterling a month, which he didn't receive until after working for a month. "I was broke. I had $58 in my pocket upon arrival. I ate lentils and white rice for the whole first month." Transportation is affordable there, but almost anything else costs a fortune. "If you go to Tesco or Marks and Spencer, a cut of meat will be 10 pounds. I would say to myself, 'I can have that, but then I won't be able to eat the rest of the week.' "

After getting good experience there, a year later he got a job in San Francisco, which wasn't much better. "I was living in a one-bedroom apartment with a tiny little living room for $1,340. Once you add in utilities and internet it was $1,500. It wasn't even anything very exciting for that price." At his one-year point there he started looking around at international jobs and six months later was employed as a financial associate in Delhi, India. Now, his rent for an equivalent apartment is $247, just a 15-minute walk from his office. He earns less, but his rent and utilities only take up 1/4 of his pay, compared to almost half when he was in San Francisco. A five-mile taxi ride went from $25 to $3. Lunch at a decent restaurant near the office went from $10 to $2.

Now if you went to India on some kind of luxury tour, you may not have realized how cheap it is there. The same goes for your vacation in the Galapagos Islands of Ecuador, or the high-end resorts of Thailand. There's a huge gulf between what tourists pay and what locals or budget travelers pay.

Ask any backpacker who has traveled around the world what kinds of misconceptions they deal with in talking to friends and family about their travels. One of the big ones is that most people can't fathom how you could travel around the world on $50 a day, and that in some countries it could average out to half that amount. For two. It simply does not compute for them that there are places with $2 restaurant meals, $10 hotels, and museums that cost a buck.

Most expatriates who have cut their expenses in half without trying very hard deal with similar misconceptions. People have trouble believing that a family can live in Mexico for $2,000 or less per month. Their impressions of Mexico are mostly of all-inclusive resorts, expensive tours, and inflated taxi costs in Cancun or Los Cabos. Their impression of Portugal is a holiday in the Algarve, which might be cheap compared to one on the coast of France, but not half of what they spend just living at home. People comment on my blog all the time that "Thailand is not cheap anymore." Usually it turns out they only stayed at resort area hotels in Phuket and never ate where the locals eat.

There are two very different sides to all the countries profiled in this book: the tourist side and the everyday living side. The two have little to do with each other when it comes to prices. The tourist side is priced for foreigners on a short-term vacation budget. The everyday living side is priced for what the local market will bear. The "invisible hand" of economics takes its cue from local wages and the local ability to pay for goods and services. Tourist prices exist in a parallel economic universe, based solely on what visitors from a richer country are willing to pay.

When you move somewhere to become a resident, you generally move from the tourist price universe to the local price universe. And those local prices can cost a tiny fraction of what you're used to. After all, the per capita annual Gross Domestic Product in Australia is more than $55,000. In Nepal it's more like $550. If you earned just half the annual per capita GDP amount in Australia—$27,500—and spent that in Nepal, you'd instantly be among the upper crust. You'd be elite, wealthy, stinking rich by local standards.

Here are the factors that impact your monthly cost of living, from housing to recurring bills to eating out.

Lower Utility Costs

In 2014 Google bought a little company called Nest for $3.2

billion. What that company does is help you control your home thermostat remotely with a phone app. Why is that such a big deal? Because heating and air conditioning together account for 56 percent of the average U.S. home's energy consumption. If one of the world's biggest companies can help you substantially lower your utility bills, you're probably going to be more than willing to pay a monthly subscription fee.

Or you could just move.

Let's say you move to an "eternal spring" climate place like Boquete (Panama), Medellin (Colombia), Cuenca (Ecuador), or one of the highland Mexican towns like Ajijic, or San Miguel de Allende. You rarely need heat, hardly anyone has air conditioning, so voila—half-price utility bills.

Even if you go somewhere hot and tropical, if you're in a place with regular sea breezes you might find that you need the A/C less than you used to as time goes by and you get acclimated. If nothing else, your utility rate—what you pay per kilowatt hour—is more likely to go down than up. In most countries, power costs are subsidized or at least tightly controlled to prevent rapid spikes. After all, if nobody can afford electricity or gas in the country a ruler is governing, he's going to have a rebellion or coup on his hands in short order. Every elected official will be blamed and booted out of office.

So in general, utility costs have a correlation with the average income in a country. It's not a direct correlation because of policy decisions: in Venezuela gasoline is practically free, in Ecuador it's half price, in Cambodia it's priced at the world market rate, in Europe it's double the market rate because of high taxes. Overall though, electricity costs in Togo or Thailand are going to be less than in Canada or Denmark. If not, the market will usually find a way to bring costs down for individuals, such as through increased use of cheap solar hot water heaters or ultra-efficient appliances. Your monthly utility bills should decrease and you'll benefit from lower prices at businesses that use energy too.

Lower Labor Costs

Close your eyes and think of ten services you spend money

on where labor is a high percentage of that organization's cost.

Now, imagine what kind of impact it would have if all of the people doing those jobs had their pay cut by two thirds or more.

Wow, that would drastically lower the costs to consumers like you, wouldn't it?

It doesn't really matter which things popped into your mind. It's a very long list to pick from. You can imagine hospitals and plastic surgery, taxis and flights, babysitters and house painters, hotels and water parks. If a person who would be paid $50 an hour where you live now gets $15 an hour where you're moving, that's a massive difference. If a surgeon makes $3,000 a day in your home town and makes $300 a day where you're going, imagine what that's going to do to your coronary bypass bill.

Where I live in Mexico, my handyman gets around $4 an hour and that's considered pretty good money. The maid cleans our four-bedroom house for the local equivalent of $15.50. A ten-minute taxi ride across town is $3. A carpenter made us an entire king sized platform bed frame with built-in drawers, in cedar, for a shade over $300. In none of these cases have we bargained people down to their minimum: we're paying normal rates or better.

The minimum wage in Ecuador is around $10 a day. In Portugal it's only twice that. In Nepal it's less than $1 a day. So if you pay someone triple the minimum in Cuenca to build you some custom cabinets, the labor part of the cost may only be $30 per day. Taking advantage of this is not exploitation. It's arbitrage. You're using your dollars/pounds/euros acquired where labor costs are high and spending them where labor costs are low. Keep doing this over and over again in your daily life, on nearly every transaction you make, and it's easy to understand how you can cut your expenses in half quite easily.

Lower Food Costs

Here's how Bryan Haines of GringosAbroad.com describes his food costs in Cuenca, Ecuador with when he travels back to Canada. "We eat at the food court at Mall del Rio for less than $8 (3 people, with a hearty meal and drinks).

We had 3 ice creams on the Halifax Waterfront for $14. Dinner at McDonalds there is around $30."

Where I live in Mexico, a sit-down "meal of the day" can easily be found for $3 or $4, a tamale on the street is never more than 80 cents, and a fresh-squeezed orange juice is a $1.20 for 16 ounces. A pulled-pork sandwich is $1.55 and I can get four pastries at the bakery for a buck. If I were to spend more than $10 on seasonal fruit and vegetables at the market I'd need someone to help me carry it all home.

Think about your last trip to the supermarket and where all those items came from. You may have bought blueberries from Chile, peppers from Mexico, pineapples from Costa Rica, and bananas from Honduras. If you're in the UK, maybe green beans, oranges, and bananas from somewhere in Africa or Asia. Assume the wholesale cost doubled along the way, there were shipping costs, and then the retailer doubled the price again. You're easily paying four times what the cost was at the source. So, when you move to the source and start shopping locally, you'll probably find your food costs are a small fraction of what you paid at home.

There are exceptions of course: coffee tends to follow international export prices for the good stuff and if you want imported products, you're back to the same mark-ups. If you mostly eat what locals of average means eat, however, you are going to eat very well on far less money. This is a good reason, of course, to pick a place where you like the food. If you can't stand Thai food or Vietnamese food makes you cringe, you're probably not going to be real happy in Thailand or Vietnam. You'll also spend far more than people who love those cuisines.

Lower Taxes

In many European countries, the tax burden on average individual income can easily reach 50 percent when you add everything together. In the United States the tax burden is significantly lower. Unless you're one of the two-percent that's a multi-millionaire, and you live in a high-tax state like California or New York, you probably don't pay out more than 25 percent of your income. When you look at what corporations actually pay (as opposed to what the rate is in theory), it's well under 10 percent.

These numbers are very high by developing world standards, however. In a place where the average wage is $10 a day or less, it doesn't make much sense to hit people with an income tax that's going to scrape off a big chunk of that. So almost anywhere you're going to move to from the destinations in the last section of this book, your tax bill will go down. You may need to keep filing and paying in your home country—especially if your income is still from there—but your local bills for property taxes, sales taxes, business license fees, and a million other things will probably be lower than where you left. When you buy something at a store, you're paying sales tax or an IVA, but it's usually included in the price already. It's not an add-on surprise at the end.

It's the indirect result of this lower tax bill that matters most in your everyday life, however. If businesses pay less in taxes, they don't have to build a big impact into their prices. If a laborer doesn't have to give 30% of his income to the government, he's going to be far more flexible on what he's charging you for a job. If the license fee to run a street cart is low or non-existent, your street tacos or Thai curry dishes don't have to have that built in. If it doesn't cost an astronomical sum for a taxi license, a cab driver can charge you a much lower fare. This, in a nutshell, is the argument for lower taxes by conservative politicians and pundits around the world. Let the market set rates, with no government interference or influence.

That ignores the other half of the equation, however. Most of that tax money does not go into a black hole or get siphoned off by the corrupt. Most of it builds infrastructure, treats water, educates children, funds safety net programs, and covers defense spending. In the civilized nations of the developed world, taxes fund health care that cures the sick and covers the expenses for a mother to have a baby—for 100 percent of the population.

So there's the eternal trade-off: what you give up in taxes, you give up in government spending. That treated water you can drink from the tap in developed countries like the one you were born in? In many destinations covered in this book, you're on your own for drinking water. It's not a given that you can drink what comes out of the tap. The wastewater flowing out of your toilet may not be treated properly either. The local schools might be terrible, with 45 kids in a class going nuts every day. There's probably a public health care system, but if you want quality care and good testing equipment, you'll need to pay for it. The food inspections may be non-existent or minimal, the regulations weak. What laws that are on the books to protect workers, keep the air clean, and protect the environment may not have enough of a budget behind them to ensure compliance. There are probably not enough police, and the ones that are in place may be easy for criminals to buy off since their pay is so lousy.

Always keep this trade-off in mind when you're ready to go on a tirade about how nothing works properly in your newfound home and how the workers are so lazy in every public service office you have to deal with. You're often getting what you pay for. The good news is, you're paying a lot less—even if you do factor in those five-gallon purified water bottles you have to keep buying.

Lower Medical Bills for Better Care

If you're moving from the USA, lower health care costs can present a dramatic change in your expenses. Only three countries spend more per capita than the United States on health care, (Luxembourg, Norway, and Monaco), and they have far superior nationalized systems. Those politicians who tell you national health care would be a fiasco haven't spent much time living elsewhere. Just ask anyone living in another country if they'd prefer our privatized, profit-oriented system. Unless they're a billionaire with a rare type of cancer that they want treated at Johns Hopkins, probably not.

If you have even two or three prescriptions, you know how much the cost of medicine can impact your budget. Most new medicines are developed in the United States, but the Big Pharma companies certainly don't do their home country citizens any favors. The average cost of heartburn drug Nexium is $215 in the U.S., but $58 in Spain, $42 in England, and $23 in the Netherlands. It's less than $20 in most developing countries: nobody would buy it otherwise. An anti-parasite medicine that's typically $5 or less in Latin American sells for more than $100 in the USA.

If you have to actually go visit a doctor or stay in the hospital, it's even worse. An MRI that is $138 in expensive Switzerland and $250 in Mexico is a whopping $1,145 in the United States. My father's hip surgery bill in 2013, in South Carolina, was $45,740. Sure, our Medicare tax dollars and his supplementary insurance paid most of that, but in Malaysia it'll be less than half that. In Mexico or Ecuador, it's half again. In India even less. Heart surgery that can literally bankrupt someone in the U.S. will cost less than a used car from the 00s in most of the cheap places to live.

For those Americans who are poor or self-employed, medical care is a huge chunk of the monthly budget, even if there's seldom a need to make use of the insurance. Before the Affordable Care Act got pushed past the congressmen receiving paybacks from the medical industry, many small business owners and freelancers couldn't get insurance at any price because of pre-existing condition exclusions. Within a year of that law going into effect, the number of Americans without insurance dropped from 18 percent to 12 percent, but that still means 12 out of every 100 citizens have no coverage at all, usually because it's a choice between that, rent, or food. While the number of mothers who die during childbirth went down 3.1 percent across the developed world since 1990, it actually went *up* in the USA by 1.7 percent.

For the countries covered in this book, healthy people often don't even carry any kind of insurance. Medical costs are so reasonable that paying out of pocket is not an issue. Even if they're in an accident and end up in the hospital, they can probably cover the cost with a Visa card that has a $5,000 credit limit. In many countries, residents are automatically covered under the national universal health scheme or they can get on it by just submitting the proper paperwork. If they do want private health insurance, it will cost a small fraction of what you would pay in richer countries and then you can use the best medical facilities available—with no waiting time.

Lower Transportation Costs

For every expatriate I've talked to who owns a car, there are another two who don't. Few countries are as geared to motorists as the U.S., Canada, and Australia. In most of the cheapest, desirable places to live in the world, a car is a status symbol more than a necessity. Cities and towns are more walkable, public transportation is cheap and frequent, and almost nobody thinks it's acceptable to put up with hour-long commutes to get to work.

If you do need a car, you will probably not find one as cheap as you can find in the USA, where margins and the number of middlemen are both compressed. There's often not much of a used car market because everyone passes an old car onto a relative who then runs it until it can't run anymore. Fuel costs may be higher or lower, but maintenance costs will certainly be lower, from an oil change to an engine repair. The American Automobile Association reported in 2014 that a person driving 15,000 miles a year in the USA spends an average of $760 a month on all car-related expenses, or $967 a month if they own a sport utility vehicle. In much of the world, that could get you a private chauffeur at your beck and call instead, all expenses included. Or better yet, a nice vacation on a regular basis with the savings.

Chapter 3: Why Move to Another Country?

A vast majority of my friends and relatives think I'm absolutely bonkers for wanting to leave my home country, much less to do it over and over again.

Many people who leave the USA, Canada, or England to live elsewhere say the biggest resistance to overcome is not internal, but external. There are a lot of doubters, haters, and envious people who have a myriad of reasons to tell you this is a dumb idea. These can range from rah-rah nationalism to envy of your freedom to the kind of fear that makes their stomach clench up in knots. We all have an innate fear of the unknown that served us well in caveman times. For many, this instinct is impossible to ever overcome without an effort to do so. They may not be happy with their life, but they're comfortable, so they can't imagine rocking the boat and dealing with change.

While some may not be able to vocalize it, your decision represents a threat to everything they hold dear. If you think the grass is greener on the other side, well, what if it *is*? What does it mean for this place they're still stuck in, which is looking worse than it used to look, with fewer good job prospects?

For those willing to research, prepare, and then take the leap, however, the post-transition time often turns out to be easier than they expected. Of course, this is not true for everyone, so do read the chapter after this on why *not* to move abroad. Some people clearly aren't cut out for this and it's better to find that out before selling the house and investing the proceeds in a foreign land.

Naturally, I wouldn't have moved abroad multiple times and written this book if I didn't think the positives outweighed the negatives, so let's look at what you gain by moving to a cheaper country.

The Ability to Hold Onto More of Your Money

The number one reason cited by most expatriates who move abroad by choice is financial savings. Simply put, they spend less on monthly living expenses than they would on a comparable life at home. This doesn't mean it's always an apples to apples comparison of course. There are things you take for granted in Europe or the USA that you can't take for granted in many developing countries. Usually those are offset though by something you can get in your adopted country that's better, cheaper, or more satisfying than you had before. It's all a trade-off, but usually one where the odds are greatly in favor of the cheaper place.

Even without taking an economics class, it's pretty easy to understand why a country like Nicaragua or Cambodia is cheaper than Canada. On pure per capita gross domestic product numbers alone, it's around $1,900 per person annually for Nicaragua, around $1,000 for Cambodia, but around $52,000 for the USA and Canada. There are inherent problems with GDP statistics, but as a rough yardstick they show you the first two countries are far poorer than the other two—as well as other English speaking countries like the UK, Ireland, Australia, and New Zealand.

If an average salary for an office worker in Nicaragua is $8,000 per year, then you're not going to find many Nicaraguan houses going for $2,000 a month (what I paid in central Tampa, Florida to rent a modest three-bedroom home). You're not going to find hair stylists charging $50, maids charging $100, or restaurant meals going for $75 each. The local taxis have to be priced at a level local people can afford or there won't be any taxis. The bus fares have to be affordable to low-wage workers or there won't be anyone on the buses.

The local income level roughly impacts a wide range of costs, some direct, some trickle-down. Taxes, home costs, construction materials, food costs, and the price of a custom piece of furniture are all directly or indirectly impacted by two things: the cost of labor and the cost of real estate. Picture a ladder with lots of rungs. Let say you have Cambodia at the bottom, then Vietnam, Thailand, Malaysia, Korea, and up it goes through Asia to Japan. You can walk up that ladder via the capital cities: a street food meal in Phnom Penh is $2, one with similar ingredients in Tokyo is $10-$15. A one-bedroom apartment in the former? For $200 it'll be decent. In Tokyo, good luck getting one for $2,000.

You can visualize this same ladder within a country as

well. The differences won't be that stark, but imagine logging costs for Dubuque, Iowa, then Omaha, then Portland, then Atlanta, then San Francisco, and finally New York City. Getting transferred from Dubuque to New York City for a job better come with a corresponding tripling of salary just to stay reasonably even. But when friends in an old job of mine got transferred from New York to Nashville with no cut in pay, they felt like sudden millionaires.

Many expatriates say they feel downright rich when they settle into living in Mexico, Panama, Hungary, or Thailand for the same reason, but amplified. Often they have cut their expenses substantially, but are able to do a lot more with their money. Or they keep their spending level the same as home and go from feeling like they're barely getting by to feeling like they've got more money than they need. All that was required was a change of address.

Money is nearly always at the top of the list for what's stressing people out at one time or another. Being short on money can take a toll on relationships, on health, and on success levels of a career or business. It can impact your children's education, how your aging parents are cared for, or whether your golden years are spent seeing the world or being stuck at home in front of a TV.

Doubling the amount of money you earn is really hard though. And in a country with a progressive tax structure, the more you earn the less you keep. But what if you could just cut your expenses in half, without giving up any of your normal expenditures? What impact would that have on how much you have left to save, invest, or spend on what's important? By picking the right place to move to, this is not a difficult feat to achieve.

For Better Weather

The "ideal climate" is not the same for everyone, otherwise we wouldn't be spread across the globe like we are. Where people go on vacation tells you that many people like to be in a warm and sunny place near an ocean. If you ask people to pick their ideal retirement spot, more are going to pick a hot place than a cold one.

If that's you, there are plenty of cheap destinations to choose from that are hot. Some of them have great beaches too. You've got swaths of Mexico, Central America, and some of South America on one side of the world, most of Southeast Asia and southern India on the other. Or you can be a real pioneer and move to a beach in Africa.

If you hate bugs and would prefer an "eternal spring" climate, it's easy to find one of those too. You can move somewhere that the daytime temperatures are always between 60 and 90, all year long. Your utility bills will be next to nothing and one or two light jackets could be all the outerwear you need to bring.

If you want to keep experiencing all four seasons, there are options in this book for that too. There are European destinations featured that go from snow to hot summers, or you could move to the bottom of South America.

Whatever the ideal climate is that's going to make you happy, you can find it in a much cheaper place than you are living now.

To Improve Your Health

The health care reason comes up more from Americans than it does for those with more logical health care systems, like, oh, every other developed country in the world. Unless you're old enough to be on Medicare in the USA and you have good supplementary insurance, almost anywhere you go is going to have a cheaper and better health care system than what you are used to experiencing. You will pay less, get far better service, and have no inexplicable surprise bills arriving in the mail months after your treatment. In most of the world, the health care system is designed to deliver a service that will make people better for a cost that everyone understands. Or no cost to the patient at all.

Despite what you may hear on Fox News, the U.S. does not have the best health care system in the world—not even close by any objective measures. What it does have is the best-paid doctors, the best testing equipment, and the latest drugs. Doctors in the United States are more likely than any other profession to be in the top one percent of earners. According to *Bloomberg News*, the actual cost of a caesarean birth is $606 in Canada, but $3,676 in the U.S. Medical device companies average a profit margin of between 16 and 20 percent; so getting an MRI and a prescription in the U.S. can cost four times what it will in France. We're talking rich country to rich country comparisons here. Imagine the drop when you then get medical care in a place where the average annual income is half or less what it is where you live now.

We have a dysfunctional health care system that benefits private corporations more than the patients and there's so much profit built in that it is easily the most expensive care in the world. We pay a lot more than citizens of almost any other country and get far less in return. For those who are self-employed or not covered by a really solid employee plan, the insurance costs can easily eat up 20 percent of your income. The Affordable Care Act is helping in many cases, but it's still just baby steps toward curing an ailing system. We have huge swaths of the population that don't have access to regular preventive care and check-ups. We're the only developed country with no mandated time off or medical care for mothers having a baby, and *USA Today* estimated that because of state budget cutbacks, some 40 percent of those with a "serious mental illness" receive no care for it.

For the countries featured in this book, you can probably have loads of health problems upon arrival, pay everything in cash out of pocket, and still spend less than you did just on insurance and co-pays the year before. It's not uncommon for some procedures to literally be one-tenth of prices in the United States, from x-rays to doctor visits to a dental cleaning and check-up.

Other expats, especially older ones, decide to get some kind of international catastrophic care insurance to cover major accidents or sudden cancer treatment, but pay for little things as they come up. In some countries you can opt into the national health care system, with varying degrees of how good that care is, only paying if they elect to go to a private hospital. Most digital nomad types who don't spend long in one place will either just wing it and treat their credit card as an insurance policy, or they'll get some kind of travel insurance that covers them in case of accident for a whole year.

Even for those coming from a country with a national health care system, the care you get abroad will often be better than what you're used to at home.

You'll get in to see a doctor more quickly, that doctor may make house calls or hand out his or her cell phone number, and if you need an operation you won't go on a months-long waiting list. You won't dread the bill you get and you won't have to hire a third-party service to decipher it.

Wendy Justice has lived in Thailand, Vietnam, and Malaysia and had this to say about the difference in care abroad when she was interviewed on Jet Set Citizen: "If I was in the US and had a serious medical condition, I would prefer to fly to Kuala Lumpur, Singapore or Bangkok to receive treatment. Not only would I save thousands of dollars, (even with the airfare), but I think that the care that I would receive would be superior—and this from a nurse-manager retired from the U.S. healthcare system! I would say the same for dental care as well—it's cheap and of a high standard."

Because health care costs are so much lower, you can afford to take better care of yourself and go get things checked out whenever you need it. If you need to get screenings, an MRI, an eye exam, or a full dermatology scan, you can probably do it the next day and it won't cost you the equivalent of a month's rent. When you get sick, you can afford to go to the doctor. If you need your teeth cleaned and a crown put on, you won't spend the equivalent of two months' rent to do it. If you need surgery, the price will be three or four digits, not the price of a new Mercedes.

Great care from western-trained doctors in state-of-the-art medical facilities is the norm in some countries, which is why they have become medical tourism hubs. If you're getting up in years and this is a high priority, you'll be in good shape if you're in or near a city in Malaysia, Mexico, Panama, Ecuador, Thailand, and India. For others, it may be great in the capital, but hit and miss elsewhere. In a country like Cambodia or Nepal, people often end of flying to another country for something serious. I've covered this in more detail in the individual country chapters.

Many expats will tell you they are far healthier than they were in the place they left. Even Canadian snowbirds who hold onto their home health insurance say they feel better knowing they can just call the doctor and get treated immediately (often with a $40 or less house call), as opposed to waiting for weeks to get an appointment or paying out the nose for private care. There's no reason to put off a trip to the dentist for a cleaning and check-up when it's only going to cost you $30. You don't have to fret over whether to take a certain asthma drug or not when it's $20 a month instead of $200.

There are many other factors contributing to better health though, often brought on by changes in climate, in habits, and in diet. It's no secret that the USA is the inventor of and chief marketer of junk food and soda. The making of unhealthy processed food is almost an art form there. Other countries have adopted the practices like we were handing out crack and the whole world is getting fatter. Still, when you move to a less developed country, you often do find it easier to eat less crap.

In Asia, the street food is healthier and "fast food" is still good-for-you food. In Europe there's a greater emphasis on slowing down and savoring, of conversation instead of a quick face-stuffing. In Latin America, food is communal and works with nutritional building blocks like rice, corn, beans, potatoes, and squash. Sure, you can buy crappy food in every convenience store, but the average "meal of the day" you get for $4 at a typical, basic restaurant is going to be well-balanced and much healthier than a McDonald's combo.

If you move to a place where most people walk or use public transportation, you'll probably get more unstructured exercise. I lost 10 pounds in four months after moving to Guanajuato, Mexico the second time, in great part because our house is on a hillside, on a pedestrian-only street with 30 steps to climb. Half the foreigners in my town don't have a car. The only reason they would need one is to drive to Costco or Walmart in another city to stock up on what they can't find locally. Taxis are $3 to anywhere in town and we can bus it to most anywhere else in the country.

If you're not spending all your time working, commuting, or watching TV, you can pursue outdoor activities as well. Walk, run, go for a hike, surf, swim, or ride a bike. Your stress level gets deflated from multiple angles.

To Experience Another Culture

Let's face it: your normal life is probably kind of boring. Every week you do the same things, see the same people, watch the same shows on the same boob tube, and then repeat the cycle. Your brain is probably crying out, "Feed me! Give me some stimulation!"

Some people are content to ignore that little voice and stick to a routine. They like routines. They'll keep repeating them until they die and be perfectly fine with that. If they need some variation, they'll take the kids to Disney World and buy a bigger TV. Or a new SUV with better built-in TVs.

Then there are the restless people, the curious people, the ones who want to see something surprising, different, and amazing. If you've thought enough about picking up and moving that you picked up this book, I'm guessing you're one of those.

When you move to another country, your brain shifts gears and everything starts moving faster, with more stimulation. Each day is a little different. The sights, smells, and sounds are all new. Different food, different names, often a whole different language. The thought of all that terrifies the hell out of some people, but for the curious ones, it's like an adrenaline injection. Suddenly the switch goes from "blah" to "bodacious." From black and white to saturated color. And you're not just getting a quick fix of this: you're *living* it! Your dinner table conversations start out with phrases like, "I saw something really interesting today..." or "I discovered this great little street food stall..."

To Improve Your Career Prospects

A lot of people are afraid to make the leap because they're afraid they won't be able to get a good job when they come back. There are plenty of well-meaning friends, relatives, and (bad) mentors who will reinforce this fear for you. The thing is, they're usually dead wrong. Seek out the right kind of advisers—people who have done what you're looking to do and returned—and you'll find they have a much more optimistic view. Most will tell you they had an easier time getting the kind of job they wanted when they returned. After all, their resume/C.V. stood out from the hundred others that all looked similar. By moving abroad and doing something different, you've shown initiative, an ability to adapt, and the means to think creatively. In today's *real* job market, those traits are far more desirable than the ability to do what you're told for years and not make any waves. Some recruiters say they actively look for people who have studied or worked abroad because those people are proven problem solvers who don't give up easily. If they've become fluent in a second language, even more doors open up.

Earlier I mentioned Michael Gans, an American on his third post-MBA job and finally feeling financially stable. He's living and working in India, at a much higher level in his company that he could have even applied for in the USA. "I am a huge advocate for going abroad," he says. "I feel that it builds your personal character and your view of the world. It advances your career and gives you a better perspective on life."

For others, the move abroad puts their life in perspective and convinces them the regular rat race wheel they've been told is a normal life is not for them. So they find a way to combine their passion with a market need and they become successful freelancers in a certain niche, or they start their own business with a newfound confidence. They can toss the resume altogether because they're making their own future on their own terms.

Many people I interviewed said they wanted to find a way to avoid returning to their own country, so they found freelance gigs or set up companies that would enable them to keep working from the road. Some of them are now pulling in more than their friends back home in "the real world" who stayed on the tried and true career path.

To Get Off the Treadmill

You hear a frequent lament from people living in developed countries that they feel like they're on a treadmill, that they're not making progress, or that they've lost control of their schedule and feel like all they do is work. Some spend years doing this and don't realize how bad it has gotten until they take a long vacation or get laid off and are forced to relax. They're working non-stop, their buzzing smartphone essentially putting them on call at all hours, and if they're a parent they've got all the over-scheduled school and sport activities in the mix as well.

Cathy Brown, a mother of three, has this to say about her move to Argentina: "I didn't want to have to work two jobs just to get by and have a crappy apartment to come home to. I can freelance here as a writer and make it, spending a lot of quality time with my family."

Expatriates in other countries are busy too, but it's a very different kind of busy. "Our schedule is fuller than it was when we lived up north," said Tim Rumsey of Mazatlan, Mexico when I interviewed him and his wife Nancy for an article. "But it's a social schedule now. We've got tee times, happy hours, dinner parties, and theater shows. They're things we *want* to do instead of have to do."

In most of the world, a workaholic is not something to be admired. Family and social groups take priority over slaving away at the office and you work to live, not the other way around. The idea of a junior lawyer or stockbroker working 80-hour weeks just plain does not exist and nobody wants it to exist. For many people who move abroad, this change in outlook feels like a big weight being lifted off their shoulders. Whether they get an international job posting or are working on their own as a virtual "solopreneur," the rejiggering of priorities in life brought on by the new environment is invigorating. Their work is a focus, but no longer *the* focus of their life.

Before you make a big move though, you have to do some soul-searching. You have to affirmatively answer the question, "Are you really ready for this?"

Chapter 4: Are You Cut Out for This Life?

There are plenty of reasons why you should *not* move abroad. There are certain people who are cut out for this kind of move and others who are definitely not. If you want the benefits without being able to bear the compromises, you're going to be a very unhappy resident of wherever you're going. In expat circles these people who moved and shouldn't have are often referred to as bitter "economic refugees."

Naturally, if you purchased this book, I'm assuming you are seriously thinking of moving to another country. I don't want to be the one to push you over that line, however, and have you cursing my name two months after arrival if you aren't mentally ready for this kind of change. Moving to a whole new country, with new customs, new bureaucracy, new standards of living, and maybe a new language can be way too much for many to handle.

Some people are stuck in a comfort zone and they like it there. Sure, they may be broke and have no real chance of their future getting better, but it's a discomfort they know rather than the risk of one they don't. Most people will dream and say, "Wouldn't it be nice to move to..." but they will never do it. They just plain don't have the initiative and they're way too scared. It will always be a fantasy for them.

This chapter could be a whole book on its own, but one valid criticism of the likes of *International Living* and *Live and Invest Overseas* is that they're very heavy on the cheerleading about moving abroad and very light on addressing the problems more than a few people encounter. The negatives are presented in passing if at all. You can understand why: they are large organizations with a staff to support and they have courses, workshops, and e-books to promote. Like glossy travel magazines that never met a luxury hotel they didn't like, these companies will either say something nice or say nothing at all. They don't want to dissuade their potential customers from plunking down their money.

Surf any expat message board though for areas you're considering, and you'll find plenty of disenchanted expatriates with real beefs. Some get downright depressed. Some try it out, then go home in a year or two because they miss the comfort zone.

What do you give up when you move abroad? Some conveniences, of course, and proximity to relatives and long-time friends. You also give up some intangible things you didn't even realize were important to you.

Many people don't realize how attached they are to certain aspects of home until they move away from it. Before you make that clean break, it's best to go live somewhere else for a while to see how strong your feelings of homesickness are. You can dip your feet in instead of diving in headfirst and staying there. Here are just a few things people end up missing that maybe they hadn't thought much about in advance.

- The greenness, the mountains, the changing seasons, or the colors of changing leaves.
- Their lush garden full of plants they know and recognize.
- Their church, their community, their local clubs, their golf buddies, their college friends.
- Their extended families they may not see so often.
- Their favorite grocery store, their local bar, their regular restaurant.
- Their 248 channels of TV in English.
- Their lightning fast fiber-to-the-home internet service.
- The ability to buy 24 types of mustard and 48 kinds of beer in their local supermarket.
- The ability to walk into a hardware store and explain exactly what they need without pantomime.

You'll find plenty of people living abroad who never should have moved in the first place. Every location has its problems—including wherever you're moving from—but some people are going to be unhappy no matter where they moved to because it's not home. It's not what they're used to, so it's inferior. They spend their days bitching and moaning about what doesn't work right and why things are screwed up. The place has its problems, but the real problem is *them*. They moved to save money and forgot that saving money cannot be the be all and end all of a relocation. As David Morrill from Cuenca Real Estate told me, "If you are just coming to stretch your savings and don't appreciate the culture or the people, you probably won't be happy. Some spend a lot of time and money learning that lesson the hard way."

In my experience, the people who have the hardest time adjusting after a move like this have one or more of the following characteristics:

- They love convenience in all its forms.
- They are super-patriotic and think their home country is the "best in the world" at everything.
- They didn't travel much internationally before they made the big move.
- They are dreadfully worried about safety in the big scary world out there. (Often related to the point above.)
- They have lived in one place most of their lives and are very connected to that community.
- They like things to be neat, orderly, logical, and well kept. (As in a suburban gated community with lots of rules.)
- They are impatient and can't stand waiting around for things to get done.
- They like to be in control of every situation at all times.
- They expect to be able to pay extra to make extra demands—like having people work on a Sunday.
- They don't want to exert the time and effort required to learn even the basics of a new language.
- They have trouble taking things as they come and expect everything to work in a logical manner.

One or two of these issues can easily be overcome and we all struggle with moving pains to some extent. Only a tiny percentage of people are naturally blessed at learning a new language as an adult and all of us get frustrated with bureaucracy at one time or another. We all get annoyed when rules and customs seem ridiculous to the point of being comical.

The people who are cut out for living abroad cope and move on, however, just as emigrants have for a couple thousand years. Others never manage and they drive themselves (and everyone around them) crazy. If you're one of them, do everyone a favor and retire in small-town USA or UK, and live frugally instead of moving to Ecuador just because it's cheap.

What Will Be Different?

When you move from a developed country to one that's further back on the development compendium, you can expect to compromise on some things you formerly took for granted. That's why in each country chapter in this book I have a "downsides" section. Here are a few that are going to be more common than not.

- You may not be able to flush toilet paper and you may have to use a squat toilet sometimes.
- People will probably be late a lot and appointment times are just a rough estimate.
- The electricity may go out sometimes.
- You probably won't be able to drink the tap water.
- Regulations will be lax or unenforced, from food preparation to road safety.
- The police may be understaffed, underpaid, ineffective, corrupt, or all of the above.
- There will be a higher tolerance for garbage, graffiti, and poor aesthetics.
- Private interests of the well-connected will often be more important than the public good.
- The judicial system may be overtaxed, underfunded, under the thumb of the ruling party, or corrupt.
- Zoning laws for building may be lax or unenforced.
- The noise level will probably be much higher than you are used to.
- People will often tell you they don't have change when you buy something, even when it's a trifling amount.

You may encounter more corruption, but don't assume the gulf is vast. A report by the European Commission estimated that corruption in the EU costs member states $160 billion a year. You don't have to read the U.S. news much to see that big business has a stranglehold on politicians of both parties there and special interest groups can easily get congressional representatives to write laws two-thirds of the electorate opposes (just look at the lack of gun control.) The five majority members of the Supreme Court have shown they are unabashedly pro-business, even granting companies the same rights as people: an open invitation to corrupt the political process with huge campaign contributions.

Can You Take a Punch?

Did you or your kids ever play with one of those inflatable punching toys with a weight on the bottom, usually a clown with a squeaking nose? You would punch it in the nose and it would fall to the floor, then rise back up straight to be punched again. Unless you busted a hole in it, the thing would keep popping back up for more.

You need to be that clown.

Especially in the early days, when you're learning the ropes and going through residency paperwork for a long-term stay, you'll feel punched a lot. You will make mistakes. You will overpay often. You will be asked for surprise paperwork nobody mentioned before and of course it will need to be stamped, notarized, or paid for in another office or on another day. Everything you attempt to do seems to take twice as many days as it should, including a simple home repair or buying ingredients for a meal. Most of these developments will make no logical sense. "There's got to be a better way," you'll keep saying to yourself. Yeah, there is a better way, but inertia and tradition are hard things to break, so the better way is not coming anytime soon. Deal with it.

Some people have a real problem becoming that clown, even when it means a big payoff at the end. Competitive, type-A personalities used to instant gratification take the punches as a personal affront and they want to fight back. They get angry, they yell, they ask to speak to the boss—and they expect to have that conversation in English, of course.

In the end, they either change their behavior and win or they get deflated and give up. Often they go home eventually, cursing the country, the people, and their big mistake. "I don't know how people keep living there," they'll say to their friends back home, exasperated.

"It's easy," I would answer, "They're just better at bouncing back."

Living in another country, among people who have different traditions, beliefs, and ways of doing things requires one major attribute: adaptation. It's evolution in the modern age. I'm not going to quote Charles Darwin here as his prose is much too verbose for this book, but here's a paraphrasing of one of his best-known theories: "It's not the strongest or most intelligent that survive, but those who can best adapt to a changing environment."

You may need to learn another language to get things done and become immersed in the culture. If nothing else, the basics for just buying things and getting a taxi will take you beyond helpless. Gord MacKay moved to Nicaragua from Canada with his wife and was thrown into learning Spanish in a hurry. "When I moved here I ordered a beer because that's the only thing I could say. They asked me 'bottle or can?' and I was stumped. I will chat with my neighbors now, all Nicas. I can have a conversation, but after an hour I have to come back and take a nap because it wears me out. I'm totally comfortable at the market, but taking a car in to get repaired is a different story."

Here are a few really cheap and easy tests to carry out in your spare time before taking the plunge. Read *The Castle* by Franz Kafka. Watch the movie *Brazil* by Terry Gilliam. Then read this blog post on what one guy went through in his quest to get a residency visa in Bolivia. If you laughed or were entertained, and viewed these stories as comments on the human condition and government absurdity, congratulations. You are ready. If they made your blood boil, gave you nightmares, and caused your fists to clinch until your fingernails made marks on your palms, you may want to rethink this whole idea of moving to a whole new country. Or bank a lot more cash so you can go live in Switzerland.

The best test is going to cost you more money but it will be a lot of fun: take your destination for a real test drive. Let's head to the next chapter to talk about that.

Chapter 5: The Importance of a Trial Run

In Mexico, they call it "the margarita effect." In Spain "the sangria effect." In Thailand I would call it "the hot babe who loves you effect" (or worse). They all refer to someone visiting a place for a week on vacation/holiday, thinking it's heaven on Earth, and deciding then and there it's time to pack their bags and move.

You see this fantasy play out often in popular culture too, whether it's a bad movie with Ben Stiller moving to Los Cabos or the dopey formula on *House Hunters International* where they make it look like it's a good thing to swoop in and plunk down $300,000 on a house based on one weekend of looking around.

Many people do buy a house abroad on impulse and do just fine. A rising market will soon erase any overpaying and if the block-by-block neighborhood situation is not very variable, it's harder to make a big mistake. Sometimes a house just feels right and so does the neighborhood, so the buyer gets lucky and is thrilled.

For each case like this though, there are probably three or four times as many where a hasty decision was a bad move. Even if you're just renting, finding yourself next to a house where people party all night until dawn and have four barking dogs will wear you down fast. Or in countries where zoning laws are lax, you may suddenly find yourself next to a dry cleaner, an auto repair shop, a music club, or worse. If you've bought the place, you're stuck.

The even bigger problem though is when the whole location is a bad fit. Often what looked great on vacation turned out to be much uglier when you are in a real neighborhood with monthly bills instead of on a $500 a day all-inclusive vacation budget. Or, it was great fun hanging out on the beach in a lounge chair for a week, but then after two months of that you get bored out of your skull. Playing golf every day might sound great when you rarely get time to do it. Like anything though, it can get old when that's all you're getting up for day after day. That "charming colonial city full of local color" may not seem as charming when you realize there's no good grocery store and there's nothing to do besides eat, drink, and stroll.

Other times, I've heard of people buying a house in a hurry without asking many questions, in a place like the Dominican Republic for instance, then quickly finding out that nearly every house in the area gets broken into on a regular basis if there aren't four levels of security and someone watching the place 24/7. Now, they have to try to unload the house to another equally naive foreigner willing to overpay.

The solution, almost always, is to try the place out first. Do at least a scouting trip, even better a lengthy trial run.

If you can go on a scouting trip during the worst part of the year weather-wise, that's great. If not, ask locals what is like then. Many people visit Mérida or Puerto Escondido in Mexico during January and think it's heavenly. Then they come back in super-hot May and ask, "How did I end up in the mouth of Hell?" People visit Cuenca, Ecuador in the dry season and think the weather's perfect. Then the overcast rainy season hits and they say, "If I wanted this weather, I would have moved to Portland." People go to some tropical beach destination in the dry season and it's just as postcard-perfect as they imagined. They come back during "green season" and get stuck in the house for a week, putting buckets out to catch the leaks in the roof from the deluge.

If you know these seasonal issues going in, you'll be ready for it with no surprises. Or you can make that the time of year when you go traveling or visit relatives back home.

Travel, then Move

Ideally, you have traveled enough to know which kinds of places are right for you and which are not. (See the next chapter on choosing a destination.) It's hard to really know if a place is going to be right for you without doing two things: inner soul searching and exterior evaluation.

The first is a matter of truly knowing yourself, while the latter is a matter of truly knowing a place.

In general, it's easier to strike a place off your list than it is to decide if it's perfect. I like Ecuador a lot and I could probably be happy living there if I had to do it. It wasn't until my third trip though when I finally set foot in Cuenca, a place that I've read 50 articles about and thought would probably be at the top of my list there. It just goes to prove though that you can't rely solely on how a place looks on paper. For me, Cuenca is a great place to visit or even spend a month, but I wouldn't want to live there permanently. After a few days there I found it doesn't meet some of my key criteria. For many who live there though, it's just the right place and they would probably feel more negatives about where I call home. The smart ones knew that before making the move because they gave the place a trial run.

The people who seem happiest where they've settled are those who have traveled enough to figure out what their key criteria are. Most of them traveled internationally whenever they had the time and money, not when they turned 65. I've met expatriates who carried out their research in a very methodical way: one actually rented places in five different locations in Mexico before he settled in Guanajuato where I live. Others have done it subconsciously over decades, asking, "Could I live here?" each time they land in a new place. Some set out for a trip through a dozen countries, looking for the perfect spot.

However you do it, once you have a place narrowed down, go do a trial run and see if this destination is really a place you can call home. Find a way to rent an apartment and stay for at least a few weeks, preferably longer. If you want to do it on a tight budget, house sit for someone through an organization like TrustedHouseSitters.com, MindMyHouse.com or HouseCarers.com.

Another option is to do a home exchange, either through a formal exchange membership program like HomeExchange.com or informally through Craigslist, word of mouth, or message boards.

Whichever method you choose, the goal is to live in a real neighborhood, not in a business hotel smack in the middle of the tourist district. You want to feel what it's like to live there, not be a short-term tourist. Shop at local markets. Explore different neighborhoods by foot or bicycle. Eat at cheap places serving typical local food. Check the prices of things you love to consume and experience regularly. Take some language classes. Ask other expats what they struggle with.

Here are some ideas on what to do to get a real feel for the area:

1) Run every possible errand you would in the future. Go to the hardware store and buy something, even if it's just an electrical adapter or screwdriver. Get meat from the butcher shop, bread from a bakery, shoes from a shoe store. Pick up local liquor or juice where your neighbors do.
2) Find a festival. Follow the noise and go see what's going on. See how the local celebrations work.
3) Try local services. Get your shoes shined or fixed, your pants hemmed, your clothes cleaned, your hair cut.
4) Take local language classes and ask lots of why and how questions of the teachers. They'll be able to explain the accumulated mysteries in English.
5) Rent a bike or scooter. You can see a lot on foot, but doing a little exploring will get you outside the bubble. If the safety worries you, take random buses to random places during daylight hours to assess the real situation.
6) Go to a local gym. What classes do they offer? What kind of shape are the machines in? Can you live with what's around? If not, find other exercise alternatives you'd use instead.
7) Go to church or poke your head in for a wedding. Even if you're not religious, this experience offers great insight into the local culture.
8) Go to a sports event. Ditto #7. (When it comes to football/soccer, church and team seem to be on an equal level, and in both cases the locals' enthusiasm can be both baffling and eye opening...)
9) Linger in public spaces. In countries that aren't car-centric, people spend much of their time outdoors, walking, socializing, and just hanging out. Join them and observe.

Now, did you love or hate this experience? Is there one factor really bugging you that could be a deal breaker? Or are the negatives manageable?

Within 24 hours of my first visit to Guanajuato, I told my wife that "I've found the place we should move to." She thought I was nuts to be that sure that fast, but the next summer we rented an apartment for a month and did all the things we needed to do to be sure about it. In addition to the steps outlined in an earlier paragraph, my wife also went around and checked out potential schools for our elementary age daughter.

Sure, there were some negatives. We found a scorpion in our apartment a few times. The dog barks echoing off the narrow canyon we were in got annoying, especially combined with early morning church bells a few buildings over. Seeing people indiscriminately tossing their garbage on the ground was disappointing. Putting toilet paper in a trashcan instead of flushing it was hard to get used to. But we could deal with all those negatives. The positives were much greater and it ticked off most of our requirement boxes when it came to climate, walkability, culture, and quality of life. A year later we made the city our home. A year after that, we bought a house. By then we knew what we were getting into and what was a good value.

The key thing to remember during your trial run is that you need to get a glimpse into expatriate life, not tourist life. That's why it's key to rent an apartment where lots of people live rather than staying in a hotel zone. Eat where you'd be eating on a monthly living budget, not on an inflated tourist budget. (Sure, go out for a nice meal now and then, but don't eat at the most expensive places every night). Drink what the locals drink regularly, not Starbucks lattes in the morning and gin & tonics at night. Shop at the local grocery stores and markets, not the Costco 45 minutes away. Try activities and performances where people who look like you are in the minority, not the majority.

After all of that, as you're coming to the end, evaluate the pros and cons. If the pros outweigh the cons and the place still pulls you in, mission accomplished. If the negatives are too great and are gnawing at you after a month, they're *really* going to gnaw at you after a year or two. Still, mission accomplished. Better to come up short after a month of fun away from home than to make a full-blown move and then be miserable. Learn from the experience and find a more suitable spot. It may be just one town over, or it may be another country at a different latitude or altitude. After this valuable experience though, you'll be better equipped to figure that out.

Get a Feel for Local Prices

Toward the end of this trial run, if you think this might be a good place to live, take one last important step: find out what the real value of real estate is. I'd strongly advise renting first, so be bold and ask other people what they're paying or find the local classified ads (they'll usually be printed, not online) and sit down with a dictionary.

If you intend to buy something, it's even more important to get a real sense of the market. If you don't, you'll likely end up overpaying because you'll be comparing prices to where you came from. If that's somewhere like California or the Gold Coast of Australia, your sense of worth will be especially warped. As Antigua, Guatemala resident Rich Polanco says, you need to take off the "dollar glasses" and start thinking in local currency terms. "Get a sense for what things cost in your new surroundings and then you'll be able to make better buying decisions."

Chapter 6: Choosing Your Destination: Head, Wallet, and Heart

There are three main criteria most pros and cons about a destination fall into. There are head items, which are factual "must-have" factors you can easily substantiate from the comfort of your sofa with a laptop or tablet in hand. This book will help with that, plus it will help even more with the wallet items: costs for basic living expenses and setting up residency. I'll help you home in on the places where you can really live well for half price.

The heart factor though is very difficult to work out remotely. Sure, you can collect e-books, watch Travel Channel shows, check out YouTube videos, and join Facebook groups or message boards for that destination. Really though, none of those things will fully prepare you for how that place will make you *feel*. This is why I often brush people off when they leave a blog comment or e-mail asking where they should move. The only person who can really answer that is you.

Let's look at each factor on its own.

Head

If a place doesn't meet your main criteria for an ideal place to live, you're probably not going to be happy living there. As a travel writer who visits ten or twelve different countries each year, I often ask myself when visiting a new place, "Could I live here?"

Usually the answer is no for some very specific factual reasons—my head reasons. It's too cold, too hot, too cloudy/rainy, too isolated, too overrun with gringos, too ugly, too unfriendly to pedestrians, and so on. For others, there may be no such thing as "too hot" or "too overrun with gringos," They may think a steamy hot place where they can speak English every day with their fellow countrymen and women is perfecto.

If you have health issues though, this may be the first place to start in narrowing down your choices. If you are allergic to mold, you may want to seek out a dry climate. If you have limited mobility, you don't want to live in a city built on the side of a mountain. If you're someone who just doesn't want to die young, you're probably not going to want to live in Beijing, where pollution levels are frequently 20 times the levels considered healthy and you can't see more than two blocks away because of the smog. If you're a retiree, you probably also don't want to be in some remote location that's a day's drive from the nearest decent hospital. In almost any area where you find lots of people in your age bracket, there will be at least one good medical facility in town and many other larger ones you can get to in a couple hours or less.

What's on your checklist? Think about climate, culture, food, air connectivity, land connectivity, and apartment/house options. What's a deal breaker?

Lisa Niver has lived in multiple countries for three months or more at a time and says it's important to listen to the signs, to be willing to scratch your plans if something better arises. "We never would have gone to Ko Samui in Thailand if a friend of a friend hadn't invited me on Twitter. Once we got there, it just felt right. Look for something that fits with you and matches your passion. If it doesn't feel right, move on. We had planned to live in Panama for six months, but after 13 days we left and were in Costa Rica. When we wrote about our feelings on the blog, we got a lot of negative feedback and people saying, 'You need to give it a chance.' But we did give it a chance. We went to five different locations and compared to Thailand where we fell in love, Panama was a big disappointment." It wasn't right for them, so they moved on. For someone else, it may be perfect.

Wallet

While you may be dreaming of retiring on the Amalfi Coast of Italy, on the beach in the Virgin Islands, or in a nice slopeside chalet in Switzerland, your bank account might not agree with those plans. You need to find a way to combine your checklist of ideal factors with places you can actually afford.

If you picture yourself in a lakeside cottage looking up at jagged snow-capped mountains, you don't have to spend $100,000 a year in Switzerland. You can move south of

Bariloche in Argentina and live for one-fifth that amount instead. If you want to be on a warm-water beach with hot weather, there are 100 choices in Latin America and Southeast Asia that are a fraction of the cost of a Caribbean Island residence.

For most of the places profiled in this book, a pair of retirees living off two social security checks or an equivalent pension can get by just fine. For $1,500 for one person, $2.400 for two, you'll be living on far more than the average middle-class local. In some countries, that may be double or triple what's considered a good local salary. If you've got more than that coming in, you can be choosier about where to go and can upgrade your living standards.

Keep in mind though that there are major variations within a country, especially a big country like Mexico. The more expatriates there are in an area, the higher the prices will probably be: witness San Miguel de Allende. The more of a tourist destination it is, the higher prices will be: witness Los Cabos.

Also, just because you can live on $1,500 a month doesn't mean the government thinks that's enough wealth to grant you permanent residency. In Nicaragua a retiree only has to show monthly income of $600 a month, but in Mexico you have to show $2,000 for you and another $500 for each dependent. There are ways around this sometimes if you can show other assets or finagle a work permit, but do keep these restrictions in mind before making big plans.

Heart

The authors of *Freakonomics* and *Think Like a Freak* do a regular podcast on NPR and in one episode they answered a listener's question about how an economist would pick the perfect place to live. Stephen Leavitt said some of his most important factors—what economists would call "amenities"—were access to golf courses, fast food drive-throughs, and houses with big yards. He didn't care much about museums and cultural activities, but he could never live in a place without easy access to a golf course. In other words, he was meant to live in the suburbs, and specifically an American-style suburb.

Steve Dubner lives in New York City and said his most

important factors were the density of ideas, people, and creativity—and the resulting spillover effect. Without being in a big city where people interact a lot, he wouldn't get any of that. "I could never live in a place without a good diner," he added.

In the end, they decided that choosing a place to live was only an economic decision when it came to finding a place with the right amenities: childless couples don't care about schools, but for parents it may be #1. Otherwise, it's a decision you make with your heart.

The thing is, your heart may be very set in its ways. For example, are you liberal or conservative?

This may seem like a stupid question to ask in a book about moving abroad, but it turns out that will probably have a big impact on the kind of place you choose and the kind of house or apartment you will want. A study by the Pew Research Center asked Americans whether they would prefer to live in a community with smaller houses close together and everything within walking distance, or a community where larger houses are spaced far apart and you drive several miles to restaurants and schools. Liberals chose the first option by 77 percent, conservatives chose the second option by 75 percent. "Conservatives would rather live in large houses in small towns and rural areas—ideally among people of the same religious faith—while liberals opt for smaller houses and walkable communities in cities, preferably with a mix of different races and ethnicities." Three-quarters of liberals want to be near museums and galleries, while this only matters to one quarter of conservatives.

You do often see this preference play out abroad, with some gravitating to city centers and historic towns where you don't even need a car, others gravitating to towns that are replicas of American suburbs, with gated communities and garages.

Most "heart" factors aren't this predictable though and they can vary a lot even between couples who are on the same page in most other attitudes and ideals. A place may feel "just perfect" to one of them, while feeling like "a total shithole" to the other. As you can imagine, this can be the beginning of the end if they ignore these differences and try to plow forward.

For all these factors, it's worth taking some quiet time with no distractions to talk them through, maybe even writing down the answers mind-map style. When I've asked people what they love about a place, there's often a mix of head and heart in the answers and the heart ones can end up being really esoteric. Some cite a specific yoga teacher, a local hike they love, or the kind of pottery they use in their kitchen. One left the first place she lived because "the coffee really sucks there. I was annoyed every day."

For couples, talk out loud when you're traveling about why a place would be a good place to live and why it wouldn't. The time to argue about what's important is before you move, not after.

Chapter 7: What's Cheaper and What's Not When You Move Abroad

How do you feel about super-cheap mangoes and super-expensive deodorant?

People who have not traveled much or lived in different places often have one very wrong assumption about prices. They think if they move somewhere that's less expensive, *everything* will be less expensive. Eventually they get a rude awakening.

Soon I'll get into some universal truths about pricing, but it's hard to say you'll automatically save money on x, y, and z if you move from one place to another. Even if your home country has a median income of $50,000 and the one you're moving to has a median income of $20,000, you can't assume everything is going to be 60 percent less. We're in a global economy now, after all, so many items have a "global price" that has nothing to do with local conditions or exchange rates. Except for places where fuel is subsidized or heavily taxed, the price of oil is the price of oil. The variables come from taxes, subsidies, or in the case of taxis, labor costs.

That's one example of a commodity sold around the world for a fairly standard price. Others are grains, cooking oil, rubber, coffee, gold, and copper. If the country you're traveling in or visiting produces one of those things, the price might be less for a kilo of flour or a set of tires for a car. If not, the price will only be lower because sales would be zero otherwise. And when it comes to tires or copper gas lines, there aren't a lot of good alternatives. So people suck it up and pay.

Many expatriates are surprised to learn, however, that some items cost far more in a developing country where many people are living hand to mouth than they do in the "first world" country they came from. Cars frequently cost 30-40 percent more than they do in the USA, despite people making half or less the salary they would there. This is even true in countries that are major producers, such as Mexico. It makes no sense and I have yet to find someone who can explain the huge mark-ups in a satisfactory way. It's just the way it is.

Another cost that varies dramatically from place to place is alcohol. I have photos from a grocery store in Quito, Ecuador where six-packs of imported beer brands like Stella Artois or Negra Modelo are $13. No, I didn't say Copenhagen, I said Quito. When I tell people what it costs to order a glass of wine in Cuenca or order a cocktail in Quito it's like a robot that's going to start smoking from the head because, "This does not compute." The sole reason anything alcoholic that's imported is expensive in Ecuador is because the president *wants* it to be expensive. Taxes were more than doubled after he took office and he'd be thrilled if nobody took another drink. You see the same situation in many countries, from Islamic ones like Turkey and Malaysia where the ruling party would be happier to ban the stuff altogether to "sin tax" ones like Thailand. More than half the price of that beer you pop open is taxes.

Often, governments are more pragmatic and are not on a moral crusade when it comes to taxes. More often the goal is to favor local industries, something that makes a lot of sense for getting votes and staying in office. So more often than not, local booze will be cheap, while anything imported carries a higher tax. Food produced within the country is subsidized or at least not penalized, while imports from abroad incur tariffs.

My home country heavily taxes imported sugar (thus the crappy high fructose corn syrup shoved into anything sweet) and heavily subsidizes domestic crops—especially corn. Corporate welfare is a much larger percentage of the budget than the kind benefitting individuals. Handing out favors to big donors gets you reelected, whether you're in Buenos Aires or Birmingham.

Giving credit where credit is due though, the United States does have the most efficient distribution system the world has ever seen. Walmart may inspire derision and scorn, but that company has done more to cut waste out of packaging and shipping costs than probably the rest of the world's retailers added together. They have the clout to make big changes happen and they know how to use it. Companies sell directly to them, Target, Best Buy, and others without the entrenched layers of middlemen you find elsewhere. On top of that, we have the most advanced e-commerce delivery system of any large country on the globe. So nobody has the ability to charge premium prices unless they are truly delivering some kind of additional premium service.

If that's not enough, we also generally have a friendly trade relationship with China, the world's cheap goods factory. Every once in a while there's some saber-rattling and some tariffs are tacked onto a particular product line, but it's rare. Usually when it does happen, it's a disaster that's short-lived. The result is that anything made in China—which means most electronics, tools, and clothing these days—is cheaper in the USA than anywhere else. Heck, even Europeans and Brazilians come to the United States with empty suitcases. They're going to fill them up with goods they can't possibly buy so cheaply at home.

So in general, shop for expensive imported stuff at home (especially electronics and brand name goods). Shop for what is made locally abroad.

There are a few universal ways to play this game that will put the odds in your favor. You may have to tweak the strategy a bit here and there after arrival, but this is a good general game plan.

- Eat what's local and in season.
- Take advantage of low local labor costs
- Hire local craftspeople to make exactly what you want instead of buying factory made items.
- Buy medicines locally, but buy expensive cosmetics in your home country

To lay this out in a more concrete way, we've gotten lots of custom things made by local craftsmen for our house. I'm talking a whole dining room set, bookcases, a desk, tables, wardrobes, a bed, and nightstand lamps. We've got cool mirrors, glasses, and pottery we've bought in Mexico. But whenever I go back to the states, I return with lots of cosmetics, sheets, clothing, and gadgets. The TV we bought locally because it's big. The phones and speakers, elsewhere. You'll know soon after arrival how to proceed in your case.

Chapter 8: Family Life and Pets Abroad

I'm guessing the majority of people who are going to pick up a book like this are singles or couples. It's much easier to take off and start a new life somewhere else when you're not thinking about schools, child care, and supporting a family.

There are a sizable number of families who move abroad while the kids are still in school though. Besides the obvious situation of one parent getting a job transfer to another country, many move abroad to have a calmer, more fulfilling life at a lower cost. There are big advantages to escaping the rat race and lowering the bar on how much you have to earn each month just to pay the bills.

Families can move to any country profiled in this book and have good school options, but in many cases they're limited to where they can live within that country. In general, the international schools are located in urban areas or at least in areas where there are a lot of foreigners. If you're dreaming of moving to a small village in Bulgaria or Argentina, you're probably going to need to home school. Or you'll have to take what you can get from the local school system—in the local language.

My daughter has been enrolled in private schools in Mexico, but they have been in Spanish only. We wanted that for her because becoming fluent in a second language was at least as important to us as what she actually learns in classes. We know her future career options will be brighter in almost any field if she's bilingual. Some kids really struggle with this though and you can't assume yours will be a whiz at picking up a new language. Plus, Spanish is quite useful later in life. Thai or Vietnamese? Not so much.

There are many advantages to moving abroad as a family, but some clear disadvantages too. It's important to be aware of these up front.

Pros

Cheaper cost of living overall
Lower health care costs
Less time in transit
More time together

Less competition in the classroom
A more family friendly culture
Fewer cliques, less social pressure

Cons

Different school rules and requirements
Communication struggles
Effort required to keep up with home academic standards
Learning a new language is not automatic
Health care adjustments
Less time with relatives (maybe)

The way schools run and the parents' level of involvement are bound to be very different than what you're used to. Seek out others already living where you're planning to go and get their advice. Also pick up a few books on moving abroad with a family. *The Family Sabbatical Handbook* came out in 2007, but much of the advice in it is timeless and was quite helpful for us.

You also don't have to look very hard to find blogs written by parents who have moved abroad. There's probably at least one for wherever you're thinking of possibly moving. Poke around on search engines with the right keywords to find them as they're in a constant state of appearing and disappearing with the writers' moves. I can give you lots of advice for where I live, but not much for other areas: your best sources are families who are already there.

I'll touch on this aspect of moving in more detail in the last section of this book.

Moving Abroad with Pets

Pets are a whole other ballgame. I'm putting them in this chapter because some people think of their pets as family.

This is going to be a short section though because the rules vary quite a bit from country to country. In some cases you just need to have the proper paperwork showing that your pet is rabies-free and has had a recent health check-up. In other cases your precious will have to go into quarantine for months before being allowed to join you—especially for islands. Any book on moving to a specific country is going to cover this in detail, or you can poke around on the internet and find the specific rules through a government website.

My American friends Ryan and Ang of JetsLikeTaxis.com have lived for stretches in Germany, Spain, Austria, Montenegro, and Mexico. For each of them their little dog Louis has come along for the ride. Wherever they live next, he'll be making his home there too.

Moving abroad with a pet is a bit more difficult than moving without one, but it can be done. For Americans heading to Mexico or Central America in their own vehicle, it's just a matter of having all the paperwork in order and tossing Fido in the back seat. It's a similar story for Brits heading elsewhere in Europe. If you're flying though, there are a few more considerations involved in the actual flight and airport immigration steps.

For wherever you are going, you'll need to check into the local laws about bringing in a pet. For some it's just a matter of getting the right certificates signed right before you depart with your dog or cat. In others, especially island nations, your pet may need to go into quarantine for months. The more exotic the pet, the more difficult it can be. Taking your python or lemur abroad is not so simple. Or with a tropical bird, getting it there might be easy, but bringing it back may be next to impossible because of your home country's import restrictions.

You will likely need to buy the proper regulation-sized crate to fly with your pet and in many cases pay extra airline fees. In some countries the regulations may be so onerous that you'll want help from a professional pet relocation service. You can find lots of great information on the website of the International Pet and Animal Transportation Association. There's more info at LetsGoPets.com.

Keep in mind too that landlords everywhere are wary of having animals in the home they own. Everyone has a very high opinion of their own pet, but reality is that there's statistically a much higher risk of damage from tenants with pets than ones without. So you'll probably have to hunt much harder for a place to live, temporarily or permanently, and you may find pet-welcoming hotels to be very difficult to find where you're going. Put some extra time into planning for this.

Chapter 9: How to Make Sure Your Living Expenses Plummet

There are those who save a fortune when they move abroad to a cheaper country. Then there are others who end up spending almost as much as they did at home. Let's call them the Wings couple and the Chains couple.

The Wings couple really takes flight when they leave home and they embrace all that their new destination has to offer. If they move to Mexico, they eat Mexican food more often than not. They eat tropical fruit and seasonal vegetables that they buy from the local market down the street. They mostly eat local cheese and drink local beer. When they have a party they serve more tequila and rum than Scotch and vodka. They buy five-gallon containers of bottled water that the companies are out delivering several times a week.

They walk and take taxis or they just keep an inexpensive used car for shopping trips and excursions. They travel a lot within their adopted country and take advantage of all the free and cheap entertainment around them.

The Chains couple didn't really move because they appreciated the culture, loved the food, or wanted to learn a new language. They simply moved because they could afford a bigger house or live on savings that would be insufficient where they really wanted to go—let's say Florida or the most British parts of the coast of Spain.

They buy or rent a house with a garage that looks just like they would get at home and they install an expensive whole-house water purification system. Rather than waiting to get custom made furniture from local artisans, they spend three times as much on factory furniture that looks like what they had before. They bring down their giant SUV and drive it everywhere they go, even though it means having scratched up bumpers the week after arrival because of the narrow streets. After a week or two of eating Mexican food and drinking Pacificos, they hit the Costco and stock up on imported cheese, wine, vegetables, and processed snacks.

When they go out to eat, it's to one of the most

expensive restaurants in town, the one with an English menu and international dishes to order. They fly out of the country every few months to visit friends and relatives in their old home and to vacation in "civilized" places like London and New York. Since all the people they socialize with each day are other gringos and they haven't made much effort to learn Spanish, they constantly feel like outsiders who are being cheated.

Know Yourself and Choose Accordingly

If the Wings couple decides to pick up and move on to Panama, Argentina, Thailand, or Portugal, they'll be fine. It's not the place that matters, but the attitude of the people moving there. If the Wings moved to Portugal, for instance, they'd eat lots of oranges and olives, drink Portuguese wine at dinner, and eat lots of fish. If they hated all those things, they wouldn't move there to start with.

In my younger days my wife and I taught English for more than a year in South Korea. Why there? We were trying to choose between Japan and Korea, the best places to earn real money as an ESL teacher outside of the Middle East. "I really don't like Japanese food," I told my wife. "I'll go crazy if I have to eat that stuff for a year straight." It may sound petty, but that's why we went to Korea, where the food is much more flavorful. Sure, I got tired of that too after a while, but we made it most of the way through before our food bill started rising from all the imported items we were buying from the Carrefour superstore and the pizzas we were buying from the takeout place a few blocks away.

Just as I couldn't stomach Japan, neither of us would be able to stomach the Philippines. There's a good reason you don't see Filipino restaurants around the world. On top of that, I place a high value on aesthetic beauty and the cities in that country are as butt ugly as they come. Many men who live there feel differently about the country and love it. But that's usually because of a different kind of beauty: hot local women who are looking for a ticket to a better life.

On the other hand, I could live almost anywhere else profiled in the destinations section of this book. In most of them I could eat local, shop local, and enjoy what the country has to offer to its fullest. Within any country there are places right for me and wrong for me—something I wouldn't know if I hadn't been there. Once again, trial runs are a very good idea before making any moves toward permanency.

Budgets and Your Consumption Habits

The Chains couple profiled at the top is not some mythical man and woman I've invented out of thin air. I've seen dozens of pairs like them and if you've spent much time in expatriate enclaves anywhere in the world, you've probably seen them too. They're the ones keeping the expensive restaurants and imported food shops in business. They're the ones who have been there for five years and speak less of the local language than you learned on the plane ride over from your Lonely Planet phrase book. They may be living more cheaply than they did at home, but you'll often hear them complaining about how it wasn't as cheap as they thought it would be and they're the ones grumbling the most about what doesn't work properly in the community or the country. When they get together with other expats like themselves, it often turns into a bitch session.

In places like Cuenca, Ecuador, there are lots of grumpy foreigners that resident Holly Walker calls "financial refugees." They're the ones who came for the sole reason that they couldn't live on what they'd saved or are getting from social security in the USA or Canada and are bitter that they had to go elsewhere.

Here's some advice I've never read in the usual living abroad sources but is a good test: go spend a week in the country you're considering, but in basic hotel in a town where there are no expatriates. There should be no fellow countrymen to complain to and nobody that shares your culture and history. Eat out, have a few drinks, shop in the local market, and stroll the streets in the evening.

If you manage to make it through the week and you still like the country, you're in good shape. If you can't wait to fly home and tell everyone how horrible it was, this is probably not the life for you.

If you did make it through that week of extremes and actually enjoyed it, then you know you'll be fine when you have more of a support system around you. One byproduct of that week though will be a crash course in language immersion. You find a way to communicate what you want, or you don't eat.

I actually had an experience like this several times, for a week here and there over the course of several years. My wife and I bought a little beach house on the Gulf coast of the Yucatan in Mexico when we were living in land-locked Nashville, TN, eight hours of driving to get to the closest beach. The house was cheap because although it was 40 minutes from the big city of Merida, it was a fishing village most of the year and a holiday weekend getaway spot for Mexicans from the city. Occasionally we would see another white face in the snowbird season, but sometimes a whole week would go by and we didn't hear a word of English except from each other. Our caretakers for the house didn't speak any, so if we wanted to tell them a water pump wasn't working or the propane needed to be replaced, we had to figure out how to say it in Spanish. It wasn't easy at first, but we got better fast.

We still liked Mexico a lot after all that. So although we never intended to live in that house (it's sold now—more on that in another chapter), we were much better prepared for what to expect when we moved to Guanajuato to live.

Both at the beach house and where we are now though, we took our leads from the locals. We ate what they ate (within reason), shopped where they shopped, and asked their advice on how to get things done for a reasonable price. This requires some faith, yes. It requires a willingness to leap into the unknown. It requires adaptability. If you can manage those things though, you will easily get by on half the budget you had before your move. If you try to live with figurative chains still attached to the homeland, your savings will be far less dramatic.

Chapter 10: Making a Living and Getting a Visa

To live abroad, you'll need some kind of visa or permit. You'll also need to have some money coming in.

If you are just going to bop around the world on tourist visas as a digital nomad, staying as long as you can and then heading somewhere else, you won't have many restrictions if you're from a developed country. Citizens of Finland, Sweden, and the UK can get into 173 countries without a visa or by getting one upon arrival. For the USA, Denmark, Germany, and Luxembourg it's 172. For Belgium, Italy, and the Netherlands, 171. Canada, France, Ireland, Japan, and others, 170. Those with a New Zealand passport can get into 168 and those with an Australian one, 167. (If you need a reason to thank your lucky stars that you were born in a rich country, consider that people from Nepal, Kosovo, Eritrea, Sri Lanka, and Angola can only get into 40 or fewer of these places without securing a visa in advance.)

When you want to stay longer than a few months, however, that's when things get tricky.

What you're going to live on and what kind of visa you will be eligible for go hand in hand. In nearly any country in the world, their main concern when evaluating your status is whether you are able to support yourself. In Country A that may be a low bar of $600 a month coming in each month or the equivalent of that times 12 sitting in a bank account. For other countries it may be several thousand dollars a month—plus more for each dependent.

If you can't meet this threshold, you will likely be hopping around on tourist visas, never being able to stay longer than three or six months at a time. If you do earn enough already though, you won't likely meet much resistance from the authorities. As Mark Ehrman says in the book *Getting Out*, "Unlike your parents, countries don't really mind if you sit around all day doing nothing, as long as you spend money and don't become a burden on the system."

When I surveyed readers of my Cheap Living Abroad newsletter on what was holding them back from moving to a cheaper country, how to earn a living was at the top of the list, with around a third of them ticking off that check box.

The funny thing is, there were another third who didn't check that box and would probably put it at the very bottom of their list. That's because they have a location independent job or business they can operate from anywhere. Whether they're in Los Angeles or London or Lisbon makes no material difference in their income. They can live almost anywhere and not miss a beat.

This is the ideal situation for a whole lot of reasons, the main one being that you have true arbitrage: you're earning money in a rich country and spending it in a poorer one. You need less to live on and if you have a really good month, it's easier to put away some savings. You can show embassy officials that you can easily support yourself while being a net positive contributor to their economy. You're not taking much from them, but you're giving a lot. Countries like to open their doors to people like this.

There can be downsides to this arrangement of course. You need to be in a place with a good internet connection and if your business requires a lot of bandwidth-heavy applications like real-time stock trading programs, video chats, or constant uploads of large files, you'll simply have to strike some destinations off your list completely. There are a lot of really desirable places to live where the pipes just aren't fat enough to support that kind of data flow.

If you need to talk or meet online with clients, you will likely need to work a very non-conventional workday to be available during their regular work hours. If you're in the Americas somewhere and your clients are too, no big deal. But I've heard of many freelancers or business owners who had a lot of sales calls in their mix that ended up having to move out of Southeast Asia. The difficulty of being on the exact opposite schedule of the people paying for their services was hurting revenue and relationships.

In the digital age we're in now, however, most jobs require more e-mail and file sharing than meetings or phone calls. One person I interviewed for this book said she blocks out two days every month for calls. The rest of the time she never talks to anyone. It's just not necessary. I've hired more than a dozen people to do one-off jobs for me, from book cover design to Wordpress installations. I have only talked to one of them on the phone and that's because we were getting bogged down in too many e-mails and wanted to hash out the punch list all at once.

What kinds of jobs do these digital nomads or location independent business owners do? It's a wider range than you probably think. In this book you'll hear from business consultants and a t-shirt designer, travel writers and a CPA, software coders and web marketing specialists. Here's a list of what people I've personally run across or read articles by are doing as they make a living abroad.

Virtual Jobs - Very Portable

Transcriptionist
Systems Analyst
Web Designer
Programmer/Code Writer
App developer
Online Teacher
Professional Blogger
Freelance Writer
Author
Ghostwriter
Technical Writer
Web Editor
Online team leader
Translator
Online Entrepreneur selling products
Online Entrepreneur selling services/info
Software as a Service Developer
Graphic Artist
Illustrator
Voice talent
SEO Consultant
Online marketer/consultant
Stock or Forex trader
Wealth manager
Tax adviser
Sales rep (when few face-to face meetings are required)

It's far easier now than it was even 10 years ago to both

look for virtual employees or to be one. You could start out with no clients and gain them through services such as eLance, Odesk, and Envato Studio. An easier route is to strike out on your own while you're still in your home country, then keep working for those same clients as you change physical locations. If you're good enough at what you do and keep meeting or exceeding expectations, you'll probably build up more clients through referrals and actually increase your income.

Shannon O'Donnell is known for her popular travel blog *A Little Adrift* and was named *National Geographic* Traveler of the Year for her approach to meeting needs on the ground as a volunteer in various locations around the world. Her "real job" though is being an online marketing consultant for businesses, helping them with their website content and search engine positioning. "While I was still living in the USA, before traveling, I asked my biggest client, 'If I keep up the same standard of work, you won't fire me, right?'" She kept that client and a couple others, and built up many more over time. "Now I'm at the point where I have more business than I can handle," she says. "I've never pitched, I don't even have a website—it's all from referrals."

Many International Jobs Are Not Virtual

Parachute into any place with hundreds or thousands of expatriates and you'll probably find a hundred ways people are making a living abroad. For many it's some kind of hands-on but skilled job that requires their physical presence. They play in the local symphony or teach at the international school. They work for IBM, GM, Marriott, or Unilever as a manager. Or most commonly, they teach English, sell real estate, or run a restaurant. Some options may be obvious through the skill set you already have. For creative entrepreneurial minds, the options may seem so unlimited that you have to reign in your idea fountain and focus.

If you're a nurse, engineer, doctor, financial analyst, or a specialist in a specific technology that's used worldwide, you'll probably have little trouble finding a job in your field and getting a work permit.

Experienced teachers can often make the leap by teaching for their own state department, for a certified international school, or by doing a short stint on a Fulbright program. For English as a second language (ESL) teacher, some jobs come through formalized programs aimed at recent college graduates, while others are filled by a network of international recruiters and online ads for teachers.

Think beyond the obvious though and dig around. When I was teaching English in a suburb of Seoul, the other foreigners in my town who weren't teachers were some fish-out-of-water contractors and carpenters from the Pacific Northwest. They were building American-style wood framed houses for wealthy Koreans. I've met tennis instructors, dive masters, fishing charter leaders, archaeologists, helicopter mechanics, and fashion designers plying their craft in a cheaper location—while still making a good living.

Here are a few occupations where the right degree or certification can be your ticket to portability.

Portable Credentialed Jobs

Import/Export Manager
Hotel Manager
Financial Industry Analyst/Manager
Personal Trainer
Dive Instructor/Trainer
Corporate Trainer
Business Team Leader
Doctor
Nurse
Dentist
Massage Therapist
Yoga Instructor
Acupuncturist
Chiropractor
Pilates Instructor
Ski Instructor
Classical Musician
Architect
Interior Designer
Fashion Designer
Film/Video Technician
Certified ESL (English as a Second Language) Instructor

School Teacher
College Professor
Engineer
Chef
Scientist

With these occupations you can generally make a good enough living abroad to enjoy a similar or better lifestyle than you had before—even if you take a sizable salary cut. Many find that their quality of life betterment makes up for a lot as well: the doctor who can spend twice as much time with patients instead of paperwork, for example, or the teacher who gets to actually teach her students something lasting instead of just "teaching to the test." In some cases, the leap abroad takes the person from being a small fish in a big lake to a big fish in a small pond. There's less competition and less stress.

There are also plenty of jobs out there that don't require any special certification or experience. Just be advised that the closer you come to skills the locals already have, the less money you can potentially make. You'll also have a much harder time getting a work visa or business visa.

For the unskilled labor jobs, if you're not bringing any special experience to the table, you're competing with locals willing to work for far less than you. Here's a good rule of thumb: if people from *that* country are coming to *your* country to do this job for more money, trying to go the opposite direction for the same job is just stupid. Mexico and Bulgaria don't need fruit pickers or hotel maids. Nicaragua and Vietnam don't need coffee workers. Colombia and India don't need people who can sew t-shirts. There can be exceptions now and then. Nobody really needs your basic bartending skills—unless it's an expat pub and they want a native English speaker. Or if you have five years of experience working in a high-end cocktail bar and the Ritz-Carlton is hiring, then you're a better match than any local could be.

For the sake of opening your mind to the possibilities, here are some no-certification (some would say no qualifications) jobs many expats are doing across the globe right now. One note on real estate agents: many are experienced and skilled. It's just that in more countries than not, neither certification nor skill is required to peddle houses for sale. Keep that in mind if you're a buyer.

Portable Non-credentialed Jobs
Organic Farm Helper
Real Estate Agent
Property Manager for Rental Homes
Musician
Bartender
Waiter
Cook
Hotel Worker
Sales Rep
Public Relations Rep
Business Consultant
Business Owner
Airline Worker
NGO/Aid Worker
Actor
Low-end ESL Teacher
Tour Leader/Organizer
Fishing Charter Leader
Construction Worker
Au Pair/Nanny
Yacht mate
Cargo ship worker
Cruise ship worker

For all of these jobs, you can't really generalize about what you can find in advance and what you can find in person after arrival. There's some correlation though between how specific the skill set is and how often the positions are advertised online. If you're a petroleum engineer or financial analyst, you can likely find ample positions to apply for without leaving your comfy desk chair. Some positions are advertised in industry-specific trade magazines or websites, which you'll probably be able to find easily if you're already in that industry.

At the other end, if you're trying to find one-on-one work for clients (personal trainer, massage therapist, etc.) you will likely need to get your feet on the ground and start hustling. That's not as hard as it sounds though since at least at first, most of your clients will probably be other expatriates. Work of mouth and getting your name out there on the local message board may be enough to get your business moving in a hurry. My wife's a personal trainer and although there are probably only a couple hundred expats in my Mexican city, she's fully booked some weeks.

There are some social and visa dynamics that come into play as you move through these kinds of jobs. For a virtual, digital nomad gig, you don't need a work visa. If it helps you stay for longer periods, then get one, but governments are generally happy to have you spend money in their country without taking any of it from them. You can come in on a tourist visa, work away on your laptop, and keep taking cash out of the ATM. Usually you don't even need a local bank account.

For jobs requiring certain credentials or education, you may have to go through the right channels and apply for a work visa...eventually. As we speak though there are plenty of ESL teachers at private language schools, dive instructors giving scuba lessons, and bartenders mixing up classic cocktails in boutique hotels on a tourist visa. That's riskier for both the employer and the employee though, so if you're not in a country like Cambodia with very liberal labor laws, sooner or later you'll probably want to go legit. There's usually more security in this arrangement too: you've got someone vouching for you with the local authorities, someone who knows how to work within the system. If you're legal, you're also less likely to get cheated out of your pay.

Think Creatively

If you don't have a professional skill that easily transfers, I *strongly* advise you to find a job you can do remotely. Or make your own. That may be a freelance job, a structured job that allows you to telecommute, or a business you can run online. There are some very good reasons this works much better than the alternatives:

1) You earn first world currency and spend it in a cheaper country.

2) You can show proof of income to immigration without needing to work locally.

3) You can set your own hours and probably work fewer of them.

4) You can hit the ground running instead of taking months to ramp up local

earnings.

5) You have zero dependence on the whims and pay rates of the local market.

If you have no earthly idea how you get from your current position to one that works like this, first start thinking of what skills and experience you already have that wouldn't require much of a pivot. Also consider ways to turn your expertise into some kind of online platform that would attract a community and enable you to sell products or advertising. There are what seem like an infinite number of e-books, websites, and podcasts out there providing advice on this subject and you'll find some that I'm comfortable recommending in the resources section.

There's one way you can get a virtual job tomorrow that can potentially pay you a nice salary: become a sales rep. These days many sales jobs are done entirely by e-mail and phone, so unless you're on the other side of the world, you can keep prospecting and selling in your home country just as you would from where you're living now. If you're willing to work on straight commission and you're a hustler, you can barge into nearly any industry and be hired in no time. Sure, you don't get paid until you deliver, but if it's a product or service that aligns with your interests and the quality is good, you should be able to get ramped up before too long.

There are also all kinds of online money making opportunities out there if you just have a little bit to invest in testing and tweaking. Read the book *The $100 Start-up* for some inspiration. There's a forum called StackThatMoney.com where members pay $99 a month to talk about how they're killing it with affiliate marketing sales. Basically that's driving people to purchase a product online and then getting paid a commission. People spend x amount on search ads or Facebook ads, for example, then get y amount in commissions. As long as y is a good bit more than x, it's a profitable campaign. Do this enough times in the right way and you can be making more money than you would have as a cubicle jockey using your college degree.

The other shortcut is to lay out a little capital to buy an existing online business and take it over. You can find opportunities on Flippa.com, Empire Flippers, and other sites geared to online entrepreneurs. Sure, you have to make an investment up front, but then you're cash flow positive immediately and it often will take less than a year to recoup your investment. Try finding a deal like that on Wall Street or your local real estate office!

By the time you read this there may be a dozen ways to make money online that I haven't touched on or that didn't even exist when I wrote this. There will be people living somewhere exotic just killing it, pulling in serious bucks while working wherever they want in the world.

The key to any of these though is actually doing it. You could find enough online courses and e-books to buy that would keep you reading and dreaming for a year. The people who really make an online business work are the ones who get out there and take action.

Types of Visas

Some countries have only three or four visa types, while others have a whole laundry list. You'll probably need to dig deeper after reading the specific destination chapters before making a move, but here are the general categories. I'm lumping all the following together as "visas," though in reality the ones that let you stay a year or more are probably going to be called a "residency permit." For those you'll have something extra in your passport and probably some kind of local identity card. All of them will have rules about how long you can stay, whether you can leave and re-enter the country, and what you can and can't do while you're a guest there.

Tourist Visa - If you're from one of the advanced countries of the world, especially an English-speaking one, you can often just show up at the airport counter and get two to six months with a *thwap* of the passport stamp. For others, such as India or Vietnam, you need to apply in advance. Sometimes you have a choice in advance too of how long you can stay: pay more to get more. In general, you are not allowed to work in a local capacity. (Earning money from abroad is fine.)

Student Visa - If you're enrolled in a formal study program, this is one of the easiest long-term visas to get. Some expatriates have found a way to get one by taking language classes or enrolling in a graduate program at a local university.

Work Visa - You usually have a job secured in advance and the employer takes care of much of the paperwork. If you have a real job with a written contract, these are usually easy to get. If you secure the job after arrival, you'll often need to go back home to apply for a work visa or at least leave the country to come back with a fresh start and a new residency status.

Freelance Visa/Residency Permit - For some countries, if you can show regular income as a freelancer or self-employed person who is a sole proprietor, this is the visa to get. Demonstrate the means to support yourself and follow the right steps to get permission to stick around for a year and probably renew to do it again.

Retiree Visa/Residency Permit - Show sufficient pension income, social security income, or a fat bank account and most countries are happy to have you. Some will even roll out a big red carpet of enticements. Age is surprisingly not a factor across the board. In some cases you can be any age, in others 45 or 50 years.

Spousal Visa - Marry a local and you'll be on the fast track to residency. Not right away of course—you'll have to be together long enough to prove you're a real couple—but you'll seldom get kicked out of the country if you've found true love and gotten hitched.

Specialist Visa - Various categories have special visas for limited use. These include professors, artists, journalists, and aid/NGO workers. In many cases though these are one year or less and are difficult to renew.

Permanent Residency - For most of the countries in this book, if you've renewed your temporary residency for years on end and have been a good boy or girl, you can be granted permanent residency. For very lenient countries it can happen much sooner. For some (like India and Nepal), never.

What You'll Need to Present

Documents required by the country you're interested in moving to vary greatly. Usually they are posted on the official government website, but only sometimes will that information be in English. You can also be sure you'll get hit up for something that's not on there too. Surf the local expat forums for the real deal and assume that if you hire an attorney he or she will be able to fill you in.

You'll be asked for things you haven't thought about for years and may have trouble locating, like your marriage certificate or birth certificate. To make things more difficult, you may have to produce an "apostille" version that has the equivalent of an internationally recognized notary seal or accompanying document.

Speaking of notary seals, you'll probably need some of those too, on things like bank statements or investment account balances. If you go teach English in Japan or Korea, you may need to show your actual university diploma, so dig it out of the frame. If you're getting a work permit, you may need to show professional certifications and you'll almost surely need some kind of employment contract or offer letter.

In general, it's better to over-prepare than to have to return to the office four times. Especially if you're applying for residency as a "solopreneur" or freelancer, the more documentation the better. Bring copies of any bank or investment statements, real estate holdings, professional memberships, and anything else that can show what you do isn't just a hobby. You want to show beyond a doubt that you're not going to need to lean on the state for support.

It may turn out you brought a lot of things you didn't need. When Jim Lynch applied for his residency permit in Nicaragua, the immigration person skimmed through his documents without seeming to really look at them, then asked Jim if he had a car. When Jim replied yes, the man asked him what kind of car it was. "A Nissan Pathfinder" he replied. Apparently that was a sufficient display of wealth, because that was the end of the interview and Jim walked out a legal resident.

A Back Door to Europe

In some European countries, you can be granted citizenship or at least a second passport if you can show a clear bloodline to that country in the past. For Ireland, Greece, Iceland, and Croatia, for instance, if you are a child or even a grandchild of a naturalized citizen of that country, you can apply to become one yourself. For Germany, if you're descended from someone who lost citizenship in the past or was forced out of the country during the Nazi period, you can apply to become a German citizen.

Even if you have no desire to live in any of the countries where you are eligible, the peculiarities of the European Union make it worth doing there. That's because once you have citizenship and a passport from an EU country, you're good to go in any of the 26 others. So if you planned it out and went through all the right steps, your Irish passport could be your ticket to a cheap life in Portugal, the Czech Republic, Hungary, Romania, or Slovakia.

Details in the Next Section

In each of the countries profiled in detail in this book, there's a section on visas. Don't take my word as the last word and remember that I'm not an immigration attorney. Not even close. So consult local sources who know far more and double-check that their advice is current.

Chapter 11: Where Should I Move To?

Just picking a spot on the globe that's cheap is easy. Picking one where you'll actually want to live for an extended period is much more difficult. After all, the cheapest cities on the planet are not exactly paradise. Karachi (Pakistan), Harare (Zimbabwe), La Paz (Bolivia), Ashkhabad (Turkmenistan), Bishkek (Kyrgyzstan), Calcutta (India), and Tegucigalpa (Honduras) are the kinds of places that are at the bottom of the cost list on Mercer's annual cost of living report for those living abroad. I want to guide you to a place that is a bargain, but is a pleasant and stimulating place to settle down in as well, maybe even a place where you would raise a family.

In this book you'll find lots of possibilities. Some may have the kind of climate you want and the right-sized community. Others will be a good fit in terms of your interests, the time it takes to get back to see relatives, or the level of English proficiency you think you need. Others may not fit any of your requirements and you can ignore them.

Unfortunately, finding the right place to live is almost as complex as finding the right mate. You can't just list a few requirements on a page and find the one that checks the right boxes. That doesn't work on OKCupid and it doesn't work for choosing your perfect destination. What you can do though is narrow it down by looking at the important factors and at least writing off the ones that aren't in the ballpark.

In the following chapters, I'm going to tell you stories, introduce some people living in these places, and give you a sense of the pros and cons of each destination. I'm not going to give you pages of statistics though on leading export products, the current state of abortion laws, or the national debt. You also won't get the kind of super in-depth details on a specific country you will get by buying a book just on that country, such as *Living Abroad in Mexico* (477 pages) or the *Wood Egg Malaysia* guide to starting a business there (420 pages). This book is an idea generator and a way for you to think through your future, cheaper life. When you settle on a place, you'll be ready for a second round of research that's more specific to that one location.

Since this is a book on cutting your expenses in half and ending up with a better life, I'm going to give you a feel for the 18 countries where you can easily live for half what you're spending now and give you a sense of how much it should cost to live there. You'll see real prices for real things you'd spend money on, like rent, utilities, a taxi ride, and a beer in a bar. I'll talk about the things that are a great bargain there and things you might want to bring with you or pick up on trips back to your original home to see relatives. There's also a section at the end on other places to consider if none of these are a great fit.

Keep in mind though that all this information can never be more than a combination of facts and anecdotes. To know if a place is really right for you, there's no substitute for going there. Jeff Johnston, whom you'll meet in the Ecuador chapter, says that after all his research, he went to Ecuador looking for "a reason *not* to move there." When he didn't find a good one, he packed his bags and made it his home.

Susan Korthase and her husband landed in Portugal for the first stop on their country-hopping trip and then didn't hop any more. They had found their place. Susan had already traveled a lot and lived other places though, so she had a good sense of what kind of place they wanted. When I first wandered the streets of Guanajuato, Mexico and decided I'd love to live there, it wasn't exactly my first time out of the country. I had lived in Turkey and South Korea teaching English and had traveled through countries on five continents. I'd also been to expat enclaves like Playa del Carmen, San Miguel de Allende, and Puerto Vallarta and knew they were not for me (or my wife).

For some people, it's like trying on a dozen pairs of shoes before finding the one that's just right. I've met some expatriates who traveled to 10 or 15 locations before settling on the one where they live now. Others distilled their 20 or 30 years of travels into a wish list they knew would make them happy and after an either/or trial run between two top contenders they made a decision.

Others make the wrong decision, sometimes after a change in the local environment, a change in their health, or just a "falling out of love" change of heart. A move abroad does have similarities with a long-term relationship in that way, but if you rent instead of buying it is more like shacking up than getting married. You can move on without suffering a lot of consequences.

The worst thing that you can do is watch *House Hunters International* on TV and think that reality TV is actually real. Smart people don't fly into a country for the first time, look at three houses over a weekend, and buy one instantly. If you want to see how the show really works, search the article "House Hunters" and my buddy "Matt Gibson," who starred in one episode. For starters, the place he "picked" was where he was already living and the "real estate agent" was an English-speaking friend who didn't really sell real estate. Shows like that are filmed as entertainment, so treat them as such.

Also, don't assume it's a good idea to sign up for an expensive seminar on location in a country you've never been to and buy something there from one of the partner real estate agents or developers invited to talk. Besides this arrangement being ripe for conflicts of interest, it's never a good idea to be under time pressure when making a big, life-changing investment. If you want my opinion, don't buy anything at all until you've lived somewhere for a while and truly know the local market—including what the locals are paying. Sure, there are exceptions, like people who have a close friend or relative in the area who knows the scene well, or savvy real estate investors who already own 50 properties and this is just one more for the portfolio. But for the average person who owns two homes at most, it's better to take your time before getting hitched.

Some people will surely quibble with my overly simplistic directive to just change addresses and cut your expenses in half. So one qualifier: I am talking apples to apples when making this "half price" comparison. So if you live in New York City or London now, you can move to any big city in the countries profiled in this book and live for half price. Heck, you can probably even move to the most touristy tourist area and still cut your expenses in half. If you're moving from Nowheresville, Oklahoma or some obscure town in the Outback of Australia though, you're probably already living pretty cheaply when it comes to housing. So you can't move to Kuala Lumpur or Puerto Vallarta from there and say, "No fair—you said my expenses would be cut in half and they're not!" If you go from one of the cheapest areas of your own country to one of the most expensive in another, your prices will still be lower, but you may not save such a fortune. The half price living refers to a mid-sized city to a mid-sized city, one resort area to another, one big metropolis to another big metropolis.

Even so, if you go from rural Oklahoma or the Australian outback to any location in the countries profiled here, you will save a lot of money and you'll be able to live a life you couldn't have lived making a similar move at home. In other words, if you move from an inexpensive town in your own country to a beach resort town in Mexico, Nicaragua, or Thailand, your costs are going to go down—not up like they would if you moved to a beach resort or big city in the country you're living in now. Keep this in mind if you're anywhere close to retirement age and are looking at making the typical move to a sunnier, warmer climate. Move to Florida and you may go broke. Move to San Juan del Sur in Nicaragua and you'll be living large.

That out of the way, you can read this next section in its entirety or skip over the countries you have no interest in whatsoever. They're not really in any order except that four of the most popular ones kick things off. Keep an open mind as you're going through: maybe a place you hadn't thought of will tick off more of your requirement boxes than the ones you're more familiar with. Many times I've visited a town or city I knew next to nothing about and said to myself, "Living here would be pretty nice!"

If you don't see a cheap destination that was high on your list, like the Philippines or Morocco, check the "Also worth considering" section at the end. Usually because of visa hurdles or a very small expat population to get info from, I've covered some in less detail.

If you find all this to be a tantalizing appetizer that fills you with questions you want answered, see the specific resources at the end of each section and at the end of the book. Beyond that, if you're not part of our Cheap Living Abroad community already, sign up there to connect with like-minded individuals and me on a regular basis. See

CheapLivingAbroad.com.

Chapter 12: Mexico

Pros: Six-month tourist visa, straightforward residency requirements, wide range of climates, wide range of locations, established expat centers, good domestic transportation options, friendly population, low stress.
Cons: Poor waste management, ineffective police, can't drink the water, high import prices, land restrictions near coasts, high income requirement for residency, noisy.

Until my daughter got comfortable going to school by herself, I would take a 10-minute cab ride to her middle school for $3 and listen to podcasts on the 40-cent bus back home. Often I'd buy a sausage and cheese baguette for 80 cents or two pastries for 50 cents on the walk from the bus stop to my house. I might buy 16 ounces (a half liter) of fresh-squeezed juice for $1.20.

If I go out for lunch, I'll get a pork sandwich in a crusty roll for $1.60 or a couple *gordita* corn patties with fillings for a shade over a dollar each. A meal of the day at the largest market is under $3, a three-course one at a real restaurant can be found for $4.

For going out in the evening, we've bought ballet tickets for $4, movie tickets for $5, symphony tickets for $6, and performances from major international acts for $15. Most of the time though, entertainment is outdoors and free. If we go for a simple dinner for three we might spend $12, if we go to a top-tier restaurant and order wine we can occasionally top the $50 mark for two—with some effort. A beer is not more than a lemonade, coffee, or juice, usually around $2. Museums typically cost a dollar or two, the most spectacular ones in Mexico City around $6. Much of our furniture is custom made for about one-third of what it would cost stateside. If we need tailoring done, it's a few dollars. Our maid and handyman are both paid around $4 an hour and we're paying above-market rates.

All in all, we spend less in Mexico for *everything* added together than we did just on rent and utilities in Tampa, Florida. We have swapped rent for house upgrades and furniture in a house we own outright our second time in the country, but when we rented the first time we also cut our expenses in half. Your experience could vary depending on where you're moving from: Mexico is not a cheap as Nicaragua or Cambodia, especially in beach resort areas that also require air conditioning. We're in the highlands where utility bills are next to nothing. On average though, most people who make the move cut their expenses by a third even if they're living the high life, but by half is easily doable almost anywhere in the country.

Our life is less stressful than in it was living in the U.S., we spend less time in traffic, and keeping the weight off here seems almost effortless because we walk almost everywhere. Our experience is shared by many, many others. Some are single mothers, some are young couples, some are entrepreneurs, and some are retirees. Mexico draws all types.

I'm making this the first and longest destination chapter because Mexico has more expatriates living in it than most of the others in this book added together. If you add just the Americans and Canadians together the total is well over a million. Add the others who come on a tourist visa and stay three or four months a year regularly, and you're probably edging closer to a million and a quarter. That's a mid-sized city's worth of people enjoying better weather and lower prices south of the border.

Besides the proximity to the North American neighbors, Mexico has a lot going for it: welcoming people, good food, interesting cities, and plenty of beaches to pick from on 5,600 miles of coastline: Gulf, Caribbean, Pacific, and Sea of Cortez. It works for city people who like culture and the arts. It works for rural people who like farmland or jungle. It works for beach lovers who want to watch the waves and walk around in flip-flops.

With a generous 180-day visa available for the asking upon arrival, this is also one of the easiest countries in the world to live in temporarily or for a year without paperwork: just leave the country and return to have five days shy of a year in one place. With a large network of expatriates in some areas and at least a few to connect with in others, it's not hard to find guidance on getting a house or apartment and getting settled.

You can spend a fortune in Mexico if you would like. There are mansions on the Pacific Ocean north of Puerto Vallarta worth more than $10 million and colonial homes in San Miguel de Allende with price tags above $2 million. Some people are surprised to learn there are lots of rich Mexicans as well. One of the two wealthiest men in the world is Mexican after all, and there's a sizable collection of millionaires in every city, fed by a strong industrial base and a middle class that gets substantially larger each year. This is not a country like Nicaragua or Honduras where a few families hold all the wealth and power. There are hotels in Mexico charging $500 a night that are filled almost entirely by Mexican families and there are upscale malls full of stores where only those making six figures a year (in dollars, not pesos) can afford to shop.

Many industries have too little competition, no doubt, and ten families have a grip on some near-monopolistic business sectors, but a rising tide is definitely lifting a lot of boats. The middle class in Mexico is for real, with a widening girth being the most obvious sign that most families are in pretty good shape financially. Fewer have headed north to the U.S. since 2008 not just because there are fewer jobs, but also because the outlook at home keeps getting better.

It's very easy to live a middle class life here for less, however, even if you don't have 10 people in the family compound. Lydia Carey lives in Mexico City, the thriving capital that's one of the world's greatest cities for museums, culture, art, and food. She and her partner share an apartment in the Roma neighborhood. Both do freelance writing, translation, and other jobs for local companies and foreign ones. They live on an average of $1,600 a month for two.

T.W. Anderson, author of The Expat Guidebook (theexpatguidebook.com), has managed to get by for cheap in some of Mexico's most expensive tourist towns: Cancun and Playa del Carmen. "We save a lot of money by living like working class Mexicans," he explains. If you live where all the tourists hang out in Playa del Carmen, you can spend as much as you would in Miami, like $800 or $1,000 for a so-so studio apartment. But I pounded the pavement for five days and found a place in a subdivision for the equivalent of $470, a two-bedroom apartment. It's 10 minutes by bus from the beach, or a 30 minute walk." Counting utilities and all other expenses besides travel, TW estimates the monthly budget is around $1,000 even in this location that's expensive by Mexican standards. Soon after this book came out they headed to Chiapas though, to live near Palenque, where they're getting more for their money.

The UK bloggers running Never Ending Voyage give a rundown of expenses when they move to a new area and they spent around $1,100 a month in San Pancho (near Sayulita) on the west coast of Mexico and $1,300 in Playa del Carmen.

For most expats who want to live what would be considered a middle class lifestyle in the USA, it's probably in the $1,250 to $3,000 range for most singles and $1,500 to $4,000 for couples or families. It can be done for less, and of course many people spend far more. When you compare these ranges to what it would cost for a city or suburban life in a desirable part of the USA, Canada, UK, or Australia though, this is still easily half for a lot of people.

I live in Guanajuato, a historic city in the central highlands at 6,500 feet. There are probably 300 or so expatriates here, counting the part-time ones. I detailed my expenses in this blog post (cheapestdestinationsblog.com/2014/03/06/my-life-in-guanajuato-what-it-costs-me), but the short summary is that for a family of three we easily spend less on everything added together than we did just on rent and utilities in Tampa, Florida—which averaged $2,500 per month. We own our house outright, so in a way our biggest expenses are voluntary ones: furniture and renovations, private school for our daughter ($300 per month), eating out and entertainment ($300-$500 per month), and travel within Mexico. We could certainly do it for less if we were motivated enough, but since we're spending so much less than we do in the United States, we tend to take advantage of that by eating out more, traveling locally, and having a good time.

We're in the interior though, paying prices that aren't inflated for foreigners. Even down the road in San Miguel de Allende it's going to cost more per month for rent. If you decide to settle down in a beach resort town, expect to pay a good bit more for rent, eating out, and taking a taxi. It's hard for us to ever pay more than $5 for a taxi ride, for instance, but in Ixtapa it's hard to get a cab for less than $8, and in Cancun what seems like a ridiculously short trip could cost you double or triple that.

The favored expatriate spots tend to be more expensive, just because foreign retirees with plenty of money in the bank will spend a lot more for property than any local will. Still, while many of us Mexpats think San Miguel de Allende is really pricey, rents there are still a quarter of what they are in San Francisco and restaurant meals are less than half. So it's partly a matter of perspective: those from California think it's a bargain, while someone moving down from small-town Oklahoma may not see where those cost savings are supposed to come from.

Where to Live Within Mexico

Nobody can answer the question of "Where should I live in Mexico" except you. The country is incredibly diverse geographically, from hot beaches to cool mountains, humid jungles to bone-dry deserts. The best way to figure out which place really speaks to you is to figure out your priorities and do some exploratory trips to try them out.

Here are some of the most popular places for expats in Mexico and whom they're good for:

San Miguel de Allende – Around 25 percent of the 50,000 population here is foreigners. Good for those who don't speak much Spanish, who like spring-like weather, and enjoy walkable, picture-perfect colonial streets where everything is nice and tidy. If you want a packed social schedule with a like-minded tribe that speaks English, this is your best bet.

Ajijic – On Lake Chapala near Guadalajara, another mild climate place where you seem to see as many gringos as locals. Good for those who want American-

style homes with garages and don't mind depending on a car for shopping and social life.

Puerto Vallarta region – Full of foreigners who came and forgot to leave, a tourist magnet with lots of beachfront condos and hillside homes with panoramic views. For beach bums and barflies, seafood lovers and those who want multiple flight choices out.

Sayulita region – The coast stretching north from Punta de Mita is full of surfers and bohemians, plus rich people who used to be one or the other. Wilder beaches and mellower towns than Puerto Vallarta, but with the same easy air access.

Southern Pacific Coast - There are pockets of expatriates who are aging surfers or retirees all along the Pacific coast south of Puerto Vallarta. The best-known spots are Puerto Escondido, Zihuatanejo, Trancones (near Ixtapa), and Melaque (near Barra de Navidid).

Los Cabos region – Southern Baja is a very hot place, a desert landscape by the sea. Favored by Californians with lots of money to spend, those who want luxury digs and golf courses. La Paz, two hours north of Los Cabos, and Loreto much further north are the more laid-back alternatives on the peninsula.

Mexico City – The world's second-largest city by population has a strong pull for those who want an urban lifestyle akin to other world capitals but at a lower price. Many come here for jobs and end up staying or they find multiple freelance opportunities through the strong local network. The best bet for culture vultures and foodies.

Oaxaca – A colonial city with a large indigenous population, this is Mexico's finest food destination after Mexico City. It offers a lot to explore in the surrounding region, culturally and for adventure activities.

Merida – Just a short hop from the U.S. in the Yucatan state, this flat colonial city near the coast gets quite hot part of the year, but attracts residents with a gorgeous historic center, easy beach access, and great Mayan ruins to explore nearby. Lots of retirees are spread along the nearby Gulf Coast beach towns.

Cancun and Riviera Maya – As with Puerto Vallarta, many come here on vacation and decide to buy or rent something more permanent, especially in Playa del Carmen, where there's a large expat community. Prices are not so cheap in Mexico's #1 tourist destination and it's a warped version of Mexico, but well-equipped condos and good restaurants are geared to foreign tastes.

Mazatlan – This west coast area offers some of the best

beach city values and is probably has the lowest foreigner-to-Mexican ratio of the beach resort communities in Mexico: most of the tourists are domestic. Foreigners enjoy the tight-knit community, great housing options, a colonial center, and golf.

If the idea of moving to Mexico only to be surrounded by people from your own country is not appealing, it's easy to find a place where you can do the opposite. This is a very big country with metropolitan cities and gorgeous "Magic Towns" that are more manageable spread from coast to coast. Schools are better in the former, prices are lower in the latter. Naturally, the smaller the town, the faster you'll need to learn Spanish.

Housing Costs

Housing costs in Mexico are all over the map, whether you're renting or buying. This is a vast country that's about as wide as the U.S. or Canada, so just imagine the disparity you see in your own country between different regions. As is normal, big cities cost more than medium sized ones, small ones cost less than medium ones, and rural areas can be cheaper still. What's different here is that foreign demand has a huge impact on prices. Besides all the free-spending expatriates you have driving up costs, real estate tends to get overvalued quickly if there's more demand than supply. So when evaluating a potential place to live in Mexico, it's worth asking, "How many gringos are there already and do they have far more money than me?"

My friend Michelle Pettit lives where I do, in Guanajuato. She is a mother supporting two girls on a salary earned playing in the local symphony. The rent for her house on the edge of town is $350 per month. I know several retirees in town paying $250 or less for their apartment and living on less than $1,000. You can also find foreigners living frugally in other colonial cities like Queretaro, Zacatecas, San Cristobal de las Casas, or Morelia.

San Miguel de Allende and Ajijic are more expensive than any other areas in the interior, however, and it would be tougher to get by on this amount there. Go an hour or two in any direction and both the rents and purchase prices can literally drop in half. The same is true on the coasts, where Los Cabos might as well be in California, but Loreto and Mazatlan are not so bad. The Punta de Mita area north of Puerto Vallarta, filled almost exclusively with wealthy foreigners, is in the stratosphere compared to Troncones, Puerto Escondido, or Melaque. Go further afield to beach towns where you have trouble spotting a foreigner and you'll find prices to be closer to what the local market will bear. I recently sold my two-bedroom vacation home one house back from the Gulf Coast beach in the Yucatan state for just $55,000. It was in a fishing village area where most homes are owned by locals from Merida. Prices have stayed reasonable on the modest homes there.

So it's nearly impossible for me to tell you what you're going to spend to rent or buy. You could find a nice house or apartment for $200 a month or spend $20,000 a night if you're a rock star. You can buy a whole house that comes with furniture for $40,000 in some areas, but in San Miguel de Allende that will only get you a building lot a couple miles from town. In Los Cabos it won't even get you that. Going one city over or 30 miles up the beach can make a huge difference.

In all cases though, unless you want to throw away your money, take the time to talk to people and look around, with feet on the street. If you don't speak Spanish, find a friend fast who does and can help you. If you try to find apartment listings in English, you'll probably only find short-term vacation rentals. In some areas you won't find much online period: the best source of listings where I live in Guanajuato is a quirky little local book-sized newspaper that comes out once a week. There you can easily find a two-bedroom apartment for less than $200 and it's hard to spend more than $500 for one with two bedrooms even in the best parts of town, furnished and with utilities included. You can easily rent a whole house with multiple bedrooms for less than $800 per month.

Lydia Carey and her partner Ercilia live in a nice two-bedroom place with lots of light in the desirable Roma neighborhood of Mexico City. They pay around $500 a month, but "it's a noisy location and we got a really good deal," she says. "Rents were definitely cheaper in San Miguel de Allende than in a nice part of Mexico City." Many people she knows in the area pay closer to $700 a month.

In even more desirable Condesa, it could top $1,000 for a really nice apartment. Still, this is the second-largest city in the world, so compared to London or New York it's a bargain. "We can live a New York City kind of life without the New York City kind of costs," says my friend David Lida, author of *First Stop in the New World*.

Utility Costs

Costs for electricity and gas are going to depend a lot on two factors: how hot it is where you choose to live and how big your home is. Mexico has progressive electricity costs: if you use more than a certain amount, your bill goes up to a higher rate per kilowatt hour. Some people who have a pool and lots of air conditioning spend more than they did in Texas or Arizona. On the other hand, if you live in a highlands town where the summers aren't all that hot and the winters aren't all that cold, you may find you need nothing but a couple weeks of using a space heater.

Where I live in Guanajuato, I have yet to get a water bill that has topped $15 or an electric bill that has topped $20. Propane tanks for hot water and cooking are delivered to our door for about $31, and one will typically last two or three months.

Those in a tropical climate closer to sea level will need air conditioning at least part of the year and that can drive the electric bill up past $100 even if you're careful. If you get a good sea breeze and have ceiling fans, that helps a lot in keeping the costs down.

There's a monopoly on land-line phone service and a near-monopoly on cell phone service and internet service. Remember that Mexican who's the first or second richest man in the world? He owns all three. So people in Mexico pay far more than they should to stay connected and broadband speeds lag far behind other countries with a similar per-capita GDP. I can't get more than five mbps at my house ($30 a month) no matter how much I'm willing to pay. To bump it up to 10 ($40) I'd have to be right in the center. In cities where there's a viable cable competitor there can be other options, but since most people get their TV channels by satellite, that's rather rare outside the big cities.

Pre-paid cell phone services are relatively cheap if you don't need data, with $20 a month being enough for most people. Double that though if you're on your smart phone all the time sending status updates.

Health Care

Throughout the major population centers of Mexico, health care is advanced and of good quality in the private hospitals. With the country being just a quick hop from the United States, many of the doctors have trained there and many hospitals are affiliated with or owned by U.S. ones. Doctors average a salary of $20,000 to $30,000 though instead of 15 or 20 times that and all the way down the line the expenses are lower, from administrator and nurse pay to costs for liability insurance and paperwork processing. Some retirees have found that paying all their medical expenses out of pocket in Mexico is less than their 20 percent co-pay would have been at home.

A visit to the dentist for a check-up will run you $30 to $50, a filling about the same. I got a $3,000 estimate from my Tampa dentist for a bunch of dental work to be done. I got it done in Mexico instead and it was $600. The care was better than I would have gotten too. My dentist actually sent a crown back and had them redo it when I came in for the permanent one because it wasn't as perfect as he wanted it to be. He's the one that does all the serious work too; he doesn't just pop in to supervise.

A friend of mine has a house in Merida and whenever he has a dental or medical issue, he hops on a plane from North Carolina to get it treated where his second home is located. Even with the cost of plane tickets and airport parking figured in, the total is always half or less. Some retirees have done the math on knee and back surgery and found that getting it done in Mexico would be cheaper than just their costs not covered by Medicare in the USA. For Canadians, they might pay slightly more after factoring in travel costs, but they can get it done tomorrow instead of months from now, with better service.

For each location in Mexico with some foreigners, you'll find plenty of stories like this that involve fractions. As in "I paid 1/5 what my doctor quoted me in Cleveland" or "my father's hip surgery with two days in the hospital was 1/3 of just what my out of pocket costs were going to be in L.A."

You'll often pay less than $50 for a visit to the doctor, even to a specialist, and follow-up visits are often included in that price. If you just want a quick diagnosis, you can go to a little storefront next to a pharmacy and the doctor will check you out for $3 or so.

If you're a legal resident, you can apply for the national IMSS health care program and after filling out the right paperwork and getting a physical, you're in for a few hundred dollars a year. This option can mean more waiting around at clinics and government hospitals, but if funds are tight you'll be covered in case of an accident. Many expats just pay out of pocket or buy an international insurance policy that covers catastrophe anywhere—including Mexico and the USA on visits back. That's what we are doing now, at about $3,200 a year for a family of three. If we didn't have to include the USA because of trips back for business and visiting relatives, it would be far less.

Medicare is not accepted in Mexico. Neither is the Canadian health care plan. On top of that, Canadians can lose their coverage if they're out of the country more than six months straight, so you see a lot of snowbirds going back and forth. There are some whole beach communities that are packed with Canucks in the winter and are more like ghost towns in June. Don't move to one of these if you want year-round action!

Food & Drink

Mexico isn't the cheapest place in the world to eat, but it's one of the best. You'll nearly always get a great value for the money and it's hard to point to anywhere in Latin America that even comes close in terms of variety, depth, and intensity of flavors. It's also quite filling food, so you can get stuffed without spending a whole lot. In small towns you'll find dozens of variations of things stuffed into something made out of corn flour, while in the capital and food cities like Oaxaca and Puebla, you'll find chefs that win international awards and are celebrities.

Although Lydia says it's easier to find a cheaper

apartment outside of Mexico City, she actually spends a lot less on food and drinks in the capital and "the selection of everything is far superior." She says the two of them probably spend $100 a week on groceries and another $100 eating and drinking out. My family of three averages out to about the same in Guanajuato. People who are being frugal spend far less, of course. If you shop at the markets, cook a lot at home, and don't drink wine and liquor much, you could cut the food and drink budget down to a few hundred a month without trying very hard. I often go to the market and pile up a bunch of fruit and vegetables on the scale, only to get a price of 30 pesos or so: less than $2.50. In season, it's common to see produce for less than $1 a kilo (2.2 pounds) and oranges can be two or three kilos for a dollar. A lot grows in Mexico with all the different elevations, so good, fresh produce is easy to find and cheap. Most foreigners and many locals soak the things you don't peel in iodine water though. The health inspection regulations aren't as stringent or enforced as they are in developed countries.

It would be harder to do that at a beach resort. In general, the more of a tourist town flooded by foreigners you're in, the more you're going to pay for groceries and restaurants. Where Mexican tourists congregate, you'll still find Mexican prices. Where foreigners come in daily by the planeload—Puerto Vallarta, Los Cabos, Playa del Carmen, Cancun—prices naturally rise to the level of what those short-term vacationers will pay.

Street food and "meal of the day" places are quite cheap in Mexico. If you eat where the locals eat, you can stuff yourself for $3 or $4 pretty easily, even in tourist zones if you find the local market. You can easily find a plate of tacos for under $2, tamales for less than a buck each, or a set meal with soup, meat dish, rice, and something to drink or a dessert for under $4. It's actually more expensive to try to buy groceries and make some of these things yourself than you can buy them for from vendors: they definitely don't have fat profit margins.

Nice restaurants can be a great bargain in places without a lot of foreign tourists, but can cost as much as at home otherwise. In general if you can eat where middle-class Mexicans eat and you're not in a resort area, your dinner and drinks tab will be roughly half of what it would be in a mid-sized U.S. city. Which means it'll be less than half what you normally pay in Canada, Europe, or Australia.

Beers are usually $1.50 to $2.50 in a bar or restaurant (higher for microbrews), cocktails are about a third or less than what you would pay in the U.S., a quarter of what you would pay in most of Europe. You can get a good bottle of 100% agave tequila for under $10 in a grocery store, or splurge and get the good stuff for under $20. Wine and most foreign liquor types are taxed heavily though and are expensive: both will cost a bit more than you pay now probably except for rum. Domestic wine producers don't get a break: they're taxed just as heavily as the ones from Chile or California.

Transportation

There's no train system left in Mexico except along the Copper Canyons in the west, though rumors of a new train service coming to the Yucatan Peninsula may become reality at some point. What Mexico does have is an excellent, comfortable bus system and an ever-improving domestic airline network.

The buses are not cheap, but they certainly are pleasant. The first class ones have four seats across, bathrooms, entertainment, and a snack. The luxury ones usually have three seats across, with more legroom, and have (cellular based) Wi-Fi that sometimes works for enough of a stretch to get something done online. The buses have built-in speed limiters that keep the driver from becoming a maniac on wheels. There's no charge to transport luggage underneath. Prices are generally $6 to $8 per hour of travel on the first class ones, $9 to $10 on the executive/luxury ones. So a four-hour ride will be $24 to $40 depending on class and an overnight bus of 12 hours can cost you more than $100.

The relatively high bus fares are partly due to Mexico's love affair with toll roads. A short trip of 10 or 15 miles might be $2 or more and a really long stretch, like Cancun to Merida, can be $25 to $30. If you're weighing the advantages of driving somewhere yourself, take these into account.

Flight prices are quite reasonable on the low-cost airlines

Interjet, Volaris, Tar, and Aeromar, while on Aerobus they are cheap before you add in all the fees. (They're Mexico's version of RyanAir or Spirit Air.) If you plan ahead and are flexible, you can often find a flight price that's lower than the bus would be. Aeromexico is a different story though, with prices more on par with what you would pay for a domestic flight in the U.S. They also use a hub system, so no matter where you're going you'll probably have to pass through Mexico City.

Mexico has multiple international airports, with loads of flights daily arriving at 20-odd airports. This is therefore, a great country to live in if you need to get back to see relatives regularly or just like to travel internationally a lot.

In the cities themselves, taxi prices are quite reasonable once you get out of the vacation resort areas. Where I live, the average fare is less than $3 and it never costs more than $5 to even get to the suburbs. Prices in Oaxaca are pretty similar. In most of Mexico, fares within city limits are going to run less than $10. There's seldom a meter, but outside tourist resort areas, few drivers try to overcharge you. If you land at an airport or bus station, you go to a pre-paid taxi booth where fares are regulated by zone.

City buses are always a bargain, ranging from 50 cents to a shade under a dollar. Local buses that go from one close town to the other range from one to three dollars.

Other Costs

Anything that takes advantage of cheaper labor costs will be dramatically lower than you're used to, from getting your house cleaned to getting some pants hemmed. Typical pay for a skilled handyman or a good maid is $4 to $5 an hour, for a basic laborer or house painter it's less. Much of the attraction for moving here for retirees with a bit of money saved is they can hire a cook, gardener, or maid without having to spend a whole lot. Here you can actually get things fixed too, whether it's a pair of shoes or a blender—for a few dollars.

Museum admissions and entertainment are very reasonable in Mexico, with some of the best museums in the world having ticket prices under $6. When we go to the symphony in my town it's $6 each, some other performances at a beautiful historic theater are less than that. Archaeological sites are very reasonable, seldom costing more than $8.

The things that cost more are the usual suspects: Asian electronics, clothing, and toys. There's no free trade agreement with China, plus the distribution system has more layers and competition and is less robust than in the USA.

Visas

Mexico hands out six months for the asking to many nationalities on tourist visas, so this is a great place to be a snowbird who flies south for the winter. The first time my family came for a year we stayed on tourist visas: we just took a vacation in Costa Rica in the middle and started fresh with six more months when we returned. If you want to try Mexico on for size, just waltz in and unpack for six months. This is not always going to work for families though. Most schools want your child to be a legal resident in order to accept him or her and will ask for the ID card.

Those who want to put down more permanent roots get a temporary residency permit that's good for a year. Provided you haven't run afoul of the law, renewing it should be easier than getting it in the first place. You just have to cough up the fee, which is around $275, and get your fingerprints done again. (Why, did they change?) There is a working version for those who have a job with a local employer, or the non-working version for everyone else. After you've had a temporary permit for four years, you can apply for permanent residency.

Mexico made major changes to its residency visa requirements in 2012 and it's tougher to get one now if you don't have sufficient income you can document. Officially, the requirement is $2,000 per month for the applicant and $500 for each dependent. Local embassy or consulate personnel have been known to look for more than this though to be safe. This is far more than you really need to live in Mexico, of course, but those are the rules. Embassies have known to cut retirees some slack if they can show a decent amount coming in and some savings or local real estate holdings on top.

The other major change is that now you must apply in

your home country before departure. You can't come into Mexico on a tourist visa and then decide to become a resident. You must apply at a Mexican consulate or embassy abroad and that's where you'll need to show up with notarized bank statements proving you have adequate income. Once you're approved on that step, you do the rest at the closest immigration office to where you're moving in Mexico, right after arrival. This will take several visits to the office for applications, payments, and fingerprints before you get your ID card and you're all set. You can hire someone who will be situated in a nearby office to help prepare documents for less than $100, or you can spend more to hire an attorney who will take care of everything and you just have to show up and sign.

There is no special visa/permit for retirees in Mexico and not any real incentives either for those of advanced age. You simply hang around long enough and eventually you get permanent residency.

You can get a business visa in this country by setting up your own corporation.

It's a convoluted affair because first you have to set it up through an attorney, then hire an accountant, then the accountant can petition for the president (you) to get a business visa. Once you have that, you're a legal resident who can get a driver's license and do most things besides vote. You can request your own visa extensions from then on out. As you can imagine, this process is ripe for fee padding and abuse, so ask around to find a trustworthy attorney and accountant, and be prepared to lay out a few grand in the process. But, it's a way to essentially buy your way in because you'll get a few years' grace period before anyone even looks at whether your company is earning money or not.

Downsides

Half my relatives probably expected me to be dead by now. If you watch enough TV, you're bound to think Mexico is a lawless failed state full of brutal drug gangs and murderers. You can read my broader take on this in the safety chapter toward the end of this book, but the short explanation for Mexico is that "some parts are bad, some parts are perfectly fine."

This is probably true in your own country too, or your own city. You know which neighborhoods to avoid, especially at night, and which ones pose no worries. There are parts of Mexico that are best avoided, mostly on the border with the U.S. but also some interior states where drug cartels are headquartered. Most expats who read the news and are aware of what's going on can tell you more and the U.S. State Department advisory keeps getting better and better about discerning which areas pose zero worries and which are best avoided.

In all fairness, there are valid crime worries in the bad areas. Even in good areas, the police are too few, are underpaid, and are easy targets for corruption. Parents are also notoriously lax with their teenage kids and it's easy to become a graffiti-spraying, pothead punk whose mother still thinks you're an angel. If you're a big fan of law and order and well-enforced rules, you may be better off in Canada or Switzerland—or at least in a gated community somewhere around Lake Chapala. In terms of safety though, Cancun has fewer murders than Edmonton, Canada. Puerto Escondido and San Miguel de Allende are about the same. Mexico City has less than half the number of murders per 100,000 people as Washington, D.C. and Puerto Vallarta has about six annual murders per 100,000 people compared to 51 for the port of New Orleans.

A more universal annoyance is the lack of quiet, which is going to be a problem almost anywhere in the country. Mexicans have a very high tolerance for noise and seem to feed off of it like an energy field. It's not at all unusual to hear fireworks going off at the crack of dawn or a mariachi band one house over playing full blast at two in the morning. It's also not unusual to be sitting at an outdoor restaurant or cafe and hear three stereos and a TV playing at once, all different. I once stayed at a fancy resort on the Pacific coast where the wedding band played until 4:30 a.m. and then the lawn maintenance guys starting running their mowers and trimmers at 7:00 a.m., on a Saturday morning. If I had complained, they would have looked at me like I had just walked off a spaceship. That's generally how a restaurant waiter will look at you if you ask them to turn the TV or music down. They'll be baffled.

Speaking of service, don't count on it being efficient or quick. I've never managed to get out of a rental car office in less than a half hour—if they actually have the car I reserved—and every time the clerk makes it seem like it's his or her first day on the job. Eventually, the guys doing work in your house will do a good job, but if you're in a hurry be prepared to be frustrated.

For More Information:

Mexperience (Mexperience.com)
Mexonline (Mexonline.com)
Mexico Mike (MexicoMike.com)
People's Guide to Mexico book (PeoplesGuide.com)
About.com Mexico (Gomexico.about.com)
Living Abroad in Mexico book
Association of American Schools in Mexico (Asomex.org)
Expat Blogs in Mexico (Expatsblog.com/blogs/mexico)

Chapter 13: Ecuador

Pros: Dollar economy, drinkable water in Cuenca, choice of climates, bountiful food, beaches & mountains, low fuel costs, ever-improving infrastructure, good retirement incentives, easy residency, low costs for nearly everything.
Cons: Very little press freedom, autocratic government, employment dependent on government, very high alcohol costs, difficult to start a business.

When Bill Bushnell decided to move to Cuenca, the reasoning was very simple, "I looked at where my finances were and where they were going to be. I didn't want to be living in a double-wide in the southern swamps somewhere, so I moved somewhere I could live really well on the same amount instead."

He and Leita Hulmes do live very well indeed. They own a luxury condo with a view of the mountains and the cathedral lights in the distance, a terrace space of 1,000 square feet going around two sides of their building, plus a walk–in closet bigger than most bedrooms. There's even a maid's quarters with a separate entrance. Nearly everything inside was crafted by local artisans, including the custom stone fountain and the made–to–order living room set: two loveseats, four chairs, and two tables made from heavy hardwood, plus ten pillows thrown in without asking—delivered for under $2,000. They were so happy with the work that they got custom wood desks, file cabinets, and bookcases. What they spent total is more than a double-wide in Tennessee, but far less than the average condo where they came from.

For Jeff Johnston, who has written about life in Ecuador on TheMobileWriter.com for years, climate was a big draw and the financial savings were a bonus. "If there were a part of Canada that was warm all year, I'd be living there," he says. "But I remember it was the first Friday of April we had six inches of snow. That afternoon I started looking online doing research, going country by country, Ecuador seemed to have fewer negatives. I stayed another year while I sold my house and paid off my debts. I came to Ecuador on a real estate tour looking for a reason *not* to move down, but I didn't find any."

He had a house built in Cotacachi, a sleepy town two hours north of Quito, where he met his American wife Lulie. After a few years there, they moved to Cuenca but have been renting. When the "winter" weather there gets the coldest, they like to go stay on the coast for a while instead.

The number of foreigners in Cuenca has swelled to around 4,500 at the end of 2014, which is still less than one percent of the population, but that compares to less than 500 of them when Holly and Brian Walker arrived from Saskatchewan. "There is a Gringolandia area here, but I'm on the opposite side of the city, immersed in the local neighborhood," she says. "I'm shocked at how many foreigners I see when I visit the center."

Holly has seen a dark side of this influx, with some "economic refugees" being bitter that they couldn't afford to live well on what they have in their country of birth. "Some don't even bother trying to learn Spanish and fit in. They get mad when they can't communicate in a store or restaurant in English."

Besides the low costs, Cuenca has become so popular because of the climate. While Ecuador's very name means "equator," its third largest city sits at an elevation of more than 8,000 feet (2,500 meters), so it has one of those cool spring climates with no mosquitoes that so many retirees crave. The daytime highs are around 70F most of the year, the lows around 50F. Pack a rain jacket and a windbreaker and you're set. (You will need the rain jacket a fair bit though: if you want year-round sun there are better choices.) Holly likes to take advantage of the great hiking opportunities nearby, especially in gorgeous Las Cajas national park.

After Cuenca, the most popular spots for expatriates are Quito, Vilcabamba, Cotacachi (near Otavalo), and beach towns on the coast. Vilcabamba, in a valley where many locals claim to be more than 100 years old, the elevation is around 5,000 feet. Temperatures average between 65F and 81F all year long and it gets more sun than Cuenca.

Can you name one beach in Ecuador? Most people can't, but there are some nice ones on this Pacific coast near the equator, with strikingly low prices compared to other coastal resort cities. Plus, thanks to ever-improving road systems, you can now get to them much faster from Quito (a few hours) or Manta (less than an hour).

What does it cost to live in Ecuador? There's no easy way to answer this because it depends a lot on how you live. Bryan and Dena Haines, who run the Gringos Abroad blog, live on a budget of $1,000 a month for a family of three, not counting travel, and live what they consider a pretty good life in Cuenca. There are other people in the city who pay twice that much for one, living in a lavish apartment, driving a car, and eating at nice restaurants for dinner several times a week. Even at that level though, they're living a far better life than they could for twice as much in the USA, Canada, England, or Australia.

Holly and Brian Walker moved to Cuenca after spending a lot of time in the country because of Brian's job as a helicopter mechanic. "It didn't really matter where we lived because his job was and still is international," Holly explains. "He's six weeks on, six weeks off in various locations. But we really liked Cuenca after visiting a few times. Eventually we went back and sold our house and most of what we had except 13 suitcases between the 4 of us." Their son was older, but their daughter had just turned 16 when they moved down in 2008. She took classes online through the Canadian school system, while also going to a local Ecuadoran school and quickly becoming fluent in Spanish. "She was still falling behind though," Holly says, so her daughter eventually went back to Canada and went back to a boarding school to finish and graduate. "The local schools have gotten a lot better since then," she adds. "In Quito there are also several international schools with high standards."

The government has put a lot of money and effort into improving Ecuador's schools the past few years and has roped in some American tech companies to help out with getting laptops into a lot of them. So if you have children of school age to consider, get the current lowdown from expat families living in the country before assuming you won't be able to find a decent school for them. You should probably assume they will be learning in Spanish though, unless you're in Quito or Guayaquil.

Otherwise, family life is pretty easy here. You can find a big house or apartment to rent without much effort, feeding a family is cheap, and you can get domestic help for a few dollars an hour.

Housing Costs

Ecuador is not the rock-bottom buying bargain it was a decade or two for real estate, partly from more foreigners arriving, but more from an improving economy and the return of lots of Ecuadorans who made a pile of money abroad. It's still a great value to rent or buy here though, with prices half or less (sometimes well less) than what they would be in a comparable city or town in the USA or Canada.

Susan Schenk, author of *Expats in Cuenca, Ecuador: The Magic & The Madness* lived in California for 23 years before moving to Ecuador at age 54. "In San Diego I was spending $4,000 to $5,000 a month," she says. "It was impossible to save as much as I do here on $1400 a month!" She bought a penthouse condo for a small fraction of what a comparable one would cost where she came from and since she owns it outright, her housing cost is just the HOA fee of $170 per month, plus $80 in utilities.

"It would rent for $900 due to the size and view and location," she estimates. "But most of my friends rent smaller places and pay around $300 to $600 a month."

"The best deals are found when you take about 6 to 12 months looking for your ideal place. A couple down the street rents a huge house for $300 a month, but the agreement was that they would slowly fix a few things."

Jeff Johnston was paying $600 a month for rent in Cuenca, "which is pricey for the area," he says. "But we've had a home of more than 2,000 square feet, four bedrooms plus an attic. Most urban houses in Ecuador don't have a back yard but ours did. It's on a double lot, by a park next to a river."

Holly Walker and her husband rent a three-bedroom home of about the same size for $550, "That felt quite expensive at the time when we first moved in four years ago," she says. "But it's a beautiful house, with some personality to it." Many singles and couples are renting apartments in Cuenca for $350 to $450 per month. Bryan and Dena pay $280 a month, but they've had the place for years. It would be hard to get the same deal now.

Rental prices in Quito start around $250 for a small one-bedroom apartment in a decent area to $1,000 for a modern three-bedroom place in the best neighborhoods. The average take-home salary in Quito is less than $500 per month though, and minimum wage is $350 per month, so it's hard for landlords to charge four-figure rents unless they are catering to the local elite or the foreign business community.

In Vilcabamba you can find a place to flop while you're looking around for $100 to $200 a month. For a real apartment or house with some size, figure on $300 to $800. Cotacachi is even cheaper, with most apartments and homes in the range of $150 to $650 per month.

Purchase prices in Ecuador can be too cheap to believe in the countryside, with many homes for sale at less than $50,000. Prices have gotten rather standardized in urban areas where condos are more prevalent. Most Cuenca houses fall in the range of $60 to $80 per square foot if in good condition. Condos usually cost more because they're better equipped. You can get a new luxury condominium in a secure building with 24-hour security and parking for roughly $90 to $130 per square foot, finished to your specifications if it's a new build or often sold furnished if not. Expect to pay less for a more modest one. In Quito, condos can actually be less than this due to more abundant competition, as in $75 to $105 per square foot instead.

In and around Vilcabamba, you can still find building lots for $3 to $10 per square foot (under $100 per square meter). Most houses—even the largest ones—are listed for less than $200,000.

This is one of the best countries in the world to build your dream home on the ocean or find a nice condo with a view for a good price. Most of the buyers of beach lots and condominiums on this coast are Ecuadorans, not foreigners, which has kept a lid on prices. You can still find a big beachfront building lot for less than $50,000 or a condo in a great area, facing the Pacific Ocean, for well under $100,000.

Property taxes are quite low throughout Ecuador. Most

people pay less than $100 per year and to top $200 you've have to have a huge mansion. If you're more than 65 years old, your rate is halved.

If you're going to buy something it's better to rent for a while and really get a feel for the different areas. "I always advise my clients who are considering moving to Cuenca to rent first for short term or one year, to make sure this is the right place for them. This way they are familiar with the different neighborhoods and they will make a better choice buying real estate," says Maribel Crespo, a local agent. Some make a hasty *House Hunters International* kind of move and then end up leaving a year or two later, put off by a couple months of rain, the exhaust fumes, or the hurdles in getting past a basic vocabulary in Spanish.

"When buying, always look around you and assume that what you see is what you get," says David Morrill, who has sold a lot of property in Cuenca over a period of more than a decade. "Don't think that things will improve to be more like you want them."

One of the false sells of moving abroad articles, David adds, is that a certain city or a big house with a maid will make you happy. "If you are just coming to stretch your savings and don't appreciate the culture or the people, you probably won't be happy. Some spend a lot of time and money learning that lesson the hard way."

"I try to always remember I'm a guest here in this country," said Leita Hulmes when I visited, as she looked out her window at some chickens pecking at the ground in the yard of the house next door. "There's a lot to appreciate if you don't focus on the negatives and learning the language helps a lot too. My comfort level increased a lot after I knew what was going on around me."

Health Care Costs

Getting sick in Ecuador is not going to kill your bank account. Modern facilities and well-trained doctors are available at costs that are a fraction of what they would be in developed countries. Going to see a specialist will likely cost you less than $50 and here a couple nights in the hospital will cost you less than a couple nights at a luxury hotel. Health insurance costs are a good indication of the differences: a policy for a 60-year-old male that would be more than $1,000 a month in the USA will be around $70 in Ecuador. The majority of expatriates don't even bother with insurance. They know that whatever comes up, they can easily foot the bill with their savings.

There are close to 20 hospitals and outpatient medical facilities in Cuenca, most staffed by at least a few doctors who speak English well. Anyone 60 and over has access to the public health care system at a discount, with no co–pays, no pre–existing conditions denials, and a monthly premium under $100. Private care is a terrific bargain compared to what most U.S. citizens pay, with many doctors giving out their cell phone number and making house calls for $25 to $40.

Options are even better in Quito, where first class medical facilities treat government officials, business tycoons, and a large population of international business executives and their families. It's a similar story in business-oriented Guayaquil.

In the smaller towns there won't be as many choices, but you can't beat the prices: an office visit to a doctor may be less than your co-pay was before you moved: $20. If you have to come back to the doctor for a follow-up, there's usually no additional charge. The local newspaper *El Comercio* listed top-range prices to see a doctor in Ecuador in June of 2014 and the very highest one was $80, for a neurologist at a top hospital. Interestingly, they also listed the number of specialists in the country and the numbers were surprisingly high: 259 neurologists, 824 cardiologists, and 1996 gynecologists.

Prices to get dental work done are generally 15-25 percent of what they would cost in the USA or Canada, and for serious procedures it can be more like 10 percent. Stories abound of travelers getting an estimate of $20,000 at home and having the work done in Quito or Cuenca for $2,000 to $3,000. The actual dentist will do more of the work too, spending time with you to get it right instead of shuttling between six patients in adjoining rooms. Back surgery that would typically cost six figures in the U.S. will be $10,000 in Quito.

The same savings show up in most drugs too, which you

can usually buy at a pharmacist with no prescription. Retirees that were spending a few hundred dollars a month on medications in the USA often find their monthly bill in Ecuador reduced to less than $40.

Legal residents can tap into the public health care system in Ecuador if between the ages of 18 and 60. Some foreigners join this as a back-up plan, paying the $70 or so a month in case of catastrophe, but visiting the doctor of their choice for routine care.

Food & Drink

Imported goods are expensive in Ecuador. Anything alcoholic besides local beer and (bad) rum is insanely expensive—as in more than double what you probably pay now in Canada or England because of taxes that are more than 100 percent. The president is reportedly a tea-totaler and apparently wants everyone else to be too unless they're rich. When I was in a Quito supermarket I saw Stella Artois and Negra Modela beers for $15 a six-pack. A bottle of Bacardi white rum was $40. "If you're flying to Ecuador and you know someone here, they'll definitely want you to bring as many bottles in from duty free as you can," Jeff says.

Otherwise, prices for most things you consume are a bargain. You can go to the market and buy a big sack of fruit and vegetables for $10. Your haul will be a great variety too. With so many elevations here and volcanic soil, they can grow most anything, from bananas, sugar cane, and mangoes on the tropical coast to coffee, apples, and berries in the highlands. It's very common to see fruit and vegetables selling for 50 cents a kilo.

Traditional food in Ecuador is not the healthiest stuff in the world: think lots of fried things with corn in them and thick stews and soups with cheese. It's pretty tasty though and if you're not on a diet (or are doing a lot of hiking), you can eat a set meal with several courses for three dollars or buy street food for a dollar or less. If you're cooking yourself, you can feast on food that's very fresh and bargain priced, including good meat and cheese. "I spend about $100 a month on groceries, plus I eat out a few times a week for an average of $5 a meal," says Susan.

If you don't order wine, high-end restaurants are a

bargain. Outside of the trendy parts of Quito and the five-star hotels, it's hard to spend more than $25 each on a white tablecloth meal with good service. I was actually taking pictures of menu prices and posting them on social media last time I was there to show people what an unbelievable value some restaurants are.

Transportation Costs

For now, taxis in Ecuador are some of the cheapest in the world, with most rides in the cities coming in between $1.75 and $6. Assume they'll double a few years down the line though when subsidies are reduced. For now, a local bus ride is 25 cents, a long-distance bus ride topping out at around $1 an hour of travel. As I write this, gasoline is around $2 a gallon, while diesel is barely half that, so transportation is cheap. This is not going to last forever though.

The official tourism people like to talk about their new roads with the promise you can "eat breakfast in the Andes and have dinner in the Amazon." And that's if you don't fly. When I went from the capital to a remote cloud forest last time, it took less than three hours. When you do need to fly, it won't cost you much. Even if you walk up to the airport counter the day of departure, a flight from Cuenca to Quito is under $80 one-way. Those on a retirement visa get discounted rates too, even when flying internationally.

Cars are imported and generally cost more than they would in the USA, but in line with what they cost in Europe. Financing is available if you have local roots and a bank account, but interest rates are high. Toll roads are not common. Many expatriates do without a car, especially if they live in the center of a city, but those further out often end up getting one for shopping and excursions.

In 2013 a major infrastructure project was completed and the train line from Guayaquil to Quito opened up again for the first time in decades. This is more of a tourism route than a transit one to go the whole way, but you can get from Quito to quite a few nearby places by train.

Domestic air connections are good, with two airlines competing on most routes. Apart from the Galapagos, one-way fares are usually less than $100. Note that there are no direct international flights to Cuenca, however, even from neighboring countries. You must go through Quito or Guayaquil.

Other Costs

One of the main reasons Ecuador converted to a US dollar-based economy in the year 2000 was to tame inflation. It has worked, bigtime. "We don't even know what inflation looks like anymore," said one hotel owner to me on a visit to Quito in late 2013. "The only things that go up are imports and whatever the government decides to raise taxes on."

As I write this, fuel is subsidized and quite cheap, which impacts the cost of utilities. The subsidies are scheduled to start rolling back in 2016 though and prices for automobile fuel and propane for cooking will rise. Since Ecuador has a lot of hydroelectric power, many people are in the process of switching to electric stoves to get ready.

The people I spoke to living in Ecuador are generally paying very little for utilities right now. Water bills average $6 to $10 per month and you can drink the tap water in Cuenca. Electricity runs between $30 and $60 per month. Propane is cheap for now, at $2.50 for a canister that will last a month or two. One resident of Cuenca told me she pays around $40 a month for gas, water, electricity, and her cell phone minutes. She splurges on the fastest possible internet service though at $80 a month, and the most loaded cable TV package available for $85.

A men's haircut is easy to find for $3-$4, a massage can be lined up for $15 or less. Many women go for a regular manicure for $8 and a facial for $20-$25. A local SIM card for your phone is $4, and roses are 25 cents each. Museums cost $1-$3.50 to enter. Many cultural performances are free and those that aren't seldom cost more than $10 for a ticket. Bootleg DVDs are commonly three for $5.

"Somehow I live on $800 a month (average) and save the rest of my pension of $1400," says Susan Schenck. She supplements that for travel money by doing workshops and classes on book marketing, raw food, and health/weight loss.

Visas in Ecuador

You can visit Ecuador for 90 days on a tourist visa and in

theory it's possible to extend that a few more months after arrival. Becoming a legal resident is the usual baffling bureaucracy encountered nearly anywhere, which can be eased considerably by paying $400-$1,000 to a lawyer. Qualifying is straightforward though, especially if you're buying property and/or are of retirement age and Jeff says you actually get faster service these days if you're not using an attorney.

Once you're in, if you're 65 or older you get a dazzling array of discounts on travel and entertainment, including 50% off all national and international airfare, 50% off all cultural and recreational events, and 50% off some utility charges. Foreign retirees pay lower taxes all around, though you have to keep records and apply for a refund on sales taxes.

There are restrictions on the residency visa. For the first two years you need to spend all but 90 days of each year in Ecuador or you can lose your status. After that, you can't leave the country and stay out for more than 18 consecutive months.

"Once you get a residency visa, you don't have to renew it if you own a house worth more than $25,000," explains Jeff. You can also buy your way to residency by getting a certificate of deposit at an Ecuadoran bank, but then you have to renew. The easiest option if you're old enough is to get a retirement visa. You only have to show $800 a month in verified income plus $100 for each dependent. Probably 98 percent of the people who apply get it. These days it takes a month or two, which is not bad. When I first moved down it took close to a year."

Downsides

Ecuador is stable now, but many feel that President Correa is turning into a dictator who doesn't deal well with criticism. The opposition press has been crushed and the country is rated the second-worst in the Americas for press freedom, right behind Cuba. Two of the people I interviewed for this book are moving on, something I didn't run into much with the other locations. Holly and her husband are exploring their options, while Jeff and his wife recently bought land in a libertarian development in Chile, where they'll move to after they sell their Cotacachi home.

"We've decided to move to where politics are a bit more stable, the government abides by the rule of law, and the entrepreneurial spirit is alive and well. Ecuador makes it so difficult to start a business, and so onerous to have employees that this country of enormous resources is stagnating. Its recent improvements have all come due to infrastructure projects. When the country has improved its roads, built all of its hydroelectric dams, and created all its new ports, there's going to be a lot of unemployment. So we're moving on, even though it's more expensive to live in Chile. We've enjoyed our four years and two months here in Cuenca though, and we'll miss it."

Virtually everyone complains about the Ecuadorans' driving habits. Holly says, "You take your life into your hands every time you get behind the wheel. They are incredibly aggressive drivers. I used to stop for pedestrians, but then people would just drive around me, which was even more dangerous."

I almost got hit twice while trying to walk in central Cuenca and Jeff says, "If a pedestrian is determined to have caused an accident, which is easy since they have no rights, the walker can be liable and sent to jail." The very best time to be in Quito is on Sunday, when many of the streets in the historic center are closed to traffic.

"Get used to less competitive customer service," says Susan. "Here, for Ecuadorians, it's not about money, but leisure time with family. So don't expect things to be as competitive as they are in the USA, consumer capital of the world."

Lastly, the country has a habit of talking up their jungle wildlife in the Amazon Basin, but then putting oil interests first every time. After telling the world that they wouldn't put off drilling in the pristine Yasuni National Park unless the international community gave them $3.6 billion to save it, the president has canceled a national referendum on the measure and is moving ahead with oil drilling in what the tourism brochures call "one of the most biologically diverse areas in the world."

For More Information:

Gringo Tree message board (Gringotree.com)
Expats in Cuenca: The Magic and the Madness book
Expats in Ecuador: Life in Cuenca Kindle book
GringosAbroad.com
A subscription to *International Living*—they cover this country almost every month.

Chapter 14: Panama

Pros: Top retiree benefits, easy visa process, great air connections, business-friendly, good banking system, good health care, beaches, nature activities, dynamic economy.
Cons: Pricey capital city, some crime, hot and humid in most areas, boring cuisine, inconsistent service.

Kris and Joel Cunningham were living in Sarasota, Florida, the kind of place many northern Americans dream of retiring to. They had no idea how they were going to make it on their earnings, however, when retired. They were paying $1,200 per month on their mortgage and taxes. Selling it and renting wouldn't help much. "The house next to us, similar to what we have now in Panama, was renting for $1,500 per month," she adds. They're not paying anything close to that though: their rent in the city of David is $385 instead. With lower utility bills, food bills, and medical costs, they are very happy with their new life and feel much more confident about their finances.

Panama perpetually comes out on top as the world's best retirement haven in publications that write about this subject every month. Most of those publications have editors who live there or business interests where they have a stake, so take that with some skepticism. No matter how you look at it though, it's a winner in almost every category except costs—and those go down drastically if you don't settle down in the capital city. Its *pensionada* program for retirees is superb, with a long list of perks and discounts I'll get to later in this chapter. The threshold to earn those perks is low from a proven income standpoint and with the permit in your hand you get lower prices on services that are already cheaper than your home country's to start with.

Panama is incredibly welcoming to foreigners. It doesn't tax money earned outside the country and a lot of items (including booze) have some of the lowest taxes in the world. This country also has one of the best banking systems in the world, a stable political situation, a good business climate, and uses U.S. dollars as its currency. Recession? They were having none of that. Try 5-10 percent annual growth while the U.S. and Europe were reeling.

The health care system in Panama is excellent, to the point where it is a medical services destination for many foreigners who don't live here. Many fly in to get surgery, have major dental work done, or spend time in a hospital for one-quarter the price they'd have to pay otherwise.

You'll make fewer sacrifices here than you will pretty much anywhere in Latin America if you want what you had at home. There's fast internet, good prices on electronics, reliable electricity, a competitive cell phone climate, and a lot of the shops and services you're used to. Of course you also get some of the same side effects of all that: consumerism, strip malls, and a culture that revolves around the automobile.

You're never too far from a beach here though when you want to go unwind. Here you could swim in the Caribbean in the morning, hop in a car, and swim in the Pacific by lunchtime. This is also a paradise for bird watching, nature exploration, and adventure: Costa Rica without the crowds and at lower rates.

As I said though, you almost have to take Panama City out of the mix if you're on a budget, the same way you need to take Ambergris Caye out of consideration for Belize if you're on a budget. It's hard to get a nice apartment in a good area for under $1,000 a month now and with the city being decidedly unfriendly to pedestrians in most areas, you spend a lot on getting around.

Panama has a high diversity of places to choose from where there is already a sizable foreign population in place. Here are the main ones, but there are plenty of other beach and mountain towns to check out.

Panama City – The closest thing you'll get to Miami after heading south (good and bad).

Coronada – A beach resort town an hour south of the capital.

Valle de Anton - Just 120 kilometers from the capital, this highland interior area has cool evenings, hot springs for soaking, and relaxed living.

David – The second-largest city, but a bit higher in altitude and not as congested.

Boquete – A popular highland area of flowers, coffee, adventure activities, and cool air.

Bocas del Toro – A string of islands popular with tropical paradise seekers, rebels, and outcasts.

Housing Costs

If you pull up apartment prices online in Panama City, you may think I'm out of my mind to even include this country in a book about living abroad for less. Most of these $5,000 a month penthouses in high-rise buildings on the water are not aimed at you though. Their target market is people like corporate VPs working for international companies, or escaping Venezuelans, Brazilians and Argentines making banking deposit trips. Yes, there are probably a few drug kingpins and tax haven renegades here and there too. For many "nomad capitalists" who roam the globe looking for business opportunities, Panama is seen as nirvana. It has low taxes, limited regulations, a strong banking system, and little bureaucracy. So there are a lot of takers for expensive condos, whether renting or buying.

That's just one side of the city, however. After all, $1,000 to $1,250 a month for a local is a good white-collar salary, so they're certainly not paying $2,000 per month for an apartment. They are living in less ritzy neighborhoods outside the central business district, with more than two people in a big apartment or house with multiple bedrooms. If you live on the outskirts of the capital it's not difficult to find a nice apartment for less than $800. That may still seem like a lot, but the closest comparison to Panama City is Miami, where costs are easily double.

Once you get beyond the capital and the prime beach developments, prices drop drastically. Kris and Joel Cunningham pay $385 per month for a house in a nice middle class neighborhood on the edge of David, Panama and they love it. "One agent's name kept coming up when we were doing research, so we booked an appointment with him to go see some houses," Kris says. The very first house he showed us was ideal. We took it right away and didn't even look at the others. We have woods and a river behind us, plus there's only one way into the neighborhood so it feels really safe. We're surrounded by local professionals who are just lovely people."

They have been living on her husband's social security payment and have a little savings from selling their house in Florida. Kris was about to start receiving her own social security payment when I talked to her, which will double their income and enable them to meet the income requirements for the pensionada program: $1,000 for one person plus $250 for each dependent. "It's already so cheap though, I feel kind of guilty getting all those extra discounts," she says.

A cursory look online at housing rental prices around Panama turned up plenty of affordable places. I found a two-bedroom house a couple blocks from the ocean in a beach community for $500, an over-water bungalow in Bocas del Toro for $700, and an apartment with a panoramic view on an island for $400, all utilities included. I also found five apartments or houses for rent in Boquete for $500 per month or less, some including utilities.

Former Texan Richard Kongable lived in a few places in Panama before settling in a rural area near Volcan, on the side of a mountain. "I tried a few other places in Panama before settling here," he says. "I like that I never need heat, I never need air conditioning, and there's always a gentle breeze. I'm on the edge of a valley, with a volcano on the left and two rivers. I can see islands in the ocean even though it's an hour and 20 minutes away."

Richard rented his house for years for $300 a month and thought he was going to have to leave eventually when the American owner put it up for sale. Instead the owner fell into health problems and needed to sell in a hurry, so with no buyers in sight Richard got the 1,600 square foot house for half price: $25,000.

Prices in prime areas keep creeping up though as Panama's economy continues to grow at a rapid pace. "A lot of what you read in *International Living* and publications like that is out of date on prices," says Richard, "or they're only showing you the outlier situations to get you hooked on coming to a conference. In most cases you're only going to find a terrific deal by being here a while and looking around. In places like Boquete there are a lot of unadvertised rentals from expatriates who are returning home or moving and don't want to leave their house empty. You're only going to find out about these by word of mouth."

If you are looking to buy in Boquete, prices are creeping up again after hitting a wall and dropping during the housing crisis in the U.S. Most fall in the $70 to $100 per square foot range, though land outside of town can make building your dream house quite reasonable.

Other areas appeal to wealthy retirees looking to build their dream home for less. This is especially true of the Azuero Peninsula region on the Pacific coast. Avoid that area if you're on a budget or plan to spend a long time searching.

One big advantage of Panama is that this is one of the few Latin American countries with a banking system that will extend mortgages to foreigners. It takes some patience, but you can finance a home with as little as 20 percent down and interest rates are not as high as in most of the region. Also, many developers have set up financing for new projects and they will have an interest in guiding you through the process.

Health Care

Almost to a person, expatriates in Panama rave about the health care they receive. From the time they book an appointment (or get a same-day house call) to the invoice they receive after a hospital stay, it's all a pleasant surprise, especially for Americans. You get the good parts of the American system—well-trained doctors who speak English, the latest equipment, and gleaming clean hospitals—but without the for-profit incentives and layers of insurance executive riches that come with all that up north. The four largest hospitals in the capital are all affiliated with major U.S. ones, including the Punta Pacifica one with John Hopkins. By most measures, it's the best hospital in Latin America.

To give you an idea of what prices are like, here are some typical ones:

General doctor visit - $20 (not a co-pay, the whole cost)
Specialist visit - $20
Doctor house call - $45
Dental cleaning - $35
Tooth filling - $50

Porcelain crown - $350
Hip replacement surgery - $12,500 total

You will get far better care than you're used to with all this as well. The doctor or dentist won't be in a rush to move on to the next patient. There will be more nurses around. You won't have to worry they're going to charge you $5 for a Q-tip or an Advil. People will actually take the time to explain what's going on and make sure you understand.

You don't need a prescription for medicines you can't abuse and in most cases those medicines will be a quarter or fifth the retail cost in your home country. Many expats in Panama joke that the price they pay out of pocket for medicine in Panama is less than what their insurance co-pay was before.

Naturally if you're moving from a country with a more civilized single-payer health care system, like Canada and the UK, you won't save as much on health care. You will get far better service though, faster, and with the doctor or dentist of your choice. There's no waiting list or mandated delay.

There is a national health care program legal residents can tap into, but it's too low-grade for most. It entails longer waits at public clinics and few choices. Another alternative is a private insurance program, especially good to avoid catastrophic care charges, or a discount program where you pay a monthly fee to get deep discounts across the board when you need care. Those retirees in the pensionada program also receive discounts automatically of 10-20 percent by showing their ID card.

Keep in mind, however, that the major hospitals are in the two largest cities: Panama City and David. Boquete and Bocas del Toro are not too far from the latter, but if you're on a beach in the far north, or in a hut on the San Blas Islands, you may have to travel quite far for non-routine care.

Food & Drink

You can drink the water from the tap in most of Panama, so that means you're less likely to get sick from the food here than you are in many other developing countries. Unfortunately, the food is definitely not the reason you're going to move here. While there are good gourmet restaurants at the high end, especially in areas with lots of expats, the everyday cuisine is boring and uninspired. Expect lots of fried plantains, beans, rice, and meat stews.

If you cook for yourself though and have more imagination, you'll find a bounty of fresh ingredients to work with. The varied altitude in Panama means you can buy both tropical fruit and mountain berries, coconuts and fresh coffee. In the Chiriqui province of David and Boquete, you'll be very close to where much of the country's fresh food is produced. I saw people beside the road there selling ten-kilo bags of mixed fruit and vegetables for $5 and it would take you quite a while to get through them all without a big family.

According to Numbeo.com, costs for food in Panama are about 60% that of New York City for groceries and about 40% for restaurants. This is highly skewed by Panama City prices though and they'll be far less in other areas. Expect to pay $3-$5 for a meal of the day in a place where working class locals eat, up to $30 for a nice non-hotel restaurant.

Kris Cunningham says she has been pleasantly surprised by low costs in Panama, particularly groceries. "Food is definitely a great deal, especially fruit and vegetables. If you spend $20 on those it will be more than you can carry. We paid two or three times more for almost everything at home, including meat and fish. If you buy what the locals buy and cook, living here is very cheap."

You won't pay much to have a drink with your meal. This is one of the few countries in the world where alcohol isn't taxed at a higher rate than other items and since taxes are so low here anyway, prices in Panama's liquor stores and supermarkets beat out the lowest duty-free prices you'll see anywhere in the world. This is one of the few countries where I've seen Chilean and Argentine wine selling for less than I could buy it on sale in a low-tax USA state and liquor prices are the lowest I've seen anywhere on the planet in my travels.

Transportation

Maybe you can blame it on the USA's long domination of the country, but this is not an easy place to get by without a car. The good news is, it has the best roads in Central America. When there are bus connections available between cities, they're not very expensive. The two-hour trip from Panama City to El Valle is less than $5 and an express bus from the capital all the way to David is less than $20.

The big news as this book went to press was the new metro in the capital. It was finished on time, roughly within budget, and is working well. Only one line is open now, but more are on the way. That one line has already made life easier though. As Chris from the Panama for Real blog (panamaforreal.com) said in his post-opening review, "It took exactly 23 minutes to get from one end of the route to the other. That's fast, man, and is a serious game changer for Panama City. You can't get anywhere in Panama City in 23 minutes by car." The fare is a very reasonable 35 cents.

There is one train in the country, plying the route between Panama City and Colon along the Panama Canal. It's not of much use for residents except to hit the duty free mall.

Domestic flights are relatively inexpensive, with the one from the capital to David being $120. Because Copa Air is based here, you also have lots of options for getting to other countries.

The smoke-belching city buses have been getting phased out, replaced by more efficient ones. Taxis in the capital are supposed to run $1-$4 depending on distance in the central area, but you'll have to ask about the fare before taking off if you don't see a meter in use. You can rent a taxi and driver for $8-$10 per hour.

Other Costs

The pensionada program for retirement age foreigners in Panama is in most respects the best in the world. Foreigners who can show an income of $1,000 per month (or buy property worth $100,000 or more) get the same discounts and deals that locals get. "I paid back the visa processing costs the first year just from airline discounts," says Richard. Pensionadas get the following lost list of (sometimes unbelievably generous) discounts:

- 50% recreation and entertainment activities, such as

movies, theaters, and sports and other public productions
- 30% off inter-city buses, trains (well, the train route), and ferry boats
- 25% off flights of national and foreign Airlines
- 50% off the rack rate of hotels from Monday to Thursday, 30% on Friday, Saturday and Sunday
- 25% discount of food in licensed sit-down restaurants
- 15% off in fast food establishments
- 15% off the total cost for services of hospitals, dentists, and private clinics, plus
- 20% off doctor consultations
- 10% discount in pharmacies for prescription medicines
- 25% discount in monthly electrical consumption up to 600 kilowatts
- 25% discount in the water bill

The Cunninghams pay $59 a month for a bundled internet and cable TV package, $10-$20 a month on their prepaid cell phones, and around $45 a month on electricity, though if they ran the air conditioning constantly that could triple. Richard Kongable estimates that he spends about $160 a month on utilities, including a satellite TV package with lots of English channels, and spends $300 a month on a son's private school. "All in, counting car and gas expenses, the three of us probably spend around $1,700 a month," he says.

Visas for Panama

Panama is one of the easiest countries in the world to get a retirement or residency visa and it's a big reason the destination is so popular with expatriates. You only need an income of $1,000 a month to qualify, plus $100 for each dependent. You get all those juicy discounts outlined in the previous section and there is no minimum or maximum age requirement. If your pension/social security is low and you want an easy path to residency, it's hard to beat Panama.

In just three months, you can convert a temporary residency visa to a permanent one, a sharp contrast to many countries where it takes years. In addition, foreign residents can import up to $10,000 worth of goods tax-free.

If for some reason this option is not a good match, you

can still apply for a permanent residency visa from the get-go, with other options to qualify. You have to deposit $5,000 in a local bank, but that's a low hurdle for most people. Then you have three options. The most complicated way to gain residency is to set up a local corporation for a business. Another way is to have a formal offer of employment from a Panamanian company—which generally requires a skill a local does not possess. The easiest way is to buy a piece of property. It doesn't matter if this is a building lot you never manage to build on or the cheapest condo you can possible find. When you're a property owner, you're on the easy track to residency.

There's even a cheap way around this low bar. The *Live and Invest Overseas* group was offering a workaround through one of their partners in mid-2014 whereby you could invest $17,000 in a teak farm plot and then with that small investment you're a property owner. Done right, this could even be accomplished through a self-directed IRA. Sure, there's some risk involved if the price of teak goes down before the trees mature, but the world is not exactly awash in hardwoods that aren't in endangered forests so it looks like a low-risk investment.

If you're interested in living here, do some poking around to find the visa/permit that is right for you. There are others where you can buy your way in by investing $300,000 to become a full citizen, a business investor visa that requires an investment of $160,000 and employing locals, or an agricultural visa that requires an investment of $60,000 for a six-year residency permit.

The Downsides

It's not all rosy in Panama, no matter how many gushing articles you read about it. This is still the developing world, with a lot of the same problems you'll find elsewhere in Latin America in terms of public services, pollution, traffic, garbage, and inefficiency. There are still corruption cases exposed on a regular basis, despite a muzzled media that has to operate under really strict libel laws.

Unless you love stifling tropical heat and insects, you may not like the majority of the country that sits near sea level. At a higher elevation, you've got the opposite problem. Some think Boquete in the highlands is perfect. Others think it's way too cold. Again, go at the worst time of year to judge for yourself.

While Panama City has a lot going for it in terms of business opportunities and nightlife, they're just now opening a subway to deal with the horrendous traffic and the taxi drivers here may just be the most unpleasant you'll ride with anywhere. You can find good dining spots in the capital and Boquete, but overall the Panamanian diet is pretty bland. It definitely doesn't take advantage of the bounty of the land and sea.

There's no lovely historic city meant for strolling here, nothing close to Antigua, San Miguel de Allende, Salta, or Arequipa. The Spanish treated the country as a transit point. Then the United States had a lot of influence in Panama while administering the canal and the banana plantations. That means this is a country better suited to cars than sneakers.

Overall, Panama has more pluses than minuses. Its easy air connections, light taxes, good health care, good banking system, easy visa process, and dollar economy make it a no-brainer for many retirees who don't want to deal with a tougher adjustment in a place like Guatemala or Ecuador.

For More Information

Panama for Real (Panamaforreal.com)
PanamaInfo.com
Expat Exchange Panama (Expatexchange.com/panama/liveinpanama)
Transitions Abroad – Panama
Boquete Living Forum (Boquete.ning.com/forum)
The Panama News (thepanamanews.com)
Best Places to Retire – Panama

Chapter 15: Thailand

Pros: Tropical weather, sunshine, great food, fun atmosphere, good infrastructure, fast internet, good social structure, good air connections, reasonable prices, good public transportation in the capital.
Cons: difficult visa situation, rising prices, political instability, corruption, very hot, tropical diseases/insects

I could start off telling you about all the incredible sights, beautiful beaches, and cultural attractions of Thailand. But perhaps this rundown of the most Instagrammed places of 2013 says enough:

1. New York City, USA
2. Bangkok, Thailand
3. Los Angeles, USA
4. London, UK
5. São Paulo, Brazil

Yes, Bangkok beat out all but New York, including Paris, Florence, Las Vegas, and Orlando. If Pinterest did a rundown on the beaches that showed up the most, I'd imagine Thailand would rank quite highly there as well. I'm not saying it's paradise, but for a lot of people it sure feels like it.

Bangkok was an expatriate hotspot before anyone else even knew there was such a thing. Men especially, lured by beautiful women that didn't have a lot of sexual inhibitions, found the sultry climate and people hard to resist. "I came here on holiday and never got around to leaving" has long been a typical refrain.

Chiang Mai probably has the greatest number of expatriates by percentage of population though; by some estimates 50,000 of the million or so residents and workers there are foreigners. This means a major support structure and a long list of activities for expats, which run the gamut from 20-somethings to families to retirees. For many, life here is less stressful than in Bangkok. "It is still a small city which takes half an hour, at most, to drive across," says Pim Kemasingki, who lived in six countries before returning to her once-home and mother's birth country of Thailand. "A mere

30-40 minutes' drive in any direction will have you in near-pristine nature: waterfalls, jungles, lakes, and resorts. With six major universities in the area, it's a young and vibrant city that's very socially tolerant and packed with cultural activities." She keeps tabs on it all with the local publications she runs, Citylife, CityNow! and the online news site CityNews.

Other popular areas with smaller pockets of foreigners include beach resort areas Phuket, Ko Samui, Pattaya, Krabi, and Hua Hin. Those who are willing to go all in and learn Thai could find a lot of smaller, cheaper towns and islands to call home.

Thailand is not the Wild West anymore though and the days of finding $5 per night beach bungalows in an island paradise you could live in for months are long gone. The tourism numbers have grown exponentially the past two decades, edging close to 20 million visitors a year now (if you count the many who leave and come back on visa runs). The population has grown steadily wealthier as the economy keeps growing. Apart from some political hiccups here and there, Thailand has marched onward and upward.

The country is still a great value though to visitors and residents and lately it has also become one of the key hubs in Asia for entrepreneurs. With reasonable rents, fast internet, and good air connections to almost anywhere, this is a good place to use as a base for running an online business. Chiang Mai is the most popular spot for this—and for expats trying to live as cheaply as possible—but there are also plenty of digital nomads in spots like Ko Samui, Phuket, and the capital.

There are some English teachers and vagabonds living for $500 a month in Chiang Mai, but that's tough to pull off long-term for most people. Shannon O'Donnell, who runs a web marketing consulting business from the road and the ALittleAdrift.com blog, got by on that amount for a long time in Chiang Mai after arrival, not counting visa run costs. She had a modest apartment with a roommate for six months and "I don't drink very much." She says if you doubled that to $1,000 though, you could live pretty comfortably in Thailand.

That's a bit too frugal for some though. As Pim Kemasingki says, "If you live in a small room, drink Thai whiskey, have no insurance, stay healthy enough to avoid hospitals, ride an old motorbike, and eat mainly Thai food, it is possible to live here on $500 per month. You can actually enjoy a lot of what Chiang Mai has to offer for that, but I think it is only for the really young to handle, and most are doing that as they stop over here to teach or volunteer. However, if you aren't a spoiled brat like me, I would say that $1,500-2,000 dollars could be easily doable. A one bedroom apartment would cost around $250-300, rental or lease of a car would be around $300 a month, a Thai lunch would be $3 each, a good dinner around $10 each...though a fine one wouldn't break the bank either at around $30-40 dollars a head. Water, electricity, and other utilities are still cheap except for air conditioning costs during the hot seasons."

Lisa Niver and her husband George of the We Said Go Travel blog spent around $1,500 a month living on the island of Ko Samui. "Every day we would work for a bit on our blog, then walk on the beach, then write part of our book, then have lunch out somewhere, go snorkeling, or go kayaking. We'd work a couple more hours, then go to where George was playing music. I kept thinking, "Why isn't everyone doing this? We also met a lot of great people. I feel like we had more friends and hung out with them more than we ever did in spread-out Los Angeles."

UK bloggers and Simon Fairbairn and Erin McNeaney of Never Ending Voyage give a rundown of expenses when they move to a new area and they spent around $1,400 a month in Chiang Mai, living what they considered "a luxurious lifestyle." Their $655 furnished apartment was new, spacious, had a kitchen, and came with a shared swimming pool. That monthly cost included their two visa runs to a neighboring country, eating out a lot, and renting a motorbike the whole time.

Of course if you're not trying to be on a strict budget and you routinely spent $5,000 a month at home, Thailand can feel like paradise at half the price even if you're living it up. Chris from the LivingThai.org blog says a monthly $2,500 budget can set you up quite well in Bangkok, including a cleaning lady, a gym membership, a motorbike, visa runs, $670 for "going out" and at least one big trip out of the country to visit the relatives or go on a major vacation.

There is one huge negative to Thailand though that eventually becomes a deal breaker for many who live here: the foreigner-unfriendly visa policy. It is next to impossible to get long-term residency here without setting up a corporation, marrying a local, being retired with loads of cash to put into a local bank, or getting work sponsorship. Even then you'll have to jump through quite a few hoops and spend a lot of time waiting. For the vast majority of foreigners, living in Thailand means making runs for the border as soon as the tourist visa runs out. That tourist visa is only good for 60 days if secured in advance, 30 days if stamped upon arrival. Even with a one-month extension done locally, you're still forced to travel to another country at least four times per calendar year. Even for people who like to travel, that's a lot of forced trips you can't postpone.

On the plus side, at least there are a lot of neighbors to choose from. You can travel by train or bus to Laos, Myanmar (Burma), Malaysia, or Cambodia.

Life is pretty easy in much of Thailand without learning a lot of Thai and the shopping is some of the best in Asia in terms of availability. "Many merchants speak English so communication is never really an issue," says Spencer Montague, who moved from land-locked Knoxville, Tennessee to Thailand and settled on the island of Ko Samui. I have traveled extensively and chose Ko Samui and specifically the Lamai area because it has everything I need in terms of shopping, entertainment, good hospitals and overall quality of life. I'm three minutes by motorbike from one of the world's most beautiful beaches, Lamai beach. Yet, there is a large Tesco Lotus grocery store here and 15 minutes away in Chaweng you will find malls, a cinema and even bowling! No one place is perfect, but this place is about as perfect as I could ever ask for, though you will need to enjoy very warm and usually quite humid weather. Considering I have air conditioning, I am a happy camper here on my little island in Asia."

Pim says this is also a great country for parents with school-aged kids. "There are six international schools in Chiang Mai preparing kids for all the standardized tests. Then there are numerous bilingual schools as well." With so many foreigners working in Bangkok, there's a large selection of quality schools there as well.

Housing Costs

Christa Romera, a person I highlighted at the beginning of this book, works at Thailand-Property.com, a site meant to help expats find apartments in Thailand. Her 2-bedroom apartment she shares with a friend is new construction. It has a big living room, a small but separate kitchen, two balconies, and bedrooms big enough for king sized beds. Rent plus electricity, water, and internet costs her around $360 per month. In New York City about half of her salary went to rent, even though she was sharing with two other people. Now she makes less, but spends a fifth of it on housing.

That's in Bangkok, the big capital city. There are some people paying more than $1,000 a month there for sure, but you can easily find a nice furnished one-bedroom apartment on the site where she works for under $650 (20,000 baht) very easily. There were more than 200 of them to pick from as I was writing this chapter, many spacious places in a building with a swimming pool. And that's what you can find in advance online. Chris from the LivingThai.org blog is based in Bangkok and says, "If you search long enough, 15,000 baht will get you a really comfortable place to live in. I know many people who rent spacious houses or impressive apartments in good locations for that amount." That comes out to around $500 when the exchange rate is at 30 to the U.S. dollar, less when the local currency drops.

Once you get into other parts of the country, prices usually go down substantially unless you're oceanside. Even in the second-largest city of Chiang Mai, expect to pay $125 to $250 for a nice air-conditioned studio or one-bedroom apartment. If you've got some friends, you can get a whole huge house for $300 to $800—the top of that range often coming with a pool. Spencer Montague likes his cost of living on the island of Ko Samui. "I rent a lovely, partially furnished one bedroom house with full bathroom, kitchen area, and a living room area plus a nice balcony. I have at my own expense added the additionally needed furniture including a second AC unit, stovetop and washing machine. I pay about $400 a month. That includes my Wi-Fi, water, and electric. There is a large pool, which is big enough for me to do laps. No one but me ever seems to use the pool so I almost always have it to myself. The pool is lit at night and even has a Jacuzzi and waterfall!"

When Lisa and her husband lived short-term in Ko Samui, they skipped the apartment scene and instead stayed in a hotel that averaged out to $17 a night, $500 per month. They didn't have to pay for utilities beyond that. "We had a gigantic place and we could hear the waves at night," Lisa says. They were right by the beach and had a kayak to use. They were in an area where they could walk to where they wanted to go.

Technically foreigners can't own land in Thailand, so it's much easier to buy a condo if you want something permanent. Most are in the $50 to $150 per square foot range. So a two-bedroom condo of new construction, 1,000 square feet, could be between $100K and $150K in a prime area. If you're willing to buy something a bit older or less ideally located, you can find quite a few listed for five digits.

Food and Drink

All those great dishes you're used to sampling at your local Thai restaurant are as good or better here, but at a fraction of the price. Coconut curries, pad thais, big noodle soups, and the like run 75 cents to $2 on the street, $1.50 to $5 in simple restaurants, even with seafood. The variety is excellent, the quality is uniformly high, and most street stalls are extremely clean and sanitary—just don't drink the tap water. There is a serious street food culture here: it is common for office workers to grab something from a sidewalk stall and few "brown bag it" since the cost to get a real meal is minimal. Some expatriates living in Thailand don't even have a kitchen where they live: they eat every meal out since the food is so tasty and inexpensive.

"It was rare that we spent more than $25 a day on food living in Thailand," says Lisa. "We could eat a good meal for 40 baht and if we spent $7 on dinner that was an outrageous splurge. I did not in any way ever feel like I was being denied. Every meal felt like I was eating one of my favorite foods."

If you like to party, that will drive your costs up

significantly here because of high taxes on alcohol, Thailand is not a country where you can drink for cheap. You might want to stock up every time you come through duty free and treat your visa runs as catch-up time. One beer or glass of wine can double the price of a simple meal. A night of partying in Bangkok can cost more than a cheap hotel room. The local rice whiskey is much easier on the budget at less than ten bucks for a 750-ml bottle. It must be said that drugs are easy to find and are inexpensive, but lots of discretion and personal recommendation is required. There are more than a few foreigners in not-so-nice Thai jails.

If you're a hedonist with some cash to throw around though, Thailand is one of the most permissive countries in the world. Whether this titillates you or disgusts you will greatly influence how excited/bothered you get about the sex, drugs, and debauchery.

Transportation

Many foreigners don't own a car in Thailand and have no desire to deal with one. You can get to most parts of the country by bus for $1 to $3 per hour of travel and though the train is more in first class, it's still very reasonable and you can sleep on the way on longer trips. The train goes to the Laos border, up to northern Thailand, and down through Malaysia to Singapore.

Internal flights are often under $100 and can be super cheap if you purchase far enough in advance.

Bangkok now has an excellent metro and sky train system that can help you avoid traffic on many routes. Most rides are $1 to $1.50, or you can get a monthly pass. If you do need a taxi though, it'll only cost you four or five dollars for a trip of half an hour. In other cities and towns, those who don't want to depend on taxis will rent a motorbike to run errands and get around, at a rate of $60 to $100 per month.

In smaller towns and some neighborhoods of Chiang Mai you could get around by bicycle, but not in Bangkok. There you may need to take a bus sometimes to get to where you're going, at prices at or lower than the metro. In less congested towns, expats buy or rent a motorbike.

Health Care Costs

Thailand actively promotes its health tourism sector and sends its doctors to top-tier international medical universities for training. You'll get excellent care here and in the major cities and tourist centers you'll usually be able to communicate easily in English. Costs are a fraction of what you would spend in Europe or the USA though, and you'll probably have more people waiting on you.

"The startup I'm working for isn't offering insurance at the moment," says Christa, "but I do still have travel insurance in case something really serious happens. I am registered at a hospital in Bangkok, (that's honestly one of the nicest hospitals I've ever been to), and health care here has a great reputation and isn't that expensive."

Many round-the-world travelers will wait until they get to Bangkok to get all the vaccinations they will need for the rest of their travels. The costs are significantly lower and you can just walk into a clinic or hospital to get them knocked out.

To get an idea of costs, here are some Bangkok averages you can compare to where you live now:

Lasik surgery (both eyes) - $1,850
Angioplasty - $3,800
Hip Replacement - $8,000
Liposuction - $2,300
Breast Implants - $3,000
Face Lift - $4,000

Other Costs

This is a great place to stay loose and limber. You can get a massage in a place that's not fancy for $5 to $10 for an hour. If you go to a real spa, it can still be $20 or less. You get similarly great rates on manicures, pedicures, and facials. A whole spa package in a place that caters to locals will cost about one-tenth of what you spend in the U.S. or Western Europe.

If you're looking for the kind of sex you would pay for, this has long been a magnet for that kind of transaction, with any type of partner. This book is not the place to find details on that, but it's a key attraction for one large subset of expatriates.

In cleaner pursuits, you can get your laundry done for about a dollar a kilo, get your apartment cleaned for $10, or get a nice suit custom made for less than $100.

Utility costs are reasonable across the board in Thailand and you'll probably pay less than you did in your home country for everything from mobile data to TV cable. Most interviews and online estimates have put all of them together in the $80 to $150 range for a decent-sized apartment or house, less for a studio. That's electricity, gas, internet, and water. If you use air conditioning all day every day, figure on more like $200 to $250 total.

Visas in Thailand

There's one factor that keeps the long-term expatriate population in check in Thailand: the awful visa situation. For the vast majority of foreigners living here, life in Thailand means a lot of trips on buses, trains, or planes to neighboring countries. The visa run is a regular ritual here, one that wastes an incredible amount of time and money on trips that serve no other purpose than to get a new passport stamp.

"It's very easy to get a tourist visa to come to Thailand for up to three months," says Christa. "Just go to your consulate with some form, pay them the correct amount of money, and pick up your passport the next day. I did that and then found a job before the three months ended. Then they helped me take care of processing my work visa, which required me to leave the country. Visa runs can be exhausting if you are only going to process the visa, but if you can time it right and stay in the other country for a few extra days you can turn it into another travel opportunity. I got an incredible little trip to Laos out of it!

There's no denying though that the immigration office totally sucks," she adds. "It's 10 times worse than the Division of Motor Vehicles in the U.S., but you deal with it because everything else is worth it."

Shannon lived in Chiang Mai off and on for a while and describes the visa situation this way: "Most people get a double entry visa that is good for 60 days. At the 60-day mark you can pay $60 to extend it another 30 days. Then after those 90 days you have to leave the country. I would walk across the Burmese border, walk back 15 minutes later, then have another two months plus one month again. I would often go to Laos to have seven-months straight in Southeast Asia." She cautions that you can't expect to do this indefinitely though. "The first two of these are easy to get, but the third one depends on the officer. When my roommate got the last one in Laos, her third, they told her not to get another one. If you get a new passport though, you start over from scratch since your previous stamps are gone."

There are a few under-the-table methods you hear about sometimes for avoiding these visa runs, but you'll have to investigate those on the ground with some long-term residents. Officially, here's how you can get a longer-term visa.

- Marry a local
- Form a corporation with a local (real or shell)
- Be 55 or older and plop a lot of cash into a Thai bank account to receive a retirement visa.
- Work for a company that will secure a work visa for you.

"If you are over 55 years old and have some money to put into a local bank, then you can apply for a retirement visa," says Pim. "This makes life very very easy." Here's the official word on how that works, from the US Embassy site in Thailand:

"Applicant's pension or other regular income must be no less than the equivalent of 65,000 Baht per month." (Nearly $2,200—quite a high bar compared to most other countries in this book. But...)

"Alternatively, the applicant may meet the financial requirement by maintaining a Thai bank account with a minimum amount of 800,000 Baht. (Applicants will need to show that they have 800,000 Baht in savings each year when they renew their visa.)" At 30 to the US dollar, that works out to around $27,000 you need to have sitting in the bank. For many retirees, that's easier than showing $2,200 coming in each month, especially if they've sold a house or taken money out of a retirement savings account.

That's exactly what Spencer worked out. "I'm on a type OA retirement visa so I report every 3 months to immigration (only to provide an address), renew my visa yearly, and at the end of the first year I must meet and maintain the financial requirements. I keep 800,000 baht untouched in a Thai bank account. "

"If you are too young to retire, then you have to start playing clever games with the law," says Pim. "Some people set up shell companies to get work permits, others do things with marriage, some get jobs. But it is not easy. Otherwise it is the regular schlep to the border every two or three months."

If you're moving to Thailand because you or your spouse has a job offer, then pop the champagne and pack the suitcases without thinking. All the visa hurdles most people have to deal with should evaporate for you and you will be living a very comfortable lifestyle even if there's a pay cut.

If you're self-employed or living off savings, however, build visa run weekends into your calendar and assume this won't be your long-term home.

Downsides

Thailand's political situation has been a mess for years and was going through a new round of protests, coups, and curfews in Bangkok as this book was finishing up. This invariably looks worse in the news than it is on the ground, but a country without a functioning government is always a bit unnerving. Many of the government problems have corruption at their heart and there's still plenty of it at every level in Thailand.

Environmental protection has been an afterthought at best in the country, so in a few short decades the beaches and rivers have gotten polluted in many areas. There's not much serious effort to recycle and garbage is a problem everywhere.

Air pollution has dogged Bangkok for decades and there's often a haze over the city. Don't move to the capital if you have respiratory problems. Also, "We have awful air pollution between March and May each year in Chiang Mai," says Pim. "Many people time their visits back home then. Traffic is also becoming a bit of an inconvenience, but not as bad as many parts of the world. There are issues such as over-building. The sleepy backwater town of old is no more in Chiang Mai; instead it is a thriving city. With this rapid growth comes other issues people don't like: horrid signs up everywhere, tall buildings, ugly streets, etc."

Overbuilding is a big problem in many areas, with few regulations or formal building restrictions enforced. On many islands, haphazard construction and too much density have quickly taken former paradise areas like Ko Phi Phi to the point of near collapse.

Sex tourism is a major industry in Thailand and for some that's a big draw. For others it's a huge turnoff. No matter what you think about it, there are clear side effects in the form of human trafficking, organized crime, and exploitation.

For More Information

Wood Egg Thailand startup guide
U.S. Embassy Thai visa information
LivingThai.org
A Family in Motion blog (AfamilyinMotion.com)
Chiang Mai City Life (ChiangMaiNews.com)
Paper Planes Blog (PaperPlanesBlog.com)
Phuket.net living section
Thai Expat Blogs on ExpatsBlog.com
Transitions Abroad Thailand section

Chapter 16: Cambodia

Pros: tropical climate, ultra-low prices, easy residency, easy work ability, good food, relatively good internet, beach getaways, attractive neighboring countries, cheap booze.
Cons: second-tier health care, limited school options, limited property purchase abilities, tropical diseases, low literacy rate, poverty.

When I visited Cambodia with my family, we got two adjoining hotel rooms for $44 a night total, including a huge breakfast. It was air conditioned, had maid service, and they baked my wife a cake when they found out it was her birthday. We hired a tuk-tuk driver for the entire day for $14. Often our family of three would completely chow down on multiple courses in Siem Reap, I'd have a few beers, and my daughter would get a fruit shake. The bill would come and it would be $11 or $12—in tourist places. We got a massage almost every day, including an hour-long four-hand one (two masseuses) for $10.

We were tourists, fresh off the bus, not knowing where to get the best deals. How do these expenses for living in Cambodia compare to yours?

A 2-bedroom apartment with a pool for $350 per month, a $5 massage for an hour, a full-time nanny or housekeeper for $120 a month, meals out for $2, taxis for a dollar or two.

How much different would your life be if your expenses were in this range? What would it feel like if you were in the top 5 percent in household income just by earning $2,000 per month?

In most respects, Cambodia is the cheapest place to live in Southeast Asia. It's also the one that is the least hassle to get set up in. You could literally pack your bags today and be a resident for a year tomorrow—if you requested the right kind of visa upon arrival.

"This is one of the easiest countries in the world to get a business visa," says Justin Garnett, a local who has been in the capital for years. "You just pay a little extra when you arrive for the upgrade. Then you can extend for a full year for $280. From there it's very easy to rent a space and open a bar, a restaurant, or a service business. As long as you don't do anything stupid, it's no problem."

Cambodia is not for everyone, of course. It's a hot tropical country with the bugs and diseases that implies. Most people fly to Thailand for serious medical care. The Khmer Rouge killed off two million people, including everyone who seemed intelligent or part of the "urban elite," which not only wrecked the country and its institutions, but also took most of the high-IQ adults who didn't flee out of the gene pool.

The country is trying hard to make up for lost time though, with minimal regulations, low taxes, and a welcome climate for foreigners. Infrastructure spending has gone into overdrive the past decade and this is clearly an economy on the rise. Many young people speak English well and the U.S. dollar is the de facto currency for most transactions. The only time you even see the local currency in the main population centers is in the fruit and vegetable market.

About the only things that are going to seem expensive here are imported items, and even among those there are some happy surprises. Sin taxes are very low, so if you're a smoker or a drinker you won't pay a premium. Many Chinese items—like cheap cell phones—come in without extra duty. It's just when you're buying items the locals don't use or can't afford that you'll really see sticker shock.

When I asked Phnom Penh resident Humphrey, who grew up in New Zealand and has lived in England and Australia, what he spends on a regular basis, he stressed that he was living large and wasn't very careful with his money. "I earn about $2,000 a month and I spend about $1,500," he said. "Even in the nicest bars, it's still 50-75 cents for a half pint of beer. Liquor here is cheaper than at duty free in an airport. If you spend more than $4 on a meal it was a very fancy place. Women are cheap, but I'm not a player now," he insists. "I have a girlfriend."

"There are plenty of dirty old men on a pension down at the beaches though," he adds, "and I know a few that easily get by on $1,200 a month. They live well on that amount."

Justin is a family man, so his story is very different. He's got his family and a few relatives of his local wife in the compound. He has a place where he spends around $750 on rent, utilities, and maintenance for a 4-bedroom house "with a huge garden." He estimates that he probably spends $3,000 a month total, including education for the kids, but can't imagine going back to his old life in Australia. "I live a good life on this amount. I pull up to the house and the kids run inside. I always know there's someone to take care of them. We've never ever paid a babysitter."

In terms of where to live, this is not a huge country and the foreign population drops off rapidly after the first few choices. Phnom Penh is the most popular choice for its wide range of apartments, nightlife, and restaurants. Siem Reap is a tourist town because of Angkor Wat, but it's also home to a fair number of expatriates, many of them lured by the boomtown atmosphere and the chance to build a business in a hurry. Cambodia's second-largest city, Battambang, has a fair number of expatriates, especially French ones.

The rest of the foreign population is mainly at the beach. There's a coast to the south of the country, anchored by Sihanoukville, with multiple beach towns down the coast from there. There are few places left in the world where you can kick back in a rental home near a nice beach for so little cash. You can find a few island paradise spots offshore, but most of the area on those is protected and there are very few long-term rental options besides hotels.

For the right kind of people, Cambodia is a land of golden opportunity. Do your homework and give the place a trial run before making a move. If your funds are limited, however, this is probably the best bargain in Asia outside the Indian subcontinent.

Housing Costs

As with anywhere you'd want to live, it pays to take your time finding a place to stay to get the best deal in Cambodia. Patience will be rewarded. If you look online though, the prices are quite reasonable even for those in a hurry.

In Phnom Penh, the most expensive places are right by the river and you can pay as much as you do now if you want. That's where a lot of the corporate expatriates and local business tycoons live. Prices go down quickly as you count the blocks back from there. It is common to spend

$250-$350 for a modern one-bedroom condo and $400-$650 for one that has several bedrooms and lots of facilities. You can spend far more in a luxury building and far less if you're willing to live in a "Khmer style" local place on the outskirts with a very basic kitchen and no air conditioning. Doubling or tripling up with others will get you more value for your money since you can get more space and split the costs.

For those willing to spend time pounding the pavement though, there are plenty of deals. Surf the local message boards and you can find people living in three- or four-bedroom houses in the capital for $400 or less.

In Siem Reap prices are far lower. If you spend $600 there you're likely going to have a swanky villa with a pool, all utilities included. Or if you spend $30 on a hotel room while you're looking it'll come with air-con, maid service, a great breakfast, TV, fridge, and maybe even a pool. Most of the condos and apartments you can find online range from $250 to $550 per month. Go to a smaller town with fewer tourists and it drops again from there.

When I was researching prices online, I found several furnished houses and condos in Siem Reap of two or three bedrooms and as many baths for $350 to $550 per month, plus there was a 4BR villa with parking for $600. Unfurnished places were less if you're coming for the long haul and will buy furniture. (You can get handcrafted wood items for very reasonable prices).

I interviewed hotel manager Hanno Stamm, who lives in Siem Reap, managing Victoria Angkor Resort & Spa. He was just plain flabbergasted at how cheap it was where he was living. "I don't know anyone who pays more than $500 a month for a nice large apartment or house here," he says, "And even if you run the air conditioning 24/7 you won't be able to spend more than $300 per month on all utilities added together."

You can spend more of course if you budget is higher and you want to live it up for less than you ever could in your home country. Some apartments come with a full amenities package of high-speed internet, security, elevator, parking, a rooftop pool, a gym, and western appliances for $500 to $1,000 per month. The latter being a three-bedroom luxury penthouse that a few playboys could share and only owe

$333 each for rent.

In the beach resort area of Sihanoukville, prices are still very reasonable for those who want to be near the water. Online you can find 1BR furnished apartments with A/C units and Wi-Fi included for as little as $200 per month, or large two-bedroom houses or apartments for $400-$500. The most expensive long-term rental I could find when I was poking around online was $1,500 a month. That was for a 7-bedroom/7-bath furnished mansion with a 2-car garage. Another simpler one a mile away was $600 a month for six bedrooms.

Buying in Cambodia is a bit tricky. Per the letter of the law, you can't buy land without partnering up with a local. There are a few ways around this though, like by establishing a local corporation with a Cambodian. This way when you "buy" a piece of property you really get a 99-year lease for the land it sits on via the partner. Since most people aren't going to live that long, it can work for a lifetime and you can still sell it or pass it on. But this requires a good bit of faith and a good attorney.

You can marry a local and then you can buy what you want as long as he/she is on the title with you. If you end up splitting up and leaving the country though, your spouse gets the house.

In general you're better off buying a condo above the ground floor. That's straightforward and easy. Transaction costs are relatively low: negligible as a buyer, 7–8 percent as a seller, including the real estate agent's commission.

Purchase prices are all over the map so it's hard to generalize about what it's going to cost you just by looking at what's listed online. Since you should rent for a good while before buying anyway, take your time to find the right place in the right neighborhood.

To give you an idea though, online listings at the beach go from $25,000 for a one-bedroom condo to $120,000 for a 4BR house with a garage and pool. Most listings are well under the $100K mark. In boomtown Siem Reap it seems easy to pay as much as you would in your home country for a house, though of course you will get more for your $150K to $350K there and everything will be close to new.

In the capital, prices are very dependent on location. A

condo in a prime spot with a river view in Phnom Penh could cost you more than $200,000. If you poke around is less prestigious neighborhoods though, you'll find nice modern condos under $100,000 and ones that can be renovated to suit for under $50,000. It's relatively easy to find a one-bedroom one in better shape for that price.

Get out of the main population centers though and prices take a nosedive. Justin rents a house for his extended family for $750 a month in the capital, but he has a getaway place in the countryside that he owns. "I bought a block of land with a 3-bedroom house that needed some improvements," he says. All told I've spent $21,000 and I have an acre of land. If you buy land somewhere, you can build a home here for 10 grand."

Beach property here is still a relative bargain compared to the rest of Southeast Asia, though again you can't buy it outright as a foreigner. You need a corporation or a partner for a lease arrangement.

Food & Drink

Hanno Stamm has worked in several other countries in Asia, including Vietnam, and can't imagine spending less than he does now on food and drink. "I cannot think of anything outrageously expensive except some imported food stuffs. I like to dine out a lot and it is very cheap here in Siem Reap."

As long as you eat what's grown in the region and don't need a daily fix of imported items, this is a place where you can eat out three meals a day and spend less than $5 if you go where the locals go. Step up to a nicer restaurant with waiters and you can still get a meal for a few bucks. If you spend $5 on a meal it'll be in a pretty nice restaurant and probably include a beer or fresh fruit juice.

A draft beer will run 50 cents to $1.50 depending on whether it's happy hour (which in some places is 24 hours). A bottled beer will be 75 cents to $2. A soda or good coffee runs 50 cents to $1.50 in a restaurant or nice cafe. A fruit shake will be about the same. Cocktails here are some of the cheapest in the world, even with name brand vodka or bourbon, at $1–$4.

Ironically enough, most of the people frequenting the most expensive restaurants are staffers at charity organizations or other NGOs. If you splurge where they dine all the time, a meal for two will be $35 – $60 with a bottle of wine.

If you buy regional food ingredients in the market, you can stock your kitchen well for $20. For that amount you could get a week's worth of rice, vegetables, fruit, baguettes, and some meat or fish.

Transportation

If you don't plan on having a car, transportation is not going to be a big part of your budget. You can get a tuk-tuk to pretty much anywhere in Siem Reap for $2 or less and you can rent one for the entire day for $14. In Phnom Penh, a taxi ride will run $1 to $4. Here are some sample prices for getting around:

Siem Reap to Phnom Penh by bus: $6 – $13 (working A/C and Wi-Fi).

Bus from Phnom Penh to the beaches: $4 – $6

Taxi from Phnom Penh to the beaches: $50 – $60 (up to 4 people)

Bus from Phnom Penh to Saigon, Vietnam: $6 – $14

Bus to Thai border from Siem Reap: $9

Taxi in Phnom Penh: If there's a meter, $1 per 2 kms, up to $4 negotiated.

Foreigners technically aren't supposed to be able to drive a motorbike here, so if you rent one ($6-$8 a day) you might have to pay a "fine" of a dollar or two if you get pulled over. You can rent a bicycle for a couple dollars though.

You'll pay more to get to and from airports of course. Only four flights a week land at Sihanoukville Airport, so it's hard to get to your hotel for less than $20 in a taxi. The drop-off shuttle bus is a better deal, with $6 tickets from a booth.

Several budget airlines serve the county, so you can usually save some time and fly to other cities in the region for $75 to $200 one-way.

Other Costs

Utility costs can be all over the map and are impacted a lot by how much air conditioning you use. Some rental units include utilities, but most of them don't. Cambodia does not subsidize fuel costs, so although this is a cheap country, energy is purchased at world market rates. So electricity costs will depend greatly on how heavily you are running air conditioning. Most locals of normal means go without, but when I visited in July because of school schedules for my daughter, the mercury was passing 100 degrees F (38c) on a regular basis. The cost for electricity was 20 cents per kilowatt hour as I wrote this, which equates to $80 to $200 a month for many expatriates. Yes, it could be possible to have a power bill that's almost as high as your monthly rent.

The rest of your utilities will be cheap though. "Water is $5 a month and that's as much as you want," says Justin. Garbage pick-up varies from $1 to $20 per month depending on the size of the house." The cable TV bill will be around $10-$20, internet $10-$35 depending on speed and location.

The local cell phone market is very competitive, so most expats get a SIM card for $5 or less and spend at most $25 per month on calls and data.

In May 2013, the minimum wage increased from $60 to $75 a month, plus a $5 living allowance. That means if you pay someone $160 a month for a full-time service like housekeeping, gardening, or being a nanny, you are paying them *double* the minimum wage.

You can easily get a massage for $5 for an hour, or a four-hand one (two masseuses) for $10–$15. A manicure or pedicure runs $3–$5. Laundry service is $1–$2 per kilo.

Taking local tours of any kind will be a minimal expense. If you want to tour remote villages or kayak on a lake with a guide, often $10 to $15 will set you up with pick-up service from where you're staying.

Visas in Cambodia

Coming in on a tourist visa only gives you permission to stay for 30 days, though it can be extended once (and only once) for another 30 days for $45. Anyone intending to stay for longer should get a business visa, which is available for the asking, regardless of whether you own a business or not.

That visa only costs $5 more when you arrive, for the first 30 days, then during that time you extend it for a full year by paying $280. With that in hand you can be a freelancer, work for a company, or start a business. As long as you don't run afoul of the (limited) rules, you will be fine. "As soon as you start f%#king with the system, it's going to come down very quickly," advises Justin. "The judicial system is not going to be your friend."

If you keep your nose clean, you can renew your business visa each year indefinitely, making Cambodia one of the most straightforward places to live long-term in the world.

When I spoke to Humphrey, he echoed the ease of getting a visa in Cambodia and not having any hassles. "When I need to renew my visa, I give them some money at a motorbike shop or travel agent and hand over two photos. The next day I have my passport back and it's done."

Plus you don't have to worry about sneaking around if you want to tend bar or take scuba divers out for PADI certifications. "This is one of the few countries in the world where you can just roll up and work," says Humphrey. "It's not like Thailand."

You can buy your way in too, by investing enough money in the country that you're granted citizenship.

A foreigner may be granted honorary Cambodian citizenship if he or she donates a significant sum of money to the Royal Government of Cambodia for the purposes of benefiting the people of Cambodia. Foreigners who have made a special impact or rendered exceptional help to the Kingdom may also be granted this honor in recognition of their expertise or altruism.

Does "significant sum" sound vague to you? In practice, it is. Some have bought citizenship for as little as $50,000. Others have paid more than $250,000.

Downsides

Cambodia is very poor, more than a little corrupt, and doesn't have a ton of money to spend on infrastructure. Some people are drawn to this lack of regulation and (almost) anything goes approach to building codes, driving, and starting a business. For others though, the lack of basic services and the deplorable condition of some roads is too much to deal with after a while. It has gotten a lot better though as tourism has increased and the government has gotten more stable, so if the trend continues infrastructure should keep improving little by little.

You can't drink the water, food-handling methods may not be up to your satisfaction, and customer service may not be super-quick or efficient. The power grid is overtaxed in most of the country, so there can be outages that last for hours or a day. Most people have backup generators. For serious medical issues, most foreigners fly to Bangkok.

This is a tropical country, with all the creepy crawlies that implies. The less urban your location, the more you can expect to see mosquitoes, spiders, and other insects. Large rats and snakes aren't uncommon either.

There are serious problems with environmental degradation, human trafficking, corrupt NGOs who use children as donation pawns, and other frequently encountered third-world problems. How well you can deal with all this without screaming will determine how happy you'll be living in this libertarian paradise.

For More Information

Khymer 440 forum (Khmer440.com/chat_forum)
Move to Cambodia (Movetocambodia.com)
Transitions Abroad Cambodia section
Wood Egg Cambodia startup guide (woodegg.com/kh)
The Phnom Pen (thephnompen.asia)

Chapter 17: Colombia

Pros: Great climate in Medellin, beaches, adventure activities, scenery, nightlife, culture, long tourist visa, easy residency, air connections, fast internet, strong economy, gorgeous women.
Cons: Medium street crime, two rainy seasons, chilly capital, long surface connections between cities, strong local currency, rising prices, expensive real estate in some areas.

I know what you're probably thinking, but today's Colombia is a far cry from the one that hosted Carlos Escobar's cocaine kingdom. As an article in the *Telegraph* said, "At the peak of Escobar's reign, in 1991, the murder rate was 381 per 100,000 people. To put that into context, the current most violent city on the planet, San Pedro Sula, in Honduras, has a murder rate half of that; 187 per 100,000 inhabitants. Simply stepping outside your front door was an enormous risk—children were not allowed to play outside, and when relatives left home for work in the morning you never knew if they would return that evening."

Now the murder rate is a tiny fraction of what it once was. The nation's economy is growing at a clip of 5 percent or more per year and many international companies are basing their Latin American operations here.

Colombia is at the top of South America, with the Darian Gap jungle between it and Panama. After decades of dealing with paramilitary separatists, drug cartels, and one of the world's highest murder rates, it is now like a whole different country. Crime is now lower than in many neighboring countries and tourism is growing by double-digit percentages as the word gets out. Expatriates who live here rave about the agreeable climate in Medellin, the culture and nightlife in Bogota, and the walled city grandeur of beachside city Cartagena. Santa Marta has even nicer beaches, on the Caribbean, while others who have moved here choose to live in a small interior town with lower prices and fewer tourists.

This is a country of varied climates, from sea level to high Andean peaks. It's one of the world's largest coffee producers, but also grows a staggering number of fruits and vegetables at different altitudes. Ask people what they like about Medellin and the weather usually comes first in this placed nicknamed the "City of Eternal Spring." There are two rainy seasons though, which can range from mild to ongoing deluges from year to year. Medellin Living and GoBackpacking.com editor David Lee says if expats complain about something, that's usually it. Bogota is higher and colder. It has the big city attributes on the plus side (museums, great restaurants, the arts), but also more of the normal big capital city problems.

Traveling around the country is not as cheap as somewhere like Bolivia or Ecuador, but it's not bad. Domestic tourism is actually most of the tourism here, so prices are geared to locals nearly everywhere. There are lots of little rustic hotels dotted around the countryside, many priced below $35 a night with breakfast. A zipline trip I did in the coffee region was $20—less than I paid in Guatemala many years earlier. A tandem paragliding trip outside of Medellin is $32.

Avianca, one of the major airline players in the Americas, is based in Colombia, so there are frequent air connections to other cities plus plenty to move about within the country, at reasonable prices. Several international airlines fly here, including Copa, American, and budget carrier Spirit.

You get a three-month visa upon arrival as a tourist and you can extend that to six months without leaving the country. That's the limit in one calendar year, but getting residency here is relatively straightforward and there are multiple visa types for different situations.

David Lee lives in one of the most popular cities for expats, Medellin. If you're serious about moving to that city or just spending time there as a traveler, he's got a great e-book out for people traveling there and the accompanying website is a gold mine of information.

American Jeff Jung lives in Bogota. He runs the great Career Break Secrets site and is author of *The Career Break Traveler's Handbook*. Jeff estimates that he spends about half what he did in the USA overall. Dave's expenses rarely top $1,800 a month, which again is about half what many people of average means spend per month in the states,

Canada, or Europe to live in a city this size. And they would go out far less on that budget in their former country.

Another Jeff who has detailed his expenses on Medellin Living spends around $3,000 a month between him and his girlfriend when averaged out over a year. The biggest expenses for them are (in order): groceries, rent, dining out, Spanish classes, vacations, and medical expenses. For two people, "This is less than my living costs were in the US where I was living alone," he says.

The rock-bottom level in the cities here is probably around $1,000 a month, or $1,500 for a frugal couple. For $2,000, a couple could have a reasonably comfortable middle-class life in the two main cities. In the countryside or small towns you could shave a bit off this budget and probably get a whole house for what you pay for an apartment in the large cities. There are a lot of very attractive places to live in this country if you don't need to have hundreds of other foreigners around you and you can pick your ideal climate: from average highs of 60F to average highs of 95F. Often that's just a matter of changing your altitude: you've got the cool Andes Mountains and the humid jungle, with lots in between. Dave says of Medellin, "You can wear a t-shirt and jeans day or night pretty much all year."

Be advised though that the country's main tourism draw, Cartagena, is significantly hotter and significantly more expensive than living elsewhere, especially if you compare it to interior locations. You're competing with wealthy Colombians and Venezuelans who have long seen a condo or home here as a solid second home investment. Most of the tourists who come here are on a short jaunt vacation budget, spending freely.

Housing Costs

Rental prices are attractive throughout Colombia, but Cartagena is in its own world. Rental prices in the historic walled city and at the beaches are geared to short-term vacation renters and this is a favored spot for wealthy investors. "Real estate prices here are on par with those in Miami," says Paul Juan of Cartagena Realty [cartagenarealty.com]. You may not be able to live here for half what you were spending at home unless you're coming from a high-priced city like New York, London, or San Francisco. Santa Marta, four hours away, is a better beach deal.

Elsewhere, you can get a lot of value. "My last apartment in the north of Bogotá ran 1,100,000 per month + HOA fees (called *administración*) of 100,000," says Jeff Jung. That comes out to about $630 US. "Renters should find out both parts of the cost when looking for an apartment. You could find something old but decent for as low as $400 and spend up to $1,000 per month for rent only. I'm quoting unfurnished prices so a furnished place might start closer to US$500. Gas and electricity will run about $15 and $50, respectively, per month. Cable and internet can run closer to US pricing at $50-80 per month. A common money-saving tactic of Bogotanos is to live with others so you can get a larger, nicer place with all common housing costs shared."

David does just that in Medellin, sharing a spacious three-bedroom apartment with a view in the most desirable neighborhood of Poblado. His share averages between $330 and $340 with utilities. Those utilities are a shade over $200 per month for the three of them for electricity, gas, cable TV, fast internet, and land line phone. The neighborhood you're in makes a huge difference: if you lived in a typical older, middle-class area of Medellin, you could find a two-bedroom apartment for $400 rather easily.

Medellin Living contributor Jeff ran a four-part series on that website about his experience in finding apartments in Medellin. His last two have been large, with great views in a modern high-rise, with 24-hour security and a shared pool. He has paid less than $600 a month for both (unfurnished), for apartments that would easily be three or four times that amount in the best neighborhood of a major city like San Francisco, Vancouver, Toronto, or Chicago.

One odd aspect of Colombian cities though is that neighborhoods are graded by income level, so if you're in strata 1 you're living in poverty, but if you're in strata 6 you've made it and are loaded. So naturally the rents are much higher in the top strata, such as Poblado in Medellin, where it's much harder to find a deal on a furnished apartment.

I saw several houses for rent around the Coffee Triangle region for less than $500 per month and buying something there is naturally lower also. It's easy to find a good-sized house for under $50,000 in the smaller towns and cities of Colombia. That's especially true if you don't mind buying something older: the resale market for existing homes moves slowly here so you can get a great deal from someone who has been trying to sell the place for years. Just take your time to look around for the right deal. If small-town Colombia appeals to you, unfurnished rental houses can be found for as low as $100 per month and $400 can get you something with a lot of indoor and outdoor lounging space.

If you really want to keep your expenses down for a while and immerse yourself in Spanish at the same time, you can find a homestay arrangement with a family quite easily where you get your own room in a private house and your meals are included. This arrangement runs from $300 to $450 and gets your two main expenses covered for cheap. You'll give up a few things though, like privacy and diet choices, plus you had better check the internet speed when evaluating places if that's important to you.

Health Care

Expatriates in general praise Colombia's health care system, which is simple, transparent, and has well-trained doctors in the cities. Care is quick and prices are displayed on signs, prices that can start as low as $15 for a consultation with a doctor. To see a specialist is $33 and an emergency care consultation from a doctor in a hospital is $51.

Below the surface there have been a lot of protests as this book went to press by Colombians against proposed laws eroding the safety net and putting more power in the hands of private sector administrators. That's more of an issue for locals than foreigners though, since as the latter you'll probably pay out of pocket for health care or you'll be covered by some kind of international plan.

In Colombia you just take a number and wait your turn or for a specialist, make an appointment and probably be in the next day. Forget reams of paperwork and medical history you have to fill out in the USA before seeing the doctor. Here they'll only ask you what's relevant for the condition you're having and the red tape is almost non-existent.

You'll seldom pay many extra fees beyond medicines and the tab for lab work is usually under $10. Just to give you an idea for comparison's sake, a full colonoscopy will be less than $100 and a mammogram less than $40.

If you have a family or are older and want to be safe, you can buy a local comprehensive health insurance plan for $250-$400 per month that will also cover you for 30-90 days outside the country. For Colombia only policies for a single person, figure on $150 per month or less.

This is not really a "dental tourism" destination like Mexico or Costa Rica, but costs here are well less than half what you're probably spending now. A crown will be $250 to $450, a filling $35. Veneers that could costs you $2,000+ in the USA or UK will be more like $400 here.

Food & Drink

A decent "meal of the day" lunch will run you about $5 throughout Colombia. You can certainly pay less at places where local workers eat, or spend a few dollars more and get much better quality. That'll generally get you a soup, a main meat dish with a side or two, dessert, and a fresh juice or something else to drink. "That can easily go up in Bogota to $10-15 depending on where you eat," says Jeff.

Naturally dinners can run the gamut, from cobbled together street food for a couple dollars up to high-end restaurants at a 5-star hotel that will cost nearly as much as you would spend in Europe. In general, the food is not worth raving about, as there's limited variety in what's traditional fare and you have to be in a city to go beyond that. You can get plenty of fresh ingredients for cooking yourself though and prices average out to half or less what you'd pay in a developed country.

Getting a great cup of coffee is harder than it should be in Colombia since most of the best beans are exported. There are a variety of quality coffee shops in tourist areas and expat zones though and the fall back choice if all else fails is the Juan Valdez chain. You can usually expect to pay about half what you would in the U.S. or Europe for a quality cup of Joe, far less for the little cups served everywhere, even on the street, for a quick pick-me-up.

You can drink alcohol on the street in Colombia, which

makes walking around the walled city of Cartagena at sunset a lot more fun. A beer in a typical bar or restaurant will often be less than $2. Dave says going out to clubs and having a blast is not going to set you back very much in Medellin compared to a place like London, Las Vegas, or New York City. In a nightclub the usual routine is for the group to get bottle service. You pay $30 or so for a 750ml bottle of rum or *aguadiarte* (the favored anise flavored local spirit) and you get ice and mixers. "Colombians go out in groups," he says, "so if there are five of you that's $6 a person. Very few places have a cover charge. If they do it's generally a couple dollars and at the most, maybe the equivalent of $12 at the very fanciest place."

You can find a whole lot of different street food (*empanada, arepa con queso*, boiled/salted potatoes) for a dollar or less when you want to refuel for cheap. For a dollar you can also get a 600ml bottle of water, a local mass-market beer in a store, couple little *tinto* coffees on the street, a glass of fresh juice from a stall, or a kilo of seasonal fruit or vegetables.

Transportation

City buses are around 60 to 75 cents one way in most of the country. A one-way ticket on the nicest "TransMilenio" in Bogota will run you about 90 cents. The Medellin metro is about 85 cents.

"Taxis are plentiful and cheap," says Jeff. "The basic fare is about $1.80 and an expensive taxi ride will cost you $10—that's traveling a long distance across Bogota. Taxi drivers are not tipped." Dave says in Medellin he generally pays 4,200 – 10,000 pesos ($2.30 – $5.50). Prices don't vary from company to company and drivers here aren't usually inclined to take you for a ride to pump up the fare.

Intercity buses are comfortable and have bathrooms: you generally won't have to deal with a "chicken bus" unless you're way off the beaten path. They start at around $8 for a three-hour trip and can cost as much as $55 for long overnight routes, so sometimes it's worth it to fly instead. The two most expensive air routes in the country are Bogota to Cartagena and Bogota to San Andres, but there are frequent specials if you book ahead. You can sometimes find internal flight fares as low as $55 and often the longest routes are going for around $100.

Colombia is the home base of Avianca, one of the two largest airlines in Latin America. Plus it has several cities on the route map of Spirit Air, one of the bare-bones budget airlines in the USA. So this is a relatively inexpensive country to base yourself in if you plan on traveling outside the country a lot or visiting relatives on a regular basis. You won't be isolated here.

Cars are heavily taxed in Colombia and it's hard to find even the most bare-bones model for less than $16,000. So if you try to buy a used car on the cheap, it will likely have high mileage, manual transmission, and no air conditioning. Gasoline is slightly more expensive than in the USA, but lower than Europe.

Other Costs

It won't cost you a lot to feel cultured in Colombia. Many museums are free on Sundays and when they aren't the cost is negligible. The Gold Museum in Bogota, for instance, is less than $2. Cultural events are often free, especially if affiliated with a university, and if not you can usually get tickets for $10 or less. When I scoured ticket prices for Bogota and Medellin as I was writing this, I only found a few concerts priced higher than this, at $12.50 for the very best tickets.

A cell phone with data will run around $25-$35 per month for the average person. As mentioned in the housing section, Colombian neighborhoods are graded by income level. So not only does your neighborhood say volumes about how wealthy you are, it can also impact your utility costs. Those in strata 6 pay a much higher rate per kilowatt hour for electricity than those in strata 3, so you don't necessarily want to be in the same neighborhood as the captains of industry unless you have more money than you know what to do with. (Supposedly those in the poorest sections don't have it easy though: their rates may be lower, but the meter works on a pre-paid card system.) Renting in strata 4 or 5 can mean not just lower rent, but lower utility costs too. If you're not in strata 6 and you're a single or couple, you can expect to pay between $80 and $150 a month for everything.

A lot of clothing is made in Colombia and if you stick to what's typically sold domestically, prices can be quite reasonable. Aspirational brands like Levis, Nike, and Adidas will cost more than you'd pay where you came from though.

Ditto for electronics, which you should bring with you or buy in duty-free Panama when possible.

Prescription medicines are drastically cheaper in Colombia and most non-narcotic items can be purchased over the counter without a prescription. That's if you can find it: I spent two hours hoofing it around Cartagena trying to find a specific allergy medicine for my wife and came up empty. The selection is better in larger cities.

Most people who can afford to have a maid clean their house or apartment twice a week for $150 to $250 a month depending on where they live.

Visas for Colombia

Is too much choice a bad thing? There are a head-spinning 17 options for a visa in Colombia, so some people throw up their hands and let a lawyer sort it out. The good news is, with that many options you can almost surely find one that will fit your situation. With plenty of patience and an ability to read forms in Spanish, you can manage it yourself in time.

Most of the residency permits cost $150 to $350, not counting what you may lay out for preparation or translations. In general, Colombia gets high marks for its visa application process. It's a lot of work, as always, but what's required is generally transparent and not subject to change every time you visit the office. With this many options though, laws do change regularly and there was a big revamp in the summer of 2013. Make sure any article you read on the subject is dated later than that.

When you first arrive, a tourist visa will probably be fine. You get three months in Colombia upon entering the country as a tourist. To extend that another three months you can either leave the country and return or go apply for an extension for about $40. But you can only stay six months of a calendar year this way, so you have to get out after that and not return for half a year. The first level of straight temporary residency visa is good for six or twelve months.

Dave obtained a business visa by showing a steady

stream of income and what he was working on. It's good for 19 months. He says some digital nomads and freelancers opt for an "independent activities visa" which is more ambiguous.

Those who have found local love can apply for a "civil partnership visa." If you're married to a local or are just declaring them as a civil partner, you can get a one-year visa that can then be extended to three years. After that, you can get permanent residency. For a work visa, you need to apply in your home country or Colombia, pay a non-refundable $50, and submit a slew of paperwork. This includes your work contract, a copy of your degree, a translation of that, and on and on. Once approved—which may take a few office visits to tie up loose ends—you then finish up with the rest of the payments.

If you're retired, $1,400 a month is the amount of income they want to see for a pensioner visa. That's good for a year and can be renewed indefinitely.

You can buy your way in to get a "resident investor" visa, but that requires a cool $100,000. A business owner visa cannot be for a sole proprietorship: you must be planning to hire local employees.

After you have been in the country for five years on temporary residency visas, you can apply for a "qualified resident visa" or a "permanent resident visa" that doesn't require regular renewals.

If you can read Spanish, here's the official word on all these and more from the Colombian government:

http://www.cancilleria.gov.co/tramites_servicios/visas/categorias/temporal/tp4

If you're willing to pay for help, try ColombiaVisas.com.

Downsides

Colombia has come a long way since its cocaine cartels made it the most dangerous country in the world for a while, but it's still not a fairytale land of peace and joy. The Medellin homicide rate has dropped dramatically, but it's still 38 per 100,000 people annually. That's lower than New Orleans and Guatemala City, but higher than all but a handful of cities in Mexico. Cali's is stuck at 86 per 100,000 though, which makes it one of the worst in South America.

Some say the official stratification of the population by level of wealth holds down mobility and the poor are likely to stay poor for life. While wages at the bottom are low ($500 a month including benefits), many local business owners complain the quality of work is low too and getting rid of someone costs more than paying them. Still, the middle class here is a much larger percentage of the population than in many other countries profiled in this book.

Many who move here are less than thrilled with the food in Colombia, so their budget creeps up as they start frequenting more international restaurants to get some variety. While there are gourmet level restaurants in the cities, in much of the country real foodies are going to be disappointed.

Punctuality is not a prized trait here, even by Latin America's lax standards. Expect to wait around a lot for everything from business appointments to appliance deliveries.

Some foreign women admit having a tougher time than usual here finding someone to date. The competition is probably stiffer here than anywhere else in the Americas—at least in the opinion of most men I've talked to who live here or have traveled here. You'll have a little easier time if you're a natural blond with blue eyes because you'll be exotic.

For More information

MedellinLiving.com (Medellinliving.com)
ColombiaVisas.com (colombiavisas.com)
Escape Artist Colombia (Colombia.escapeartist.com)
Colombia visa information (Cancilleria.gov.co)
Expat Exchange Colombia forum

Chapter 18: Vietnam

Pros: cheap prices, three-month tourist visa, ample short-term rentals, great food, decent internet, different climate options.
Cons: communist bureaucracy, heavy traffic, heavy rainy season, tropical bugs/diseases, hot and humid.

For many potential expatriates, Vietnam is not the first place that will spring to mind. For many digital nomads though, this has become an entrepreneurial hotspot. In Ho Chi Minh City (Saigon) especially, there are lots of people with laptop jobs you can bounce ideas off of and get advice from about settling in.

This country is one of the best values in the world for travelers, especially when it comes to lodging and food. Naturally that makes it a great value for residents too. You can land one day and have a short-term apartment for a good price the next. Many foreigners who live here don't even care if there's a kitchen or not. They eat out every meal and just use the fridge for beer and sodas. (For juice, they just get it fresh squeezed from a local stand.)

Forget the image of a war-torn country or a bleak communist wasteland. This is not some sad and downtrodden place anymore where a lot of people are struggling to get by. It's a thriving economy where motorbikes seem to sprout from the ground each time it rains. When you say, "Everybody and his brother has one," it's really true. This is a business-friendly country where regulations are lighter than you would expect, though the "soak the rich foreigners" attitude is unfortunately still alive and well. Getting the local price for goods and services here sometimes takes a lot of effort and patience—and the willingness to walk away when the difference is really blatant.

With a coastline as long as the US west coast, there are plenty of beaches to choose from. You'll also find soaring mountains, waterfalls, jungles, and hill-tribe trekking areas that aren't as commercialized as Thailand's. Most of the beauty here is of the natural type: the older architecture was wooden and most has long since vanished, outside Hué anyway.

Many educated locals speak English in Vietnam, especially in the south. The local language is tonal (like Chinese or Thai), but the writing uses Roman letters with accent marks. So with a little effort, you should at least be able to learn to read menus and navigate street signs.

Despite the madness you'll encounter on the streets and barely passable sidewalks, there's a lot to uncover in Vietnam, the food is interesting, and one study found the locals to be the second-happiest people in the world behind Costa Rica.

The most popular spots after the largest city are Hanoi, Danang, Hoi An, Hué, and Nha Trang. Others have found their bliss in cooler highland areas like Sapa.

Ho Chi Minh City (Saigon) - Huge, spread-out, chaotic, and hot, this is also clearly the business center of Vietnam and a hub for virtual entrepreneurs. This is the place with the best health care, shopping, and air connections.

Hanoi - The second largest city is calmer but more compact, with architecture from the French and an old quarter great for strolling. This is a traveler base for excursions to Ha Long Bay and the northern hill tribe areas, so there is plenty to do and see nearby. It's cooler here than in the south much of the year, though summers are equally brutal.

Danang - Vietnam's cleanest city strikes some as boring, but it's close to beaches, islands, Hoi An, and beautiful countryside. Two golf courses are nearby, one of them frequently tagged as the best in the country.

Hoi An - This popular tourist spot is the center for getting clothes custom tailored, so you'll be well dressed if you live here. Historic Chinese and French buildings vie for attention and there are stunning beaches nearby. Danang is about 30 minutes away to hit big supermarkets.

Hué - Vietnam's most interesting historic area is an easy city to navigate. It sits on a large river and has train connections north and south.

If you want to live a frugal life, it's quite easy to do here. Hanoi resident Wendy Justice writes about her experiences often in Live and Invest Overseas. She and her husband live on an average of $1,000 a month, including a furnished apartment that they moved right into after arrival and have stayed in.

Or you can choose to live large on what's not really a large salary by developed world standards. "I probably spend a lot more than most people," says John Myers, who does software interface design and runs several online businesses. "I'm higher maintenance I guess." He estimates he spends $2,000 to $2,500 a month, which includes a luxury apartment with twice-daily maid and laundry service, a gym membership, and lots of socializing. "Also, there are a lot of good food delivery places here connected to the restaurants," he adds.

Housing Costs

As in most countries, cities cost more to live in than small towns and rural areas, but Vietnam is a good value no matter where you choose to live. You can get a 900-square-foot apartment in the best area of Danang for around $600. Apartment prices can be half that in smaller towns, especially if you're content with the kinds of places most locals live in, but almost anywhere you can find something nice and reasonably roomy in the range of $400 to $800 per month.

James Clark and many other digital nomads who have settled in Ho Chi Minh City find that there's an easy network of short-term rentals to tap into upon arrival. "Every time I've returned, I've found a place within one day for a short-term rental. I'll book a guesthouse room for one night and the next day I've found a place," James says.

What you get for your money is generally quite good. "You can get your own private furnished one-bedroom apartment in District 1 where I am for $500 that will be decent," he says. "That includes a maid who comes three times a week and does your laundry. All of them include internet. Electricity is never included though, which is $20 a month if you're not there much, three or four times as much if you have the air conditioning running all the time."

If you want to get a modern apartment like you would find in a big city in the USA or Europe, expect to pay $450 to $1,200 for a furnished one in a good district of Hanoi or Saigon. Jon Myers pays $1,050 for his "big one bedroom with floor to ceiling windows on the corners that open up." He has a good work-space for his home office and there's no long-term lease. "I have a relationship with the owners and have been there a few years," he says.

To put things in perspective, the crowdsourced cost of living site Numbeo.com says average rental costs in Hanoi or Ho Chi Minh City are less than one-fifth what they would be in New York City or London. So if you're paying $3,000 a month for an apartment there, you can probably get something comparable here for $600.

In other cities, you can take your time looking around while sleeping in a value-priced hotel. Vietnam may just be the best accommodation value in the world. Western toilets, hot water, clean sheets, and fresh towels are pretty standard even in cheapie backpacker places running $10-$20 double per night. You'll say "Wow" more often than "Ugh" when opening the door to your room the first time.

Food and Drink Costs

Most expatriates who don't try to live on a western diet or eat at fancy restaurants constantly easily get by on a food budget of $300 a month eating very well. Some do it for half that and have a well-balanced, nutritious diet. Figure on $300 to $500 a month for a couple if you're not on a strict budget and you frequent nice restaurants now and then. This is a country though where you can get a big filling bowl of pho soup on the street for $1.50 in a central business district, half that in most other areas. If you spend more than $5 on lunch it was probably in a nice restaurant with uniformed waiters.

Tropical fruit is a bargain, often $1 or less for a kilo. Parts of the country are at higher elevations, so there's a good range of vegetables too. This is one of the world's greatest producers of coffee, rice, shrimp, and multiple other staples, so prices on those are quite good if you go to the right stores. You'll pay $1 or less for a kilo (2.2 pounds) of rice, tomatoes, potatoes, peppers, or onions. For that dollar you'll probably get two kilos of lettuce or cabbage. Because of the French influence, this is one of the few Asian countries where you can get good, inexpensive baguettes.

This is one of the cheapest countries in the world for beer, which gives it a huge edge over Malaysia and even Thailand if you like to tip one back on a hot day. Almost every day is a hot day here. A big liter glass can be as little as 50 cents at a sidewalk *bia hoi* stand, with a bottled beer averaging a buck or less in a restaurant or bar.

Sodas and basic coffees are 30-50 cents, though you can spend $2 on a really good coffee at a cafe. Fruit juices and shakes are 40-80 cents. Ice cream and coconut popsicles can be a welcome treat in the heat and they're not much of a splurge at 50 cents to $1.

A cocktail will run $2 to $5 in a bar. Rice wine and Russian vodka are inexpensive, but vary greatly in quality. Foreign liquor here is about the same retail price as in the U.S., so you can drink your Jack Daniels or Tanqueray in a cocktail without breaking the bank.

Transportation Costs

You can easily get by without a car here unless you live in a suburban or rural area and need it for a commute or hauling groceries. Most of the population gets around on buses and motorbikes within the cities, so if you can get used to going with the flow, it's cheap and easy to follow their lead. If you don't want to buy a motorbike ($800 to $2,000), you can rent one for $100 a month or less.

Taxi rides range from 50 cents to $4 for most distances around the big cities, though it will cost more to and from the airport. Local city buses are 15-20 cents once you figure out the routes. To travel the long distance between Hanoi and Saigon will cost anywhere from $50 to $125 by bus, train, or plane. Shorter trips, such as the scenic three-hour train from Danang to Hue, are more like $3 - $5.

Although crossing the street on foot in Vietnam takes some getting used to because of the sea of motorbikes flowing around you, many neighborhoods are easy to navigate on foot. Some expatriates get almost everything they need in their local area, so their transportation costs are just occasional taxis and costs to leave the country on a visa run every three months.

Health Care

In a nutshell, Vietnamese health care is better than Cambodia's, but worse than Thailand's or Malaysia's. The system is government run and tightly controlled, without the plethora of gleaming private hospitals dishing out medical tourism care that you find in some other Southeast Asian countries. This doesn't mean you'll get terrible care though: the government hospitals in the cities have modern machines and people who know how to run them. The doctors may earn a measly government salary, but that doesn't mean they're not well trained.

The main obstacle is often language. Some expats learn to hire an interpreter to bring with them to the doctor (or get a favor from a Vietnamese friend who speaks English) because even counting that payment the total will be less than a private clinic. It's not uncommon to pay $5 or less for a doctor consultation, about the same for many tests like an ultrasound or EKG, and less than $2 for an x-ray.

If you need a doctor who speaks English, you will often pay for more to go to a private hospital or outpatient center, though compared to your home country the costs will still probably seem quite reasonable. Hospitals in the largest cities are good enough now for most issues, but some foreigners feel more comfortable grabbing a cheap flight to Bangkok for major treatment or surgery since the service and communication there are some of the best in the world.

Other Costs

John Myers pays an average of $75 a month extra for electricity, $20 a month for a phone plan with unlimited data. His internet is included in his rent and "goes through fits," but when it's on it's really on, at 32 mbps on average. If you have to pay for your own internet, expect it to be between $12 and $25 per month depending on speed, which probably won't be that fast outside of urban districts.

Water can range from $4 to $20 a month depending on usage, garbage pick-up is a dollar or two a week if it's available. Electricity is around 50 cents per kilowatt hour, but ramps up after a certain amount if you have a big house with lots of air conditioners running. Cable/satellite TV starts at $4 and can rise to $25 with lots of premium channels. Bottled propane gas canisters for cooking and hot water will average out to $5-$10 per month.

It's inexpensive to get cultural stimulation in Vietnam. Admission charges at most museums are between 15 cents and $1.50. The outliers, such as the Hue royal tombs, still rarely top $4. Most cultural performances, even if geared to tourists, are between $1.50 and $5. The rare exceptions are grand operas or symphony performances in the big cities, often with foreign troupes on the bill. Still, they'll be a fraction of what you would pay for tickets in your home country.

There are three cell phone companies battling it out in this market, so costs are very low to pick up a new SIM card ($4 or less) and get pre-paid service for voice and data.

As you'd probably guess just looking at the staff at your local nail salon, the Vietnamese have plenty of experience giving manicures and pedicures. Here at the source you'll probably pay around a dollar or two for either. Services like waxing and facials will be a few dollars, an hour-long massage $10 or less if you're not at a resort.

When you fly in to Vietnam you can get a one-month visa on arrival. If you apply ahead of time though, you can get a three-month multi-entry visa instead. With that you just need to leave the country every three months to get a new one and start the cycle over again. Unofficially though, it's possible to renew it without leaving at all. John Myers lived in Thailand for a year and hated the constant visa runs he had to do. "Vietnam's visa situation is very friendly, even if it doesn't seem like it on the surface. I just hire a service, show up with US dollars, and a hundred bucks gets me a three-month, multiple entry visa again."

If you do have to go and come back, Cambodia, Laos, and Thailand are nearby and inexpensive to get to for a break. There are also frequent flight sales to Malaysia, Singapore, and Indonesia.

It is possible to get a business visa, but that's more complicated. In most cases you either need to show that you will be employing locals or you need to be sponsored by a local company to do a job a foreigner is required for, like teaching English or running the local division of an international company. You'll be expected to show a copy of your university degree and pass a criminal background check.

Others have claimed success getting a work visa for a freelancer/business owner just by showing sufficient proof of income that's earned in another country. If you manage this, it only has to be renewed every six months and you can go on like this for years.

Downsides

What people usually think the downsides of living in a communist country will be turn out to be not such a big deal. There's far more surveillance, snooping, and rule navigation to deal with in the UK or USA than there is in Vietnam. You do have a lot of state-owned enterprises though (basically any company starting with "Vina"). This can stifle competition and keep standards low. There is some banning of certain websites and social media, but the government is really bad at it. Most foreigners figure out a way around the blocks in a few minutes and most coffee shops use some kind of proxy server to reroute traffic.

You can look around and see that capitalism is running at extreme speed here, so where you really feel the lingering effects of communism is the attitude that those who have more should pay more. It's often next to impossible to get old ladies selling fruit in Hanoi to give a white face a price that's even double what the locals pay—never mind parity. This gets a little better each year though as fixed-price supermarkets proliferate and younger food stall owners find they get more repeat business by being more even-handed.

As mentioned in the health care section, most people go through a government-run, centralized system here that is perpetually underfunded. If you want the best equipment and an English-speaking doctor, you either have to pay a lot more at a private center or head to Bangkok.

Navigating the traffic in Vietnam's cities and trying to cross the street are both learned skills that seem insurmountable when you first arrive. From a third-floor building in Saigon you can see a sea of motorbikes 1,500 riders deep, flowing around the smaller number of cars like a stream moving past the rocks. As a byproduct, noise and pollution are both a big problem. Environmental controls are lacking throughout the country. We stopped counting the dead fish in the lake in central Hanoi when we passed 50 the last time I was there.

Lastly, the further south you go, the hotter, muggier, and buggier it gets. Some people thrive on that kind of heat, but be advised that for part of the year it can routinely top 100 degrees F, even in Hanoi.

For More Information

A comprehensive guide to Saigon street food on LegalNomads.com

Wood Egg Vietnam startup guide

ExpatExchange Vietnam forum

Expat blogs in Vietnam on Expat-Blog.com

Chapter 19: Argentina

Pros: Vibrant capital, European attitudes, great wine, good food, good beer, beautiful scenery, fashion, arts, culture, easy visas, gay-friendly, sensible drug laws, fast internet, free-to-cheap health care, good infrastructure.
Cons: frequent financial crises, fragile banking system, wacky politics, petty crime, long distances, long way from other continents, expensive flights, very late dinner/nightlife hours

Cathy Brown was looking to escape the boring, predictable life of a mother in suburban Michigan and wanted to find somewhere that was exotic but safe, cheaper but with decent infrastructure and education. Her kids were 4, 6, and 8 at the time and she wanted their view of the world to be broader. She wanted their life and their options to be more flexible. "So I bought one-way tickets to Buenos Aires," she says. "I figured that if we were going to learn a second language, Spanish would be the most helpful. I had been to Peru before and liked the Latin culture, the warmth and hospitality. People actually smile and hug constantly. Argentina seemed like a good choice and if it didn't work out, we could always move on."

She quickly decided that Buenos Aires was too big and too congested, so the family went to Mendoza. "That still didn't feel like the right place," Cathy said, and everybody who knew me well kept mentioning this town of El Bolson in Patagonia, saying that's where we should go. They were right."

She and her kids, now a few years older, are settled in El Bolson, an "artistic, hippy mountain town" that's a center for hiking and is the microbrew valley of Argentina. "Living here is about as laid-back as it gets," she says. There's gorgeous scenery, with mountains on all sides, and a really welcoming community. People get together on weekends to do projects. It's very safe: you see old ladies out hitchhiking to get to town and back"

A large number of people who visit Argentina seem to dream of living there for a while at some point in their life.

The capital, Buenos Aires, is a major tourism magnet, but that's just the beginning in a country that has more land than Mexico or Indonesia—but with a much lower population density.

There's no shortage of iconic images you can associate with this country: tango dancers, gauchos, soccer champs, the Mendoza vineyards with the Andes Mountains behind them, and the glorious peaks of southern Patagonia. There's a lot of diversity in these landscapes. Up north you have a dramatic desert on one side and Iguazu Falls on the other. There are seasides, cities and farms in the middle, down to glaciers and freezing cold in the jumping off point to Antarctica.

I could hear birds singing outside the window when I interviewed Leigh Shulman, a mother who moved with her husband and child from Brooklyn to Argentina. Eventually they ended up on the outskirts of the northern city of Salta. "We lived in Panama for a while and didn't like it so much," she says. "We went to Costa Rica and actually had a job offer from a friend who ran an organization, but we had planned a trip down here anyway after we arrived we wanted to stay. We were originally looking at Montevideo in Uruguay. We stayed in Buenos Aires for a while, but some friends were moving to Salta and we ended up following them. We liked it so much here that we bought a big house and stayed."

The distances here are vast though, so getting around the country or returning from your remote home somewhere to see relatives in the country you left is no easy task. Driving distance from Buenos Aires to El Bolson is more than 1,000 miles (1,695 kilometers). Buenos Aires to Salta is almost as far in the opposite direction. Internal fights are both expensive and nonsensical: you must fly through Buenos Aires when going between cities, yet each leg gets charged as a full flight instead of a hub stop. You can take a bus, and it may be quite nice, but on many routes you'll be on that bus for 24 hours or more. Round-trip flights to the U.S. or Canada from Buenos Aires are rarely less than $1,200 and to most cities in Europe they're even higher.

Once you get settled in though, prices can be very reasonable, especially if you have a way of bringing in lots of U.S. dollars or euros in cash. That's because there are two exchange rates in Argentina's fragile economy: the official rate and the "blue rate" you can get on the street from money-changers. The latter is typically 20 to 35 percent better than the official one and both are printed in the local newspapers. Getting to your money electronically is almost like a weekly hobby here though: many banks limit ATM withdrawals to around $150, so you end up hopping from one bank to another or using a service like Xoom to take out larger amounts of pesos. Hold onto your home country Paypal account because the banks here are too unstable to work with that service locally; the best bet is to get a debit card you can use to pull money from in Argentina using your original country account. It's not unheard of to get counterfeit money either. Leigh has even gotten a bogus bill from her bank teller!

The good news is, they're not real big on rules in Argentina and that includes visa rules. It will probably cost you a lot to enter for the first time because this is one of those countries (like Brazil and Bolivia) that has a retaliatory visa fee policy. Whatever Argentines pay to enter the country on your passport, that's what you'll pay to enter theirs. It's good for 10 years or the life of your passport, however, so after that you can come and go without paying again. Many renew their tourist visa indefinitely, leaving the country every three months for a short hop to Chile or Uruguay.

There are also no nanny rules about drugs either, especially marijuana, which is essentially a non-issue for personal use. (Neighboring Uruguay is even more lax, currently setting up a way for it to be sold in taxed shops.) This is also one of the most friendly countries south of Mexico for LGBT couples or singles.

Housing Costs

Lisa Besserman lived in New York City most of her life and was facing the prospect of looking for a new apartment in Manhattan because her lease was up. "The rental prices were absolutely ridiculous, super-expensive," she says. "My company was going through some changes and my job position didn't feel stable. I didn't want to be spending thousands of dollars on rent without being secure about my job. I was up for a promotion though and proposed a deal with my boss where I would work remotely for a few months instead, at the same pay rate, and I would go live somewhere cheaper. They said yes, so I looked at a map for places with a similar time zone and ended up in Buenos Aires."

She did her three months of work for her old company, then decided not to come back. She left the job and now she runs her own company in Argentina: Startup Buenos Aires. "I pay $700 a month for my duplex apartment in Palermo Hollywood, a great neighborhood, and it's a doorman building with a pool. If you transplanted this place into Soho in Manhattan, which is a pretty similar kind of neighborhood feel, it would easily cost $10,000 to $15,000 per month."

Naturally the prices drop when you settle in a smaller city or town. While it may be hard to find a nice apartment for less than $500 in the capital, that will get you something furnished and modern in Salta, Mendoza, Cordoba, or Rosario. Where Cathy lives in rural Patagonia, $350 gets her a four bedroom, two-bath house on 15 acres, beside a river.

Lining something up ahead of time is quite difficult though; hardly any agencies list prices online. The best plan is to rent a short-term apartment or stay in an apart-hotel at first so you can take your time looking around. Get recommendations from others (both locals and expatriates) on which agencies are trustworthy and look at plenty of apartments to assess what's a good value.

If you're going to buy a house or condo here, figure on paying the whole amount in cash, in dollars. People literally bring bags of money to a closing. In theory you can get a mortgage, but with interest rates running at 18%, you probably don't want to. You can't find the bargains here you could 10 years ago since Argentines view real estate as one of their reliable places to put their cash and there have also been buyers from Brazil coming in too. If the financial system collapses again though like it did in the early 2000s, who knows?

Land can be surprisingly expensive in many areas, but construction costs are not. "You can hire a skilled workman for $40 to $50 a day," says Cathy.

Health Care Costs

Get ready to see a dramatic drop in your health care costs when you move to Argentina, from emergency care to elective care to medicine. "Despite having company insurance, I was paying nearly $800 per month for health care in New York City," says Lisa, "and I was a healthy 20-something. I'm terrified of moving back there and feel like if I do I have no choice but to base where I work on who has the best insurance plan."

Here she rarely even thinks about it. She had an ankle injury that required going to the emergency room, getting x-rays, and seeing a doctor. It cost her the equivalent of $60 at a private hospital. Getting adjusted at a chiropractor will cost $25-$30.

Cathy Brown's son was kicked by a horse and suffered several broken bones. He was in the hospital for days. Although they had just arrived in the country on tourist visas, when it was time to go there was no bill to pay. It was completely free, no questions asked. Whether you're a citizen, tourist, or legal resident, health care in public hospitals is gratis.

Dental work comes with a cost, but is still a fraction of the cost of the U.S., Canada, or Europe. A cleaning may be $25, getting a cavity filled $50 tops.

"To give you an example of the difference in drug costs," Lisa adds, "birth control pills used to cost $30 to $50 a month in the U.S. even with insurance. Here the same package is $5-$8 without insurance, just walking in and buying them."

If you do purchase health insurance in Argentina, that won't set you back too much. A full-blown family plan that makes use of the best private hospitals and clinics will run about $300 per month. "If you pay $60 more you can get plastic surgery done once a year," Leah adds with a laugh. If you do want to have a nip and tuck—very popular here—you will find some of the best rates in the world, performed by doctors with plenty of daily experience.

Food & Drink

If you like a good steak dinner accompanied by a nice bottle of wine, you'll be in heaven here. They take their grilled meats very seriously in this country and it's considered a God-given right to sip wine with every meal. Prices are quite reasonable on both, to the point where a group of people can go out and eat to their heart's content for $10 a person or less. The things Argentines do well they do very well: barbecued meat, wine, Italian food, coffee, ice cream, and pastries.

The recent financial problems have wreaked havoc with prices and supplies though. When the peso fell by 19 percent in January of 2013, many store shelves were bare and prices for what was available skyrocketed soon after in local currency terms.

This is a farming nation, so it's easy to find local meat, fruit, and vegetables at good prices. The closer to the source you are, the less they'll cost. "I'm a real foodie, but I still probably only spend $60 a week for food and wine for the four of us," Cathy says. "I get most of our food from neighbors who grow it. The flour is from locally ground wheat and we can get honey, milk, vegetables, and meat from neighbors who produce it. I can get really high-quality microbrews for $2-$3 a liter. We do a lot of bartering in this area, which keeps the costs down. You can have a really nice family life here for $1,000 a month. It's a huge part of the reason I live here."

Cathy fully admits she could not live on even twice this amount in the capital. Also, if she were further south in Patagonia where transportation costs of goods are higher (and there's a shorter growing season), it would be more expensive. Then again, in Buenos Aires it's easier to find a real job, as opposed to where she is, which really requires having a virtual job paying the bills.

Keep in mind too that $1,000 a month is higher than the average Argentine salary and high inflation can hit food prices hard, especially for workers whose wages don't rise at the same rate. Most expatriates have it much easier since they're cashing in dollars instead of working in pesos.

Transportation

If you only move around the city where you live, transportation costs in Argentina are minimal. "Most taxi rides in Buenos Aires cost me what I paid for a subway ride in New York City," says Lisa. "The local metro is less than 30 cents."

If you're riding a long distance in a taxi, your fare may creep up to $4 or $5. When Cathy rides the 25 kms into the closest city from her house, it costs around $10. Local bus rides are generally 25 to 75 cents.

This is a big country though, so when you want to take a trip to another city, that's when your costs are really going to be substantial because of the long distances. A bus ticket from Bariloche to Buenos Aires can cost $100 per person one-way and a flight will be twice that much.

Visas

When it comes to visas, most foreigners in Argentina assume they're going to have to leave the country every three months. With Uruguay and Chile on their doorstep though, that's not really a big deal. People who have come to work for an international company tend to get a work visa, but many others just leave four times a year—indefinitely. If something happens and they overstay their visa, it's not the end of the world. "Argentina is one of the most lax countries for visas," Cathy says. "I don't want to do anything wrong because I've got kids, but I've heard from a lot of people that if you overstay your visa, you just have to pay 300 pesos (less than $40 at the official rate), whether you overstayed a day or five years. They sign off and you're on your way."

If she's not leaving for her travel writing job and the kids haven't gone back to the USA, they make a quick crossing into Chile. "If we really wanted to we could do it on foot, but my oldest daughter is not excited about that," she says. "So we rent a car, cross the border, and can be back in the afternoon."

If you're only going to stay six months at a time, you may be able to renew your tourist visa locally without leaving the country. That's generally only going to work once though, so it's best for people not planning to spend the whole year here.

Getting a business visa requires a letter from an employer, a specified time period, and the employer's acceptance of financial responsibility for the traveler. For obvious reasons, the employer really has to want you to make this happen. If you get one though, multiple-entry business visas are valid for four years.

There are various long-term residence permits valid from one to three years, but you'll probably need to hire a lawyer and be prepared for a long slog. The Argentines love bureaucracy and paperwork and you'll need to navigate a dizzying array of papers and people. The financial requirement is not daunting though: proof of income of $900 a month that you can transfer into an Argentine bank. For those of retirement age, it's even lower. Once you do manage to secure a one-year residency visa and have renewed it twice, you can then apply for permanent legal residency. You are then allowed to work legally. Two more years and then you can apply for citizenship if you plan on sticking around permanently.

In a country like this, there are ways around the rules. If you buy property under a corporation you have formed, you could offer yourself a job and get a business visa. Invest enough money in the local economy, and you could get on the fast track. If you spend enough time in the country asking questions, and you have some capital, you can certainly find other options for speeding things along.

Other Costs

Thanks to subsidized electricity, Argentina has some of the lowest monthly utility costs in Latin America. Lisa pays $5-$8 a month for her apartment of around 1,000 square feet. "I thought it would go up a lot when we were running the air conditioning in the summer, but it was only a couple dollars more," she says.

Cathy Brown pays even less in her small town. "My last electric bill was around $4," she says. "And that was for two months." Houses are heated with wood there though in the winter, with a trailer load being around $25. Her water is free and comes from a well, while cooking gas is $2 for a tank that will last a couple months.

Leah and her family live in a large house they own in Salta, but still only pay $10-$15 per month in electricity and $8-$10 per month for gas and water combined.

Cable and internet together are $15-$18 per month depending on the package. "In New York City I paid $150 per month for about the same bundle," says Lisa. Internet in

Argentina is not pokey either: the country has twice the world average for internet penetration and most of it is fast broadband.

Private school costs for the kids range from $120 to $350 per month, with only a few elite international ones in Buenos Aires charging more than that.

Downsides

In many ways Argentina sounds like paradise, but of course like anywhere there are problems. The economy could collapse at any moment and nobody has much faith in the government to get anything done. People are used to fending for themselves and finding ways to get around the system. (Check out the Oscar-winning movie *The Secret in Their Eyes* to see the country's typical bureaucrats in full public service glory.) Leah had to give up on the first internet company they contacted after weeks of calls and waiting for someone to show up. Promises are often not kept, customer service can be non-existent, and times to show up to do work are treated as just suggestions.

The import restrictions imposed in desperation by Cristina Kirchner to protect domestic companies has meant that getting any products from outside Argentina has become difficult and expensive—from electronics to perfume to tropical fruit. With the banking system in disarray, it's hard to take the local currency seriously.

If you ask what expatriates complain about the most, it often comes down to the lack of variety in the food. Argentine cuisine is kind of a one-trick pony and it's difficult to find ethnic food from other countries, especially outside of Buenos Aires. Partly because of demand and partly because of import restrictions, there's not much variety in the local supermarkets. Finding Asian spices, hot sauce, peanut butter, or maple syrup can be an exercise in frustration. "Can you bring something back for me?" is a common request when a friend is visiting another country.

Some expats with family in other places can feel like they're a long way from loved ones, which they are. Getting back to the northern hemisphere can take a whole day or night at best, longer with connections, on an expensive ticket.

For More Information

Transitions Abroad Argentina Living section
Wander-Argentina.com`
Expat Blogs from Argentina on ExpatsBlog.com
Startup Buenos Aires

Chapter 20: Nicaragua

Pros: Very cheap prices, low bar for retirement visa, variety of landscapes, strong (but not overwhelming) expatriate population, relatively cheap airfares, lots of opportunities to start a business.
Cons: Still a lot of poverty, very basic public transportation, unattractive capital city, internet is mostly wireless, advanced health care limited to Managua.

"If you make $1,000 a month, you can drive a small car, take your family out to decent restaurants sometimes, and visit a place like this on the weekends." That was an offhand comment from my Nicaraguan guide Pablo when we were at the overlook area checking out Lake Apoyo between Managua and Granada. "On that salary, you are middle class here."

A lot more people are stepping up to that level in Nicaragua, as the economy keeps improving and its relatively low crime rate makes it a place where international companies want to invest. If you're coming from a developed country though, it's an incredibly cheap place to live.

In most respects, Nicaragua is the cheapest place to travel in Latin America, which makes it the cheapest destination in the Americas period. Since it's also close and easy to get to for a reasonable airfare, at least for those of us in the U.S. and Canada, moving to Nicaragua and getting set up here is not going to set you back very much. When it's time for a break, you've got a lot of options here or you can make a quick hop to Costa Rica.

If you're American or Canadian and you ask me where you could pack a few suitcases and take off with just a grand or two in your bank account, this is where I'd tell you to go. You can stay a while on a tourist visa, there's a good expat support critical mass in place, and you can coast along for cheap while you get established. You'll probably pay more to fly your surfboard down than you will for your first week's meals and groceries. The average after-tax salary in this country is around $600 a month, so if you've got just an average social security check to live on, you're still going to be relatively well-off by local standards.

"My pension alone is 3-4 times what the average Nica makes," American Jim Lynch told me over coffee in Granada. "We spend around $1,800 a month, which is extravagant by local standards. We live in a big air-conditioned house with a swimming pool. We eat out whenever we want, wherever we want. Medical care is so inexpensive here we don't even have insurance. We just pay for things as they come up. I had to go to the best hospital in Managua for surgery and it was cheap enough that I put it on a credit card."

This is also a country on the rise—from a low base to be sure—but there's a real feeling that it's a land on the upswing, including in the foreigner-friendly tourism sector.

Don't come to enjoy ruins from ancient civilizations or go sightseeing in the traditional sense. Come to take pleasure in the great, unspoiled outdoors and explore a land where there are few signs of mass tourism. If you're the type that yearns to be a pioneer and don't like being tied down by a lot of rules, Nicaragua is a great "blank slate" destination. If you're looking for a laid-back lifestyle, it's hard to beat San Juan del Sur. "There are people here from their early 20s to their 70s from all over the world," says Gord MacKay, who moved to Nicaragua with his wife Elisha several years ago. "There's a very relaxed vibe. Even the real estate agents are surfers; it's hard to find them in the office."

The main expatriate center is the colonial city of Granada, which is a short drive or shuttle bus ride from Managua, where most of the business population lives. Granada is a clean, picturesque small city that's easily navigated by foot or bicycle. It is by the country's largest lake and has plenty of outdoor recreational opportunities nearby. With a fairly large number of expatriates established there, you can find good restaurants, coffee shops, a bookstore, and holistic health centers.

Leon is the other city attracting a fair number of foreigners, though the number is much smaller. This is a university town closer to the coast, north of Managua. Apart from San Juan del Sur and some nearby communities, no other locations have more than a handful of foreigners in place. You'll have to be a pioneer in those, but you'll also benefit from the lack of a "gringo effect" driving up prices.

Housing Costs

The price of renting an apartment or home here is probably going to make your previous place look like Tokyo in comparison. The crowdsourced site Numbeo.com says the average price of a one-bedroom apartment outside the capital is $175 and the average for a three-bedroom is $350. On their scale where New York City is 100, Managua is a 10.

Gord and Elisha MacKay have a better perspective than most because they have lived in Leon, Granada, and San Juan del Sur. They've detailed their living expenditures to the penny on their InNicaNow.com blog. They paid $300 for a one-bedroom apartment in Leon and $550 for a swanky furnished apartment in a building with a pool in Granada. They are now are back to $300 a month in San Juan del Sur—but for a two-bedroom furnished house that includes cable and water in the rent.

Jim and Carol pay $650 per month for that big house they're in. They pay another couple hundred in utilities, much of that electricity for the air conditioning, pool, and "a 55-inch flat-screen TV."

As is usually the case, you're going to find much better deals after arrival than you will if you're trying to set up something in advance. This is a country, after all, where less than half the population has internet access, even in urban areas. It's best to get a short-term rental or hotel room at first and start asking around locally about rentals.

Despite more than a decade of non-stop promotion in the likes of *International Living*, *Live and Invest Overseas*, and *House Hunters International*, not enough foreigners have arrived in Nicaragua to drive prices to crazy levels. When the housing crisis hit in the United States, home prices here declined due to lack of buyers and are pretty much at the same level they were a decade ago. Sure, if you want a beautifully restored colonial home in the heart of Granada, you may have to cough up a few hundred thousand dollars. Those are the exceptions though, not the rule. When a luxury travel website my media company owns did a story on high-end real estate in that city, we had serious trouble finding homes listed higher than $500,000.

For the most part, Nicaragua hasn't attracted a lot of high rollers. Whether they were scared by the political climate or felt more confident investing elsewhere I don't know, but fortunately for anyone heading there now, prices are still quite attractive—and have good upside potential in the future if you're willing to be patient. Prices are highest in Granada and the coast near San Juan del Sur. If you're willing to look beyond those areas, you can really find some rock-bottom bargains. Several gated housing developments with sweeping views of Lake Apoyo have lots of an acre or more going for $35-$40,000, and building costs are very low.

Condo prices, where there is such a thing, are only $400 to $650 per square meter, so we're talking an average of $50,000 to buy a 1,000 square foot apartment. I saw whole houses for sale for that amount in several locations in Nicaragua both times I was there, even in popular Granada. You can own property free and clear here with no restrictions. Just do the usual due diligence with an attorney to ensure there's a clear title. Because of the civil war and the Sandanistas appropriation of property, the ownership history of some buildings is murky to say the least.

Food & Drink

This is one of the cheapest places to eat in all of the Americas. You can get a market stall lunch with several items for $1.50 to $3, a simple restaurant lunch for $2.50 to $7. Often you'll find all-you-can eat buffets meals for as little as $4. A fancy restaurant meal with cloth napkins will seldom top $15 and if you spend $20 per person you're really living it up.

The good Flor de Caña rum will only run you $3 - $10 per liter and a rum cocktail in a bar is often $1- $3. Dollar beers are more common than not in bars and restaurants. A cup of coffee from good export quality beans will be 50 cents to $1.50.

Seasonal fruit is often $1 or less per kilo, so if you go to the market alone with $10, you are going to need a taxi and some help. (Probably not a problem at your local organic farmer's market, right?) A buck will get you a meal or two's worth of tortillas or baguettes for a large family.

"Anything Nicas use often themselves is going to be cheap," says Gord. "Rice, eggs, beans, oil, vinegar, and beef are bargain priced. You can get a really nice filet that's good for eight steaks for $10. And it's excellent, grass fed beef. The steak was probably butchered that morning. The seafood you buy was caught that day. The fruit and vegetables were probably on the branch or vine two days ago."

Many expatriates in Nicaragua talk about how healthier they feel, about how they've lost weight without really trying. It's not that the Nicas are all eating health food, but there's far less processed food, packaged food, and fast food here, especially outside Managua. People eat what's fresh and local because it's less expensive to transport, so those who move here often follow the locals' lead, at least part of the time.

Transportation

Probably a higher percentage of expatriates own a car here than most other destinations in this book because while Granada and central San Juan del Sur are easy to navigate on foot, getting from city to city in Nicaragua is not so easy. You either pay next to nothing to endure a "chicken bus"—retired school buses from the USA now jammed with intercity passengers—or you pay a hefty $15-$30 to take a tourist shuttle that's only a couple hours. You can only find these on a few routes though, running just two or three times a day.

There is a middle ground on some popular routes. Sometimes you can find an "express bus" that still stops to pick up anyone who waves, but it's only 60-80 cents per hour of travel. It's around $1 from Managua to Granada, around $2 Managua to Leon.

On the plus side, car prices don't seem to be as inflated here as they are in Mexico or Belize. If they were, hardly anyone local could afford one. Gasoline is on par with U.S. prices or less, depending on what kind of deal is in place with Venezuela at the moment.

Taxis are very inexpensive. Except for an airport ride, 50 cents to $4 will get you around most of the time—$6 would mean a long ride across Managua. A city bus will be 15-25 cents.

Internal flights run from $40 to $140 on a puddle jumper prop plane. A flight out to the gorgeous Caribbean Corn Islands is $68 from Managua at the time of writing.

Health Care

Nicaragua is one of those countries where even elderly retirees often don't bother with insurance. Costs are so low they just pay out of pocket when something comes up. When a doctor's visit seldom tops $15 and a trip to the dentist is $25 or less, it's not going to tax your budget much. The doctors will often give you their cell number in case a problem comes up.

Residents of San Juan del Sur have only a small hospital in Rivas to go to for simple things though. "There's an English speaking Cuban doctor in Managua that we go for anything serious," says Gord. "We pay him $15 for a visit; I heard he does house calls for $20. My wife had to go to the hospital for two days at one point. She had a private nurse just for her. They ask you what you want to eat there and will prepare it. There are flat-screen TVs on the wall. For lots of work she had done and the recovery it was only $1,300."

The good news is, Managua is not very far from Granada, Leon, or San Juan del Sur, so it's not difficult to get to a good hospital from one of these three locations. Both the service and the amenities you will find there are excellent and there are some doctors who speak English. Ask around or check the message boards. If you're in rural coffee country though or out in the Corn Islands, try to stay healthy and maybe get some kind of medical evacuation insurance in case of a bad accident.

If you want to buy national health insurance, it won't set you back much. Figure on $50 to $120 per month for the very best plan, depending on your age.

Other Costs

Any costs that are labor-based are quite cheap in Nicaragua, from getting custom furniture made to having someone clean your house regularly. The per-capita GDP is around $3,000, which is the lowest in Latin America apart from Haiti. Things are improving each year, but you won't have to pay much to exceed the local norm for a maid, gardener, baby sitter, or caretaker.

Admissions, cultural activities, and entertainment are all bargains, with prices in the low single digits in dollar terms.

Internet and phone charges are low, but the whole country has pretty much bypassed the fixed line system and gone to mobile only. Outside the capital, it's hard to get a wired broadband connection and you'll be waiting quite a while for someone to install it. If you can rent a house that already has this, it's a big plus.

Electronics are costly and not high quality. "If you're looking for a TV or computer, it's what you would have bought in Canada two or three years ago, and 30 percent more," says Gord. The local clothing that's available is either cheap and poorly made or imported name brands that are very expensive. There's not much middle ground, so most save the wardrobe upgrades for when they return to their former home for a visit.

To import a vehicle requires a 50 percent duty unless you have a retirement visa. With that, every six years you can bring in one vehicle worth up to $20,000 in value, not more than 10 years old.

Visas in Nicaragua

If you come in on a tourist visa, you're allowed to stay three months before you have to leave. For those in San Juan del Sur, this means a short hop to Costa Rica and back. "I'm there for five minutes and I come back with five bottles of duty-free booze," says Gord. He hasn't bothered to apply for long-term residency, as it seems you can keep going on this three-month cycle without anyone raising an eyebrow.

"Legally you can't work with that though," he adds. "There's 20 percent unemployment here and probably most of the other 80 percent are under-employed, so they don't want people coming in on a tourist visa from other countries to do short-term work." He adds that most of the foreigners working in San Juan del Sur have gotten a business or investor visa, which just requires you having hired at least one person. "It's easy enough to get an investor visa. If I owned a house I would call it a yoga studio and I'd be an investor."

Technically the investor visa requires a real investment of

$30,000 or more, but housing counts if it has a commercial aspect and once you get approved you have permanent residency.

If you do want to stay long-term, Nicaragua doesn't put up a lot of obstacles, assuming you're not broke. They're glad to have you and your money come stick around for a while. You can get a temporary resident permit that's good for a year at any age, or if you're just 45 or older you can get a retiree/pensioner visa. You only have to show $750 in income per month for the "rentista" visa, or $600 per month for the retiree one. (To put this in perspective, Mexico requires $2,000 per month plus $500 for each dependent.) There's no tax on earnings from abroad and you can bring up to $20,000 worth of household goods into the country without paying any duties. You can drive your own car down for personal use with no duty and as long as it's not more than 10 years old, you can sell it locally after five years with no taxes to pay.

After three years of temporary residency, you can apply to be a permanent resident. Once you have that, you're set for five years before you have to renew again.

Downsides

Nicaragua is slowly but surely growing its middle class as the dependence on Venezuela's help dissipates and formerly reluctant foreign investors are more confident in dipping their toes in. This is still a nation where the wealth is concentrated in very few hands, however. The middle class may be growing, but the family behind the Grupo Pellas conglomerate—best known for owning the Flor de Cana rum empire—supposedly has an asset value equal to half the country's entire gross domestic product.

Internet penetration is reportedly the lowest in the Americas and the best you can get in most areas is 3G-wireless.

Nicaragua falls somewhere in the middle in terms of environmental protection. It's not as trashed as Mexico or Honduras, where it's hard to look anywhere without seeing garbage and graffiti, but it doesn't have the resources to be as diligent as Costa Rica. The reasonably clean state of the towns and countryside are due more to cultural norms and a still comparatively low prevalence of throwaway packaging than to any government recycling and waste disposal initiatives.

The government has successfully kept the country off the drug smuggling corridor for the most part, but they have done it by cracking down hard on anyone selling or possessing even small amounts of drugs. If you're a stoner, this is not a good place to live. It's also not a great environment for gays, with a generally intolerant society and no legal protection for partners.

The food is tasty and filling, better in most respects than what you'll get in Panama or Costa Rica, but it's not going to win any culinary awards for complexity or variety. You'll probably want to hone your cooking skills and have a healthy budget for some better restaurants now and then.

For More Information:
In Nica Now (innicanow.com)
NicaLiving.com (nicaliving.com)
Expat Exchange Nicaragua forum
The Nicaragua Dispatch (nicaraguadispatch.com)
Living in Nicaragua book

Chapter 21: Honduras

Pros: Low interior prices, coastal reefs, adventure activities, good roads, easy air access
Cons: Worst homicide rate in the world, election fraud, weak institutions, weak environmental protection,

Julie and her husband hadn't really planned to live in Honduras. They were backpacking around Central America when she got pregnant and "There was just something about Honduras that drew us in." While working for a hostel they met the owner of a local mine at a trade show and he ended up offering Julie's husband a job. They lived in the nearest town for three years, enjoying a laid-back life and putting money away since many of their expenses were covered.

"We really wanted to get to the beach though, so we moved to Roatan Island and now my husband is a construction manager. We live on $42,000 a year, which includes sending my son to a great private bilingual school, $700 a month to rent a three-bedroom, two-bath house near the beach, and $20 a day for a nanny/housekeeper. It doesn't compare to what our life in Dallas would be like on that kind of salary. We'd be poor."

Honduras offers a wealth of geographic beauty, including some stunning island beaches that are postcard perfect. The Bay Islands offer some of the best scuba diving in the world, with the planet's second longest reef right off the shore.

Adventurous travelers can also find plenty of hiking, white-water rafting, and sea kayaking options. The country also boasts the impressive Mayan ruins at Copán, as well as some dense jungles full of wildlife, especially birds.

There's just one catch: thanks to drug runners having their way with a coast and river system that's hard to defend, this is now the most dangerous country in the Americas. It probably doesn't help that guns are "limited to only five firearms per person." The stats look worse on paper than they are is in practice for most expatriates though. Most of the violence is gang-on-gang and despite years of this violence, very few foreigners have been affected. It is a valid deterrent for many though, so this chapter is shorter than some others. Forget the talk about Mexico—this is where the narcos are really in control. If you're an inexperienced traveler who gets spooked easily, you're probably wise to steer clear of Honduras for now. If not, at least avoid the two main cities and be very wary about touring the Miskito Coast. It's a jungle out there in more ways than one.

The homicide numbers and the size of the drug shipments have both dropped the past two years as the U.S. government has stepped in with equipment and training to help. Eventually the situation may turn around like it did in Colombia, but keep an eye on the news before making grand plans to invest your life savings in property. Meanwhile, by any means necessary, avoid the capital city of Tegucigalpa as well as San Pedro Sula except for essential business. There's no "must-see" anything there anyway and drug gangs are a serious problem. The larger the town/city, the more precautions you should take, especially after dark. This is especially not a good country for single women to stroll around late at night, swinging their purse.

Honduras, the original "banana republic," is a poor country, right behind Haiti and Nicaragua. This is the second-largest country in Central America, but much of it is undeveloped or set aside as barely managed nature reserves. This means that there are plenty of bargains, but the most developed tourist and foreigner-friendly living facilities are in a rather narrow range of locations—namely Copán, Tela, La Ceiba, Trujillo, and the Bay Islands—with the islands putting forth a far more luxurious face than the interior. Even if you stick to these spots, you'll find Honduras to be a great value. Venture further afield with a good command of Spanish and you'll find idyllic colonial towns with prices too cheap to believe.

The West End of Roatan Island is known as Gringo Central. It's the most expensive area in the country, but this is a relative term. Compared to Ambergris Caye in Belize it's still a good value and compared to better-known Caribbean islands or the Caribbean coast of Mexico, it's a screaming bargain. Also, unlike in Ambergris, the beaches here are really stunning: you don't have to go below the water to enjoy the beauty, plus the reef is very close to the shore, so it's good for snorkelers as well. With a whole range of troubles hitting Honduras over the years—from a coup to fishy elections to drug violence—property prices in some prime spots are lower than they were a decade ago. The downside of that, of course, is you can't assume your purchase will appreciate in the near future.

Be advised that we're almost talking about two countries here when it comes to the cost of living. As Canadian diving instructor Rika says on her Cubicle Throwdown blog, "Roatan is not mainland Honduras. Honduras is a dirt-cheap, third world Central American country. Roatan is a touristy island. Touristy + island = expensive."

Outside of the Bay Islands, prices for almost anything you would spend money on are low and have stayed low since I put out the first edition of *The World's Cheapest Destinations* book back in 2003. The exchange rate of the local lempira currency is pegged to the U.S. dollar in practice, at a rate of 20 to 1. To give you an idea of what travelers are paying, the most expensive hotel in some towns is $40 a night and it's hard to pay more than $250 a night anywhere, even on the most popular beach in Roatan. You can drink piña coladas 'til you're legless and you'll be out $10 or $15.

You don't have to live on the Bay Islands to have a beach life. Trujillo and other mainland coastal cities are much more Caribbean, with lots of seafood, great music, and all-night dancing. Prices are lower across the board in those areas because items can arrive by truck instead of boat.

If I were moving to Honduras, I'd head to the west, near the Guatemalan border. The town of Copán Ruinas, near the great archeological site, is one of the nicest towns you could ever chill out in. Nearby Santa Rosa de Copán is a center for growing coffee and making cigars. It can get cooler away from the coasts because of altitude, with Julie saying it would get down to 50 at night where they lived in the mountains and much of the year the house was wide open to the breeze. Most parts of the country where foreigners live are tropical and hot, however. Do some climate research before you go: temperatures and rainfall can vary drastically according to location, time of year, and altitude.

It's surprisingly easy to get to Honduras, partly because there's a lot of export business here. Air connections are good to three international airports. Honduras is only a two-hour flight from Houston or Miami and direct flights to Roatan are available from those airports as well as Atlanta and New York. The highway infrastructure on main routes is good too, thanks to a few rounds of international aid after bad hurricanes hit.

Housing Costs

In most of Honduras, you can just show up and start looking around to find an inexpensive place to live. Long-term rentals are available in a lot of areas for $100 to $300 a month. At the top of that range, you can probably get a monthly rate on a hotel room while you find something more permanent.

Trying to find something ahead of time is tough, especially on Roatan, since much of what you'll encounter online is vacation rentals for people coming to dive for a week or two. A lot of local owners with long-term rentals available don't have internet access or the foggiest idea of how to post something online. The good news is, once you find them there's a good chance they'll speak some English.

You'll pay a premium on Roatan because there are so many foreigners and on Utila because it's so small. If you can find a two-bedroom place for $600 near the water, it's a good deal. Julie pays $700 a month for a three-bedroom, two-bath house with an ocean view. Some people pay $400 or $500 a month for a small apartment in the busiest tourist area. If it's low season though and you only need something for a few months, you could score a bargain from a snowbird who just doesn't want to leave their place empty.

It's a whole different story in the interior. "We have a friend on the mainland who rented a house near where we worked and he paid $125 a month for a place with two bedrooms and two baths," says Julie.

You can own property outright here and there's a lot to choose from on the islands and on the mainland. Prices have flatlined or declined in many spots in the last decade as the U.S. housing crisis, a coup, and rising crime really put a dent in demand. It's a buyer's market if you're convinced you're here for the long term or can buy a good property for rentals.

Health Care

This is not a medical tourism destination like Panama or Costa Rica. "Adequate" best describes what you get here. The issue is further complicated by the fact that most people try to avoid the two largest cities whenever possible, but that's where the best medical facilities are.

Plan on making use of the best private doctors and hospitals, as this is not a place where you want to be under the national health care system. In late 2013, 670 doctors went on strike because they hadn't been paid for months and their salaries hadn't been adjusted for inflation for years. At the same time, staffers for one hospital in Tegucigalpa staged a major protest to bring attention to a lack of medicine, supplies, and food for patients.

So as you can imagine, private doctors are happy to see foreigners who walk in with ample funds to pay the bills and you can see one for $20 or less in many areas. In areas where foreigners congregate, you can find English-speaking doctors who studied abroad and they will be able to take care of most of what ails you. For serious conditions or surgeries, however, you'll need to travel to Tegucigalpa or San Pedro Sula, where your costs will probably not be more than $60 a day for a hospital bed and care. For serious surgery that can be planned in advance, some foreigners choose to fly to Cancun, Panama City, or Mexico City for care.

Food & Drink

As in the rest of Central America, you don't move here because the food is fantastic. Expect the staples of tortillas, beans, rice, eggs, and potatoes, with plenty of seafood anywhere near the coast (including lobster dishes for well under $10). A fish soup with coconut milk is a standard dish, as is a similar concoction with vegetables served over rice. The yucca vegetable finds its way into a lot of dishes here, and there are Honduran versions of burritos.

You'll also find plenty of burgers, pizza, and kebabs. There are fast food options for the homesick in the cities and plenty of international choices in tourist spots. Vegetarians won't have much of a problem in the tourist centers, especially on the islands. The influx of expatriates in the Bay Islands has given birth to a huge variety of international cuisines there, with good bread and dessert to boot. You'll pay more to eat out on Roatan Island, but you'll get much higher quality as well.

The problem with the Bay Islands is that they're, well, islands. Whether you're talking about the Bahamas, Hawaii, or the Azores, it just plain costs more to get supplies to islands by boat or plane. "My trips to the grocery store cost as much as or more than my trips when I lived in Washington, DC. And let's just all agree that DC is not exactly a cheap place to live," says Amanda Walkins, who lives on Roatan and runs the blog A Walk on the Run. "Average grocery store trip? I'd estimate $100. That's for two of us, and we spend about that once a week."

"Food seems expensive, but then we return to the USA and it's even more expensive there," says Julie. "Staples from the mainland are a decent price, but it's the import items the foreigners want that really drive up the total."

Breakfast out is usually a tortillas/eggs/beans concoction, with some fruit here and there, often for less than $1.50. Other meals range from a dollar for a quick burger or burrito to $6 for a three- or four-course meal or pizza at a local eatery. A set meal in a basic local joint is often just $2 or $3. It's hard to even find a main dish in most interior towns priced higher than $12.50, even if you're at the restaurant of the best hotel in town. On the touristy Bay Islands the restaurants are serving those on a vacation budget, so it's very easy to spend $20 a person on dinner.

A beer in a restaurant or bar will average a dollar or two depending on how fancy the place is, with the price dropping below a buck during the numerous happy hours. Salva Vida is the most popular, but some others similar lagers pop up here and there. Rum is a good alternative for those on a budget and fruity cocktails are commonly $2-$4 or so on the coast.

Transportation

There is an extensive bus system and it's easy to find a connection from one point to another. Finding a comfortable one can be another story, however. You can sometimes find an "executive" bus that costs double the normal fare. Since this only amounts to, say, $2,50 instead of $1.25, it's well worth it. In general, the regular buses run about 80 cents to $1.50 an hour. A city taxi ride will rarely top $5 (not metered) and local buses are usually less than 30 cents.

You need a vehicle to get around in many parts of the country, as the only other choice is a packed and slow local bus. Some decide to get a scooter and fill up the tank for $5 a week.

Internal flights are quite inexpensive ($30 to $100) and can be a reasonable splurge to avoid a long bus trip or ferry ride.

The boat trip out to the Bay Islands is $16 to $20 and a flight may be $50 or $60. Island hopping boats run regular trips or you can hitch a ride with someone making a supply run.

You can easily cross to Honduras from Guatemala by land, with Copán being a short hop from the border. A nice bus or van shuttle from Copán to Antigua, Guatemala runs $12 to $20. There are also land crossings to Nicaragua and El Salvador, as well as boat and land connections to Belize.

Other Costs

"The kicker here is electricity," says Julie. "We pay 43 cents per kilowatt hour. Last month our bill was $150 a month, just running the air conditioning at night in our son's room. But five months a year we run it in our room too and we've had electric bills as high as $400. There's a wind farm going up on the island, so hopefully that will bring the costs down a bit."

Most people use a pre-paid cell phone plan and spend anywhere from $10-$50 per month depending on if there's a data involved. Internet is on a pre-paid system too instead of a monthly subscription, whether it's wired or through a 3G mobile USB stick. So if you use lots of bandwidth you may have to keep feeding the meter. Figure on $25-$75 per month. Cable/satellite TV can be anywhere from $30 to $100 a month depending on the number of channels, but bootleg DVDs are $2-$3 each.

If you've always wanted to get your scuba diving license, you can do it on Roatan or Utila islands for less than $300 for a five-day open water PADI course. If you're already certified, it will be $20 to $25 per dive, with volume discounts available.

"The one thing that's really cheap here is labor," Julie says. We had a maid on the mainland that we paid $10 a day and were told we were overpaying. She also took care of our son. Here on Roatan we pay $20 a day for a combination nanny and housekeeper." Others report having a full-time maid for anywhere from $150 to $300 per month. Expatriates praise the cost of car repairs, a gardener, or a handyman to be a great value and fixing up or adding onto a house here will cost very little in terms of labor costs.

You can get your laundry done by a service for a couple dollars a kilo if you don't want to wait for things to dry in the high humidity. When you need to relax, lots of places offer a one-hour massage for $10 to $15 on the mainland, but figure triple that at least on the islands.

To give you an idea of how inexpensive living costs are, here's what you can buy for $1 or less on the mainland: simple breakfast, a burger, a beer, a hand-rolled cigar, two or three cups of coffee, three sliced pineapples or huge mangoes, a fruit shake, two coconuts with a straw, a kilo of oranges, a small wood carving, a half-hour or more of Internet access, admission to some museums, more bananas than you can carry a long distance.

Visas in Honduras

Most developed country nationalities can get a one-month tourist stamp on arrival and extend it twice for a maximum of three months. Or you can request a three-month visa upon arrival and hope they'll grant it. Hop to another country and back and you can start over. You have to choose that country carefully though from among the neighbors. The other four in the Central American Alliance don't count: Guatemala, El Salvador, Nicaragua, and Costa Rica. Belize and Panama are not part of that alliance.

The long-term visa options here aren't complicated. You

either get a residency permit for a "rentist," pensioner, or investor, or you get a work permit if you're employed by a Honduran company. There's not a whole lot of paperwork: a passport, proof of income, and a recent clean police report are the key items. But documents need to be in Spanish and need to be authenticated through apostilles in your home country. For the work permit, you'll need the usual documents proving you have a job and they employer needs your skills. Or you can buy a local company that's profitable and hire yourself as an employee, with a bit of help from a lawyer

A pensioner needs to show an income of $1,500 a month, a younger person $2,500 a month, and an investor needs to put at least $50,000 into a local business. There are no additional charges for dependents, though you will have to pay an extra fee for them and you may need a birth certificate or marriage license as proof. Fees for residency permits are $300 per year for the principle person, $200 for each dependent.

Residency visas have to be renewed annually in one of the mainland immigration offices, though you may be able to have a lawyer do it without you making regular trips. This can all be arranged after arrival and you'll get better info locally than you will online.

Downsides

Stats don't tell the whole story, but parts of Honduras enjoy the dubious reputation as being some of the most dangerous non-war-zone places on Earth. For the past three years, San Pedro Sula has been named the murder capital of the world. That city leads the globe with 187 murders per 100,000 people. The capital city isn't far behind. The drug gang violence in those two cities badly skews the overall rate, making Honduras the most dangerous country in the world. It may be quite calm on the islands of Roatan and Utila, but the overall average of homicides in the whole country was 90.4 per 100,000 in 2013 according to the United Nations.

In the areas where lots of expatriates congregate, robbery is more of a concern. Most people who are in remote areas or who leave their houses unattended for months pay a local watchman to keep an eye on things.

Blackouts and brownouts are frequent due to an overtaxed electrical grid in some areas, so many homes have a back-up generator. It's also wise to have some kind of combo surge protector/batter pack for expensive electronics.

On this health side, there is some risk of malaria and dengue fever in some areas and sanitation is poor.

There are very few good schooling options for families outside of international schools in the two largest cities, and the two largest cities are not very conducive to family life otherwise. Track down parents who already live here and ask lots of questions.

The government of Honduras is far from stable and every time there's an election there are loud cries of vote rigging and obstruction. Protests can get ugly and the most common tactic is to block roads to get attention.

For More Information

Roatan Net (RoatanNet.com)
A Walk on the Run Blog (AwalkontheRun.com)
Cubicle Throwdown Blog (CubicleThrowdown.com)

Chapter 22: Hungary

Pros: European lifestyle and architecture, great wine, good food, inexpensive public transportation, easy access to other parts of Europe, culture and the arts, bike-friendly, clean.
Cons: Difficult one-country language, cold winters, weak institutions, visible racism, anti-Semitism, dour (but improving) service.

Imagine visiting your local wine bar and ordering three different varieties from assorted regions, being served by someone who can explain the climate where the grapes were grown and what awards that vintner has won. The chalkboard list behind the bar has over 100 wines by the glass to choose from and there's something for every taste. The interior is elegant and the location is perfect, right across from a busy pedestrian plaza fronting the city's huge historic cathedral. It's the kind of place you could linger for hours, but how much is it going to cost you when the bill comes? $8.50 with a tip.

That's what I spent at the best wine bar in Budapest. For three glasses that took my taste buds on a terrific ride, from three distinct wine regions of Hungary.

I bring that up first because it's emblematic of the appeal of Hungary. Not super cheap in every way, but a good value in most ways. Budapest is thronged with tourists that are firmly in the middle of the pack budget-wise. After all, the Hungarians consider themselves "Central Europe" and they are right next to expensive Austria. They're on the Danube, with docking river cruise ships a defining feature of the waterfront. So this may be a value destination, especially outside the capital, but not the place you go just to find the very cheapest food and lodging.

Estimates of how many expatriates live here range from 30,000 to 50,000 and there are enough in Budapest to support a business newspaper in English: *Budapest Business Journal*.

Gary Lukatch was earning around $60,000 gross in New Mexico working in the financial industry, after having lived in a lot of other states before that. "When I moved to Budapest and began teaching English, my monthly net earnings after one year were around $600 per month, increasing to around $1,500 per month after, say, five years," he says. "In short, I took a *huge* pay cut, but was 1000% happier."

After teaching English in Budapest for eight years, he is retired, living a much better life than he could elsewhere on what he has to spend. "The cost of monthly house payments or rental, plus car costs alone, would be more than my monthly income, which is around $2,100 net," he explains. "Here in Budapest, my monthly flat rental, plus utilities, averages around $400, right in the middle of town." He says public transportation is excellent, so he doesn't need a car. "I eat out several times a week and I still have enough money to travel wherever and whenever I want; I have now been to 53 countries, with at least five more trips scheduled this year."

Australians Karen and Neil came to Budapest because her husband got a job offer in his industry and they thought it would be a great adventure. They had already lived in Poland and the Czech Republic though, so they didn't have to make a huge adjustment going to Hungary. "Hungary has been the cheapest of the three," Karen says. They've watched the city get easier and easier as the years have gone by, partly through them adjusting but also because the level of English fluency locally has gotten steadily better.

They also love how everyone is outside and mingling, even in the dead of winter. Instead of being couch potatoes, Hungarians will gather in a coffee shop, in a bar, in a park. "I love that there are so many outdoor festivals," she adds. "And Christmas is not all about presents. People aren't spending all their time shopping. Instead they're making homemade food and mulled wine to share, spending extra time with their families and friends. It's not a stressful time, but is very relaxed. People are singing carols, walking in the snow, enjoying each other's company."

Hungary joined the EU in 2004, but the country still uses the forint, which is a volatile currency. Prices in this book are based on 220 to the dollar, but I've seen it as low as 198 and as high as 250. So check the current rate before cursing my name because prices have changed.

Just be advised that integrating into the community here by learning the local language is a much tougher proposition than it is in countries where Spanish, French, or Portuguese is spoken. One press release on Hungary's government website started with this:

A mezőgazdasági termelés biztonsága magában foglalja az élelmiszer-termelésre alkalmas környezet hosszú távú fenntartását is, az agrárkörnyezet védelmét, különösen termőföldjeink megőrzését, a talajvédelmet és a fenntartható, integrált növényvédelmet, növényegészségügyet – fogalmazott köszöntőjében Kardeván Endre, a Siófokon megtartott Növényvédelmi Bizottság ülésén.

I have no idea if they're talking about the price of wheat, provincial elections, or the decline of morals among today's youth.

As has happened from Vietnam to Peru to Turkey though, anyone who wants to make a buck from tourists or to move up the ladder of business is learning English. Hungary has gotten a huge influx of tourists the past decade so if you go where they are, you will probably find someone who speaks at least a bit of your language. The further you get into the rural areas though, the less that's true. There are only 10 million people in this country, so you get into the countryside pretty quickly.

Few expats live in the rural areas though unless they're in the wine industry. Most choose to live in Budapest, around Lake Balaton, or in one of the smaller cities like Eger or Pecs.

Hungary got hit hard in the European economic crisis like many other nations on the continent, but has recovered faster. The official unemployment rate was 8 percent in mid-2014, which looks downright glorious compared to Italy, Spain, Greece, or Portugal. In many ways, this feels like a nation on the rise and the young are displaying something not seen much in the past couple hundred years of Hungary's history: optimism.

Housing Costs

The residents of Hungary give their rent costs in low

hundreds, not thousands, and you won't find many single people or couples paying more than $500 a month, even in the capital. When you get into smaller towns, you can get a large house for that. When I was last in Budapest, I asked several locals I talked to what they were paying per month for an apartment and the answers came in between $150 and $300. In the southern wine region I visited on my first trip a few years earlier, there were houses with a nice garden going for the same. I met an expat from New Zealand working for a winery by Lake Balaton. He was paying $210 a month for his two-bedroom apartment with a lake-view balcony.

The site Numbeo.com uses New York City for a price basis and compares costs of living around the world to that, using 100 as the NYC average. For rent prices, Hungary comes up a 10 and Budapest is 12. This will vary greatly by location, of course, but on average you can expect to pay one-eighth to one-tenth of what you would in your current situation if you're living in New York.

Gary pays a shade under $300 for his apartment in District 5, one of the most desirable and central areas of the city. (If you've come to Hungary as a tourist, you've been there to see the sites.)

If you decide to buy something eventually, which you can do freely as a foreigner, "a typical apartment in Budapest will cost between 90,000 and 130,000 euros for 100 square meters." Karen says. It's a buyer's market right now for a very bad reason: a lot of Hungarians took out loans to buy property in the pre-EU days and did it in Swiss Francs because that was a stable currency. Now they owe far more than what the property is worth because of the Swiss Franc's rise. "So there's a mass selling of properties because of exchange rate changes," Karen says. Combined with the high unemployment so prevalent in much of Europe now, there are far more sellers than buyers.

You can get financing, but it requires a significant down payment of 30 percent or more and interest rates are 8-10 percent.

Health Care Costs

In this country, the medical care is good and the dental

care is great. With the rise of cross-border medical treatment happening in many places in the world, Hungary has jumped on the trend with both feet. Many Europeans come here to have dental work done or to receive good medical care at a discount. I was actually having some dental problems while in this part of the world two years ago and started asking around for prices to get a new crown. I ended up not getting it done because of timing, but prices I was quoted ranged from $250 to $350 all-in. (In the United States or Canada, this can easily top $1,000.)

Getting a cleaning and check-up at the dentist is around $30, getting a set of x-rays about that much again.

The one time Gary had to have serious medical work done, the total bill was about one-tenth the price of what it would have been in the USA. For serious care, it's best to make the trip to Budapest if you live elsewhere. In the provinces, the doctors are often not as well trained and the hospitals not as well-equipped.

If you become a legal resident, proof of health insurance is required. It's usually cheaper and more comprehensive to get an international policy covering Hungary than it is to buy a program within the country.

Food & Drink

You can normally have a very fine cloth-napkin dinner with wine for $15. If you eat at more humble places, a soup will be a dollar or two and main dishes range from $3 to $7.

When you shop in the market, prices are at the low end for Europe. You can get rolls for 10-25 cents each or a huge baguette for a dollar or less. Get 100 grams (around one-fifth of a pound) of good cheese for a dollar, 100 grams of good local sausage for $2, and a jar of pickled veggies for another dollar or so.

For a buck or less, you can generally buy 100 grams of any of these things in the market: raisins, peanuts, sunflower seeds, banana chips, or dried apricots. Or you can get a kilo of seasonal fruit or peppers, cabbage, potatoes, radishes, or carrots. I saw a big bunch of white asparagus for about a dollar when I was there. How much do you pay for that in your local Whole Foods?

"We probably spend $80-$100 a week on groceries, not

including wine," says Karen. "In Australia we could spend $300 or $400 a week easily."

Hungarian wine should be known around the world, but the Soviet occupation days seriously hurt its reputation and the recovery will be a long one. So for now it's one of the best quality-to-price values in the world. In many countries profiled in this book, expats complain about the difficulty of getting decent wine for a decent price, so if that's a big priority, put Hungary on your list. (Along with Argentina and tropical duty-free Panama). You can find a decent table wine bottle in a store for $2, something quite good for $4 to $8. If you spend over $10 you might end up with something from a "winemaker of the year" who has adorned local magazine covers.

This once being part of the Austro-Hungarian Empire, you can get a killer coffee and pastry here just as you can in Vienna—but for literally 1/4 the price. After you do a double take at your low bill in a wine bar, finish with a coffee and dessert for another nice surprise.

Transportation

Getting around Hungary is relatively cheap by bus or train when you want to get out of town. Figure on $10-$12 for a trip of two hours, or $30 to go as far as you can possibly go within Hungary. Seniors and young children travel free. The longest ride on the suburban railway out of Budapest (30 kms) is just $2.50.

Budapest has a metro and while it's no real bargain on a ride-by-ride basis (around $1.55), a monthly pass that also works for the trams and buses is a good value at less than $50. If you're of retirement age, you might squeak by for free. "Technically senior citizens who are Hungarians or EU citizens can ride for free, not Americans or Canadians, but they never ask me where I'm from," Gary says. See more on the Budapest transportation options here.

Apart from the ride from the airport, taxis in Hungary are a bargain. In general you can get around the center of Budapest in a cab for $3 to $7. It's around $2 to start and $1.25 for each kilometer, so it's hard to spend $10 anywhere unless it's a long haul. Like much of Europe, this country is set up well for those on a bicycle and some expatriates use a bike as their main means of transport. In Budapest there are lots of dedicated bike lanes and in the countryside there's not nearly such an abundance of cars as you see in the capital.

Some expatriates keep a car here, but they use it mainly for shopping, commuting to an office job, or short jaunts. With gasoline costing nearly $2 a liter, it's cheaper to take the train or bus for long distances. Car purchase prices are in line or slightly higher than other European countries, making them more expensive than ones in the USA or Canada.

Frequent promotions on the train system and Eurolines bus make international travel from here a bargain. If you plan ahead you can get to Vienna for less than $20 or to beach locations of Greece, Bulgaria, or Croatia for around $60.

Other Costs

Karen says when they were renting, each month the landlord would come around and collect cash from everyone for utilities, determined by the size of the apartment. For her large place of 170 square meters, it averaged 280 euros for internet, gas, and water.

If you pay your own utilities they can vary greatly by the season. Gary's utilities vary widely, from $30 to $200 a month. "My place is not the best insulated in town, so I pay more in the winter for heat. In the summer, it's very low." Utility costs are significantly lower in the south of the country, where the winters are sunnier and milder.

Internet is $15 to $30 depending on speed and if you want a great connection, you can usually get it in the cities. The lowest-priced speed is generally 5 mbps, which is fine for a lot of people.

The land of Liszt and Bartok has an abundance of cultural performances going on at all times, from high-brow opera in the capital to an annual festival of wine songs in the south each year. Performances that aren't free are very cheap by European standards. The theater is amazing here," says Karen. "The cost of going to a ballet or opera can nearly bankrupt you in Australia. Here it's for everyone. Tickets usually start at $5. If you buy really great seats on a weekend for a popular show it might cost you all of $25."

Visas in Hungary

Hungary is part of the Schengen Agreement covering much of the European Union, which means you can't just stick around here on a tourist visa. You get three months upon entering the zone, but after that you have to leave the whole Schengen area for three months before returning. No problem if you're only coming for the summer. Terrible if you want to settle down for longer.

To get residency without being tied to a specific employer, you generally have to show you're doing work a local can't do, like teaching English, or you have to show that you're self-supported by income from abroad. You can see a sample of costs and documents needed at this site, which also warns you that requirements may change at any time: http://washington.kormany.hu/entry-for-long-stay

A work visa is good for a year and renewable. Expect to endure a lot of bureaucracy and if you don't have a college diploma, it's going to be even tougher. You will have to apply in your own country and will then have 30 days after entering Hungary to get the local paperwork sorted out.

Most people who want to stick around either get a work permit connected to a specific job and company, or a residence permit that's not tied to one employer. "Americans can only get residency for two years," says Gary, "then they have to renew." He's now looking into permanent residency though, which you can apply for after being in the country for three years. This costs money for a lawyer and requires a lot of additional paperwork. Most of the items need to be translated into Hungarian as well, plus you have to show proof of health insurance or buy into the Hungarian health care plan.

Do you have Hungarian blood? If so, you could be on the fast track to residency. If you have ancestral roots in the country, you can get real citizenship without giving up your original one, making you one of those enviable people with two passports. You have to speak Hungarian, but you can take intensive language courses while you're living there and collecting paperwork. This is a back door into the EU, which would give you the ability to live elsewhere too if you decide to try out another place.

Downsides

The political winds are blowing strongly to the right as I put this book together, with overt racism, anti-Semitism, and discrimination against minorities all rearing their ugly heads on a regular basis. The party most blatantly espousing these views won 20 percent of the seats in Parliament in the last election and the less-radical right has pushed through constitutional reforms that critics say basically keep it in power and remove needed checks and balances.

This is Central Europe, next to Austria, so you get four distinct seasons here. This is not a retirement destination you move to in order to escape the cold and gray unless you leave here every winter and go south.

While many people speak English in Budapest, fluency drops off rapidly in smaller towns and cities. Seek out other expats our tour around the country (it's not all that big) to gauge this for yourself and see how much trouble you will have. Hungarian is a tough language to pick up with just a couple weeks of language classes.

Last, you don't want to get behind the wheel here with even one drink in your system. Any alcohol at all (rumors abound that cough medicine is too much) can get you a drunk driving conviction.

For More Information:

Budapest Business Journal
Expat Blogs in Hungary at ExpatsBlog.com
Hunglish.org
Expats Hungary (ExpatsHungary.com)

Chapter 23: Guatemala

Pros: Gorgeous scenery, variety of locations, colonial and Maya history, close to USA, cheap real estate/rent, colorful indigenous population, all-ages expatriate community.
Cons: High crime rate, corrupt/ineffective police, poor infrastructure, unattractive capital, ownership limits on waterfront property.

A beautiful lake surrounded by conical mountains, the greatest Mayan city of them all in a thick jungle, a Spanish colonial city surrounded by hills and coffee farms, and cheap prices on nearly everything—what's not to like? Guatemala sounds like paradise!

Well...Guatemala is a perpetually troubled country whose stark divisions between rich and poor have sometimes gone from simmering to erupting. No government seems to be able to get a handle on its myriad problems. The most visible one since the civil war ended in 1996 has been crime. With Guatemala being a natural conduit between the cocaine-producing countries of South America and the lucrative market up north, it's hard to keep people who would normally make $2 a day from turning to a life of crime that pays 10 or 20 times that amount. To put things in perspective, the way our right-wing politicians want to repel poor Mexicans from the U.S. border, Mexico's right-wing politicians want to do the same with "those poor Guatemalans." The Mexicans are rich in comparison. Guatemala City is where most of the gunshots are ringing though and few foreigners live there unless they're working for a foreign organization and got transferred there.

Despite the problems though, tens of thousands of foreigners come here on vacation or to take Spanish lessons and then end up returning for good. Luke Armstrong was backpacking north from Chile when he stopped in Antigua, planning to volunteer for two weeks. He ended up signing on for a year after the director quit right after he arrived. "The executive director and founder somehow thought offering me the position was a good idea, even though I was only 22 at the time. I ended up managing a staff of 50 employees and 500 annual volunteers. The project provided education and health resources for people to break out of poverty and had a program to rescue victims of human trafficking, so it was eye-opening, but also came with a feeling of accomplishment."

To give an idea of what you can get by on in Guatemala though, Luke was earning the local equivalent of $250 a month as one of the staffers, and eventually as director he got them all bumped up to a living wage of $400 a month. "That's enough to live on and go out a bit," he says. "On $600 to $700 a month you can live reasonably well in Antigua. For $1,500 a month you could live like a king—unless you have expensive tastes." He says there are loads of single retirees living in gringo communities on the outskirts of Antigua and are getting by fine on just social security payments—often around $1,200 per month.

Richard Polanco runs a useful blog about living in Guatemala that's filled with resource links, advice, and sample prices. He moved to the United States when he was nine and didn't have any real plans to move abroad. Then he met the love of his life from Guatemala. He visited the country with her several times and after getting frustrated with the interminable wait to get his wife's visa sorted out in his home country, he gave up and moved to hers.

"I don't have any regrets about moving here and I really wish we had done it sooner," he says. "We have a much better life here and it's a really inexpensive place to live."

Any expatriate you talk to in Guatemala will have a crime story for you, though most will say being smart and aware of your surroundings goes a long way. "Antigua is not unsafe if you play is smart," Luke says. "Always carry at least 100 quetzales: you never want to have nothing to hand over to a mugger in a hurry. I carry a broken Blackberry just in case: be prepared to give away something and be done with it. Reporting it won't do much good: the police are really inept. Calling them is like calling another set of bandits." (Here's his full article on how to stay safe.)

"I was more worried when I first got here," says Rich. "The worst thing that has happened to me was having a bike stolen. I feel fine going out, but the issue is kind of always in the back of your head." He notes that the main adjustment is getting used to the idea that everyone is integrated and living together. "In the USA you can live in the suburbs and you're always in your car, so you don't have to interact with people that aren't like you. In Guatemala you can be in a really nice condo and have poor people right outside. It's very hard to put yourself in a bubble. If you're from NYC or Miami—or are at least well-traveled—it probably won't bother you as much, but if you're coming from a suburban town where nobody walks anywhere, it can be an adjustment."

The largest concentrations of expatriates in Guatemala is in the lovely colonial city of **Antigua**, which is not too huge or overwhelming and can be navigated by foot and taxis quite easily. It's also the place to go if your Spanish skills are negligible as there are plenty of local English speakers and a lot of bars and restaurants owned by foreigners. The real estate and rental markets are well established and you can find plenty of your own kind to lean on for advice.

The next most popular area is **Lake Atitlan**, which is more isolated but offers stunning views of the water and mountains and even lower prices on a place to rent. Here you can get a million-dollar lakeside view for a few hundred dollars a month. The main town is Panajachel and that's where the most action is, but there are several smaller towns around the lake with lower prices.

Quetzaltenango—better known as Xela—and Rio Dulce are other areas where foreigners tend to congregate. The former is the county's second-largest city, with a population of 225,000. It attracts adventure lovers and those looking to get involved in helping the local community. It gets plenty warm most days, with highs ranging from 78 to 86°F, but can get quite cold at night, with lows throughout the year ranging from 36 to 48°F.

Rio Dulce is a hot and tropical river port that leads to the Caribbean. It attracts people who live on their boat, those involved in shady business deals, renegades, and outcasts.

Guatemalan beaches are underwhelming and don't attract many foreigners who want to put down roots there. Head north or south to another country for palm trees and hammocks by a gorgeous white-sand beach.

Housing Costs

Guatemala is a cheap place to rent an apartment or house, even in popular Antigua. Go further out and prices drop even more. As usual though, you'll find far better deals on the ground after arrival. "The big mistake many people make is to try to book everything in advance," says Rich. "It's much better to go to a hostel or cheap hotel for a week or two and ask around, talk to people who live there." A lot of business is done by word of mouth and many landlords don't even know how to use a computer, much less how to post an ad on Craigslist Guatemala.

Luke lives right in the center of Antigua, a block from the central park. "I have three rooms off the main room, a kitchen, and a courtyard, and I pay about $220 a month for rent," he says. "When I lived here before I paid less for a larger house with more bedrooms a bit further out. If you're alone, you can rent a bedroom from a family and pay $300 a month with all meals included."

Rich lives in Antigua also and says inexpensive housing is one of the best reasons to move here—as long as you do it right. "The biggest mistake I see is people trying to set up a place to live in advance and have everything settled in two days. They end up paying twice as much. They should have just chilled out in a cheap hotel for a week or two and looked around."

When he first moved down his family rented a big house in a gated community with a pool just outside of town for $500 a month. It seemed like a great deal, but only about a quarter of the houses were occupied full time and it was hard to feel any sense of community. They then moved five minutes away to a smaller house in a less ritzy neighborhood, but they enjoy it a lot more and their rent is now only $125 per month.

Andy Graham the Hobo Traveler has spent a lot of time living in the Lake Atitlan area and has frequently found nice apartments for going for very little money. On his blog he has pictures of where he paid $150 a month for a furnished room with fridge, TV, and internet. He says a furnished apartment with more space would be $180 and "I've seen $200,000 houses renting for $300 a month because there's just not much demand." He called the $7 a night hotel room he got on a lovely town by the lake the best value he had found in 14 years of travel. Take $7 a night times 30 days and your shelter is $210—in a hotel with maid service and internet included. Because of the cheap housing, Andy was easily able to get by living here for $500 a month.

In Rio Dulce, Andy lived in a hotel room for $249 a month that had a nice pool with lounge chairs and fast internet. He says if you didn't need internet for your business, you could find a short-term apartment rental or basic hotel room for $125 to $150.

Buying something requires some capital and some time to look around. Maybe some legal maneuvering too: foreigners cannot buy waterfront land direct: you must form a corporation or partner up with a local. Otherwise you're in what's really a long-term lease of the land. This is the case in Mexico too, so it's something many foreign investors are used to, but what's different here is "waterfront" also refers to lakes and rivers. That pulls a lot of prime real estate out of consideration if you're looking for something to keep in the family for generations.

Also, be advised that while you can find a house and a couple acres of land for the price of a BMW in the countryside, in Antigua prices are high because of a limited amount of inventory in the center and restrictions on new construction.

Health Care

As in a lot of Central American countries, the medical care quality drops off rapidly once you get beyond the capital city. There are seven large hospitals in the capital that have good equipment and some English-speaking doctors, but pickings are slim elsewhere. In Antigua you have some good doctors who cater to the foreign population and there are clinics to take care of the basics, but most people make the short trip to Guatemala City for something serious.

There are actually even some assisted living centers for the aged around Antigua, obviously pegged at a much lower rate than those in the USA or Canada.

In smaller cities and towns, however, the only local option may be a poorly funded government clinic, so if you're moving somewhere remote it can pay to have some kind of evacuation insurance. If you're in a place with an airport, keep some cash aside for an emergency flight.

Food & Drink

Eating out in Guatemala is not going to set you back much if you go where the locals go. You can sit down and get lunch for as little as $1.50 and if you double that you'll get several courses and something to drink.

If you step up to a nicer restaurant, $5 or so will get you the kind of meal local business owners will be eating. Naturally, the tourist restaurants can be several times that.

If you drive to the big city every week just so you can shop at Walmart, you're going to spend a lot more money on food and the produce will be of worse quality. If you shop in the *mercado* instead the food is very cheap." Rich outlined his regular expenses in one of his blog posts and here were a few examples from the market:

Two pounds of tomatoes - 80¢
Head of broccoli - 25¢
Head of lettuce - 40¢
One eggplant - 40¢
Cilantro bunch - 15¢
Kilo of onions (2.2 pounds) - 85¢
Kilo of strawberries - $1
Kilo of blackberries - 90¢
Pound of chicken cut up - $1.15

As in many developing countries though, you buy what's in season to maximize your budget and maybe do without when it's not the right time: no constant supply of blueberries from Chile here. When things are in season though, supply and demand forces kick in. "I paid a visit to the Mercado yesterday and discovered limes were back in season," said Rich. "Sellers couldn't give them away fast enough. Limes that we had just bought last week for 1.25Q each could now be had at five for 1Q." (That equates to almost 40 for $1).

Transportation

In Guatemala there's a vast range of transportation prices

depending on how much you value comfort. To give you an example, a taxi from Antigua to the airport in Guatemala City costs around $25. The direct shuttle van is around $10. If you pack yourself into the local bus that stops every 100 meters, it's a dollar.

There are very few bus lines offering "luxury" bus trips outside the most popular routes. The local buses are cheap, but are merely converted school buses on their second life—often after living out their usefulness hauling U.S. school children. Combined with some rough mountain roads, it can be trying. But at least they're cheap. Most of the time you'll want to make use of the shuttle vans plying the popular tourist routes. Antigua to Lake Atitlan for example is $8 there, $12 coming back.

Taxis are (in theory anyway) metered in Guatemala City, with official fares $1.50 upon entry and $2 for each kilometer. In other locations you have to work out the fare before taking off. You should be able to get around almost anywhere outside the capital for $4 or less. On Lake Atitlan you get around on public boats that drop passengers off at various villages. These run $1.40 to $3 in local currency depending on distance, though if you're carrying a lot of bags you may get charged more.

There are only a few internal flight options. The most frequently used one is Guatemala City to Tikal (Flores), which is generally around $160 one-way. International flight prices from here often defy logic: a trip to nearby El Salvador or Chiapas can be more than one to Chicago. Thankfully there are good, relatively inexpensive buses running to neighboring countries for when it's time for a visa run or a cheap vacation. Antigua to Copán should cost you around $16.

Visas

Most citizens of developed countries get a three-month tourist visa upon arrival. Technically you have to leave the country for at least three days to renew it, which isn't such a big deal the first time or two if you want a vacation in Mexico or Belize, but if you are ready to endure a day of bureaucracy in Guatemala City you can extend it for another three months without leaving. You can only do this once, however.

A trip to the Central American Alliance countries doesn't count for these purposes, so you can't go to Honduras or El Salvador unless you fly and go through airport customs. The easiest overland option is a trip up to Chiapas in Mexico. To do any kind of paid work in the country though, you need a work visa, which requires a contract, a few documents translated into Spanish and officially stamped, and a clean police record.

Not so bad, right? But here's the word from the U.S. Consulate for Guatemala on what you need to prepare for:

Applicants should be aware that while the following requirements appear straightforward, applicants for residency often report that unexplained delays in the issuance process makes obtaining a resident visa very difficult. Delays of one, two and even four years are common. During such delays, an applicant's residency status may be uncertain, requiring regular departure from and re-entry into Guatemala in order to re-establish temporary status.

For a residency visa that doesn't involve work, you need to show a documented income of $1,000 a month, plus $200 for each dependent. This is a country though where you can double-check and triple-check everything you're supposed to get done in the USA before arrival, then find out at local immigration that it all has to be done over because...who knows? It's probably best to assume you're going to have to return to your home country get more documents with one certain notary stamp approved by one certain department of your government in order to proceed. Build it into your plans if you want to retire here.

There are some countries where you should hire a well-connected local immigration lawyer to speed up the process and save you a few trips to the immigration office. This is one of them.

Other Costs

If you ask expats what their utility costs are in this country, the answer can be anywhere from $50 to $300. Electricity costs per kilowatt hour are actually higher than in many parts of the United States, so if you're running air conditioning a lot the costs can rise fast. Much of Guatemala is at a high enough altitude that you don't need this much though, especially around Lake Atitlan.

Propane gas tanks of 35 pounds are around $25 and they can last two or three months depending on how much you cook and shower. Water only costs a few dollars a month and cable packages are generally half what they cost in the USA. High-speed internet averages about $40 a month, though some people get by with a USB stick and use wireless.

Having a full-time maid (five days a week) averages around $250 a month. Naturally, if you just have someone come in a couple days a week it will be significantly less. Automobile prices in Guatemala are on par with those in the United States and gasoline prices are similar as well. "Electronics prices are about 40% higher though," says Luke. "You definitely want to wait until you leave before you buy those."

Downsides

Expatriates here do all have to have their crime radar up more than those in Mexico or Nicaragua, but most of what anyone deals with is petty crime. "It's always in the back of your head that you need to watch out for things and have your guard up," says Rich. "I've gone my whole life without being robbed, but somebody took my bicycle last week. But maybe I was just lucky the rest of my life. Part of the difference is, you can't wrap yourself in a bubble here like you would in suburban USA where you just go from the house to the garage to the car to your office and back. You're integrated with the community."

"There's a high tax on imported goods in Guatemala so clothing and shoes are actually far cheaper in the USA than they are here, of better quality," says Rich. "Cheap clothing here is truly cheap—it'll fall apart in two days." Electronics and appliances are also far more expensive.

This is a tough country in which to run an online business unless you're willing to pay for redundancy. In other words, you need a DSL land line, a USB wireless stick from a cell phone company, and maybe a second USB stick for when both those fail. Or a regular chair at the local internet cafe. It's hard to get high-speed cable connections in many places in Guatemala, so it can be tough to run webinars, upload long videos, or do intensive stock trading.

When I asked Luke and Rich what expats usually complain about, both mentioned government bureaucracy and the inconsistent rules. "You go in one day and they say you need color photos with your application. You go in the next day with those and a different person says, 'you were supposed to bring black and white photos,'" says Luke. A lot of patience is required. "*Guatever*" is the common sigh.

For More Information:

Expat Exchange Guatemala
Travel Write Sing (travelwritesing.com)
Unwire Me Antigua (antiguaguatemala.unwireme.com)
Atitlan.com (atitlan.com)
Hobo Traveler – Guatemala section (hobotraveler.com)

Chapter 24: India

Pros: Very low costs, good train system, cheap labor, landscape variety, climate variety, interesting food, abundant local produce, unique culture.
Cons: Creaky infrastructure, layers of bureaucracy, endemic corruption, low broadband penetration, poor sanitation, repressive caste system, lots of petty crime, above-average sexual assault instances, constant badgering, and more "cons" in the other sense of the word than anywhere.

Jon Linnemeyer, the author of *How an Average Man Lived an Adventurous Life*, lived in a few different places in India on and off over the years. He still longs for the "beach shack" he had in Goa. "Really, if you have a shower, sink, light bulb, desk, bed, and a place to sit that looks out on the ocean, what else do you want?"

Young American Michael Gans was longing for a more interesting life when he moved to India, but another big motivator was his lack of disposable income while living in London and San Francisco after he got his MBA. "The price basket of goods here in Delhi is minuscule in comparison to the last two places I lived. For example, my one-bedroom apartment in San Francisco Bay was $1,340 per month. Here in Delhi, my one-bedroom apartment of comparable quality costs me $247 a month. A five-mile cab ride in San Francisco would be about $25, while the same distance cab ride in Delhi would be about $2 at the most."

India is a place where many people have decided to shed their baggage—physical, mental, or spiritual—and start anew with a fresh outlook. There's a long history here, dating back before the Beatles and *The Razor's Edge*, of people coming to find enlightenment or at least do some soul-searching. What they expect and what they find are usually quite different though. This is not a country where anything is simple or easy. Almost everything is cheap in monetary terms, but extremely taxing in emotional terms. Outside the biggest cities, you can live in India for less money than almost anywhere else in the world. It takes a certain kind of person to do that, however, without wanting to scream or strangle someone on a daily basis after dealing with the non-stop annoyances.

Let's cut to the chase and say that India is about the wackiest place you can choose to live. The less you have to spend, the wackier it's going to get. This is a country in the midst of massive changes, with its economy lurching forward quickly, then pulling back just as quickly by a crumbling infrastructure and a government that can't get out of its own way. If the country's economy were a train, it would be a third class one lurching through the countryside, occasionally picking up speed before having to clear cows and make small station stops.

There's an incredible amount of technical talent and education in place, but a maddening bureaucracy and stubborn inertia that together seem to stifle any real momentum.

Then there are the Indian people themselves: the hustlers, the cheats, the liars, the beggars, the gropers, and the scammers that seem to be around every corner, waiting to pounce on the next foreign face that drifts by. Ask anyone who has spent a month or more in the country for some stories about maddening experiences and they will regale you with entertaining tales for hours on end. Liz Scully recently moved back to the United States to give India a rest for a while because it was wearing her out. "I began to lose my sense of humor. The corruption, bribery, and being fleeced all the time didn't amuse me anymore. I need to live in the west for a while so I'll appreciate it again when I go back."

So why move here? Well, for starters India is one of the world's greatest bargains. You get more for your money here than nearly any other spot on the globe you can point to. Liz says most people could pretty easily get by for $1,000 a month. "For $1,500 you're living an amazing life."

People will tell you otherwise though—including expatriate executives—because there are really two sides to India. There's the side the tourism bureau likes to emphasize, of $1,200 a night hotels, luxury train trips, and spectacular restaurants. This coincides with surveys listing Bombay as one of the most expensive cities in the world for expatriate business executives—if they want to live the same kind of life as they had at home, with the same kind of apartment and appliances.

If you're not trying to live the life of the top two percent though, it's a different story. There are backpacker types living in Goa, Kerala, and the Himalayan regions up north for $250 to $300 a month. Total! Spend $600 a month outside of the largest cities and you will be living better than a middle class local. You'll probably have more space than their whole family too when you come home.

Janet Hasam had a high-paying job for a British organization when she first moved to India, but now lives with her Indian husband in Hyderabad, after a fairy tale wedding at the Taj Mahal. Her husband is a university professor and they're better off than many, but they only spend around $250 a month for the two of them. "We live in a family compound, so our living expenses are limited to paying utilities and food," she says. "That helps a lot. Still, we just bought a huge batch of groceries for the equivalent of four British pounds and that will go a very long way. We have a regular maid and a cook." Their biggest expense is electricity, at about $80 a month, and "cosmetics seem far more expensive here than in England," she says.

Typical local wages tell you a lot about how little it requires to just get by here. "When I ran our charity organization in Chennai, I used to pay workers between 6,000 and 10,000 rupees a month," Janet says. "That works out to around $100 to $170 at current exchange rates. One of them, his mom worked in a hospital and only earned 4,000 a month ($67)."

The Indian rupee has continued to decline the past few years and does not look likely to reverse. That's good news for those earning or pulling savings in a hard currency like dollars, pounds, or euros, but you do have to factor in high inflation. That inflation could easily come down with more efficient distribution systems and a more open import climate, but populist forces in the government wanting to protect the current system keep striking both down. So it's doubtful the rupee will suddenly go up in value anytime soon.

If you can navigate the legalities, there are a lot of opportunities here to open a business that fills a hole in the market. An article in EscapeArtist.com on Manali up north explains why: "The establishments that really seem to know what they're doing are invariably run by foreigners who've settled here, and do a brisk business in the absence of serious competition. With very little investment, you could own a profitable restaurant or bar." This becomes much easier to pull off if you have an Indian spouse or at least a local partner to deal with the hurdles: both above the table and under it.

There are high hopes by many after a mid-2014 election toppled the reigning Congress party and ushered in a new one led by business-friendly Natendra Modi from Gujarat. He's best known for turning his home state into the most dynamic and successful one by cutting red tape, fighting corruption, and building infrastructure. He's from the Hindu Nationalist party, which doesn't bode well for religious tolerance, but on the economic front his rise to Prime Minister should mean progress for a country that keeps promising but not delivering on the world stage.

India is a big country with vast distances, so you'll find other expatriates scattered all over the place. The ones working for a big company tend to be in Delhi, Mumbai, Bangalore, Hyderabad, or Chennai. These are not the most pleasant places to live though for sure, with an abundance of noise and pollution. Foreigners who live here by choice and have money coming from elsewhere tend to gravitate to quieter, less hectic places. You can find them on southern beaches, northern mountains, and many places in between. The personalities of Shimla and Hampi are as different as separate countries would be; so much of where you would go depends on what feels like a good fit. Kerala is progressive, tropical, and has a lot of vegetarians. Gujarat state is more conservative, drier, religious, and has a lot more meat on the menu. Rishikesh is "the yoga capital of the world," cool at night, and full of restaurants catering to health nuts. Dharamsala is Buddhist, wet, and full of Tibetan food.

Some areas are easy to get to, others are popular in part for their isolation. (India attracts a fair share of renegades, runaways, and outcasts.) To give you an idea of how this can play out, the popular mountain town of Manali is 193 miles (310 kms) from the closest real city and getting to Delhi requires a long overnight bus ride or flight. Other towns in the Himalayan region can only be reached on foot. If you want to be close to civilization, a mid-sized city with an airport or first-class train connection might be a better bet. The only way you're really going to know is to travel around the country for a good bit of time, soaking it all in.

One thing's for sure: life won't be boring after your move. "Old friends at home can't wait to hear what I've been up to the past week," Janet says. "My life is so interesting compared to what it was like in England. Life is so different all the time and I never know what a new day will bring."

Housing Costs

You can rent a penthouse with a waterfront view in Mumbai for as much as you would pay in Hong Kong or London, but in most of the country rents are too cheap to believe. Spend some time on message boards like IndiaMike.com and you'll find people paying $67 a month for a two-bedroom apartment in Goa or $50 for a one-bedroom with a kitchen and mountain-view balcony in Manali. Others hike into the Parvati Valley with a backpack on and decide not to pick it up again until five months later because they've found a whole house to rent for under $100 a month, loads of cheap restaurants, and yes, lots of bargain-priced hash to smoke.

It's not going to cost you much to stay in a guesthouse while you look around for an apartment. Many people check into a cheap hotel and find that'll do just fine. This is a country where you can still find rooms for as little as $2 a night in some areas and for $5 a night there's a good selection.

There are lots of regional quirks though, especially in cities where demand is high from workers making a decent salary. In Bangalore, for instance, you need to put down a deposit for six months rent. Liz Scully lived in Kerala before Bangalore and says, "It was much cheaper there and I didn't have to put down as much."

She notes though that in India, you often get what you pay for, with more expensive places having screens on the windows, plus a better bathroom with a western toilet. "In India," she adds, "It's hard to find a place without loads of bathrooms and bedrooms: houses and apartments are set up for extended families. Most have at least 3 bedrooms, often a maid's quarters too. Sometimes you can find two-bedroom places, but more common is three bedrooms, three baths."

Liz paid 47,000 rupees per month for her last Bangalore apartment "It had three bedrooms, four bathrooms, in a complex with a swimming pool, squash court, gym, 24-hour security, and parking. My expat colleagues thought I was paying a tiny amount, my Indian friends thought I was paying an outrageous amount." She says you're almost sure to get some nasty surprises though, or downright cheating. "I had to pay a fee to move out. When I asked what that fee was for, they told me, 'Because the committee that runs the home owners' association has to make money somehow.'" Plus there's that hefty deposit she had to pay up front, which the owners often use as an interest-free loan. "A ditch digger in Bangalore makes 200 rupees a day—around $3. So giving a landlord the equivalent of almost $6,000 up front is just nuts."

Health Care

"Pharmaceuticals cost 4 percent of what they do here in America, and for most things you don't even need a prescription. Doctors are excellent, and their fees are pocket lint compared to the cost of medical care in America," says John.

India is a major medical tourism destination, with the best hospitals having western-trained doctors and great facilities. Patients will fly from a high-priced country like the USA to India for major surgery, getting a knee replacement or a heart operation for one-fifth or less. From check-ups to shots to lab work, you can expect to pay far less than the rates in your home country, with little to no waiting. Complete hip surgery here can be well under $10,000: typically one-fifth of the U.S. cost and with one-tenth the waiting time in the UK or Canada. Want to get a facelift to get rid of some of those sags and wrinkles? Your bill will probably be $1,250 instead of the $10,000+ it would cost in New York or California.

Naturally, all the doctors speak English in India. Even though they may know another dialect, English is the language of government, education, business, and medicine. It may take a while to get used to the accent, but you won't have any trouble communicating your symptoms.

This assumes you're in or near a major city, however. If you're out in a rural village somewhere, expect care to be rudimentary at best. There's a reason the life expectancy in this country is only 67. Most locals can't afford the doctors who paid six figures to study abroad or the gleaming air-conditioned hospital with a high-end clientele. This is a country, after all, where you see dentists who don't look much wealthier than the beggars set up on a blanket on the sidewalk, a hand-scrawled sign advertising their ability to yank out your bad tooth on the spot for the equivalent of a couple dollars.

If you're living far from a city you can get to easily, you are better off being young and healthy than retired with failing body parts. If nothing else, keep money aside for a last-minute flight and a MasterCard with a large credit limit. The other option would be to sign up with an evacuation insurance company like MedJet Assist, but you need to really be a tourist (and not a long-term resident on a work visa) for that to apply.

Food & Drink

India is one of the world's greatest bargains when it comes to food, whether buying it at the market, eating at a simple restaurant, or going for a fine dining meal. "I just bought three tomatoes and a few onions for 25 cents," said Michael Gans the day I interviewed him. He probably overpaid too.

This is a country where you can still stuff yourself for a dollar. In a *thali* restaurant where you'll get heaps of different curries with rice or chapati bread, you can ask for seconds if you're not satisfied. Just don't expect the huge variety you see on Indian restaurant menus at home. Those usually cover the whole country, while in reality there are regional differences according to tradition, religion, and what's easiest to grow in the area. In some spots the food is really spicy, in others it's more likely to use milder spices and coconut. Naturally on the coast there's more seafood and in the northern mountain regions more lentils and potatoes. In general terms, the areas with more Muslims will have a lot of meat—though when you see the open-air butcher shops in the 95-degree heat (35 Celsius), you'll probably decide to be very careful about where you partake.

In general though, unless you're really on a super-tight budget, you will eat very well in India and your taste buds will seldom be bored. Just understand that if you want food that tastes like what you're used to from the home country, you'll have to seek it out (often in an international chain hotel) or make it yourself. Even the McDonald's menu is going to look very foreign.

Transportation

Getting around is quite cheap in India, once you figure out what's what and get a sense of real prices. The 14,000-kilometer train network tops all kinds of lists, from being the largest employer in the world (1.6 million people) to having the most continuously running routes. Almost 14 million people travel on the train every day.

An overnight second-class sleeper can be as little as $3, and the 17-hour trip from Delhi to Jaisalmer is around $6 for a bed. Air-conditioned first-class is roughly 2-1/2 times the price of second class, but you get what you pay for and you'll be far less annoyed, especially on journeys that can last all night and half the day. All train prices are set according to the number of kilometers. You can go 2,000 kilometers (1,240 miles) on an air-conditioned sleeper train for less than $50, including bedding. On the one-day A/C express trains ($13 from Bangalore to Chennai, for example) and on all Rajdhani Express trains, multiple meals are thrown in as well.

Buses can be dusty, crowded hulks crammed with people and a pig or two on the roof, or can be a "luxury" bus that at least has assigned seats. Prices are comparable to the train (in 2nd non-A/C class), but the buses are more direct for some routes. As a rule of thumb, a cheap bus is a dollar for 2-3 hours, while a private express bus costs 70 to 90 cents per hour traveled and it's unlikely you'll want to stay on board for more than 12 hours. Long distance night buses have "sleeper" options as well (usually for a 25 percent extra), but avoid those buses whenever possible as they are not the safest option. When the number of passengers plus the age of the bus is over 100, you have discovered the real rural India. And it's a good time to get off.

Apart from a cruise down the backwaters in Kerala, there aren't many opportunities to get around on a boat. Internal flight prices have come down in recent years with more competition. A flight can shave days off a long trip: India is a big country. Delhi to Mumbai (Bombay) can take at least 24 hours on the train, so $65 to $120 for a flight can be money well spent. Budget airlines can get as low as $40 to $70 one way.

"There are something like two hundred thousand bicycle rickshaw and auto-rickshaw drivers in Delhi," says Michael. "You can't go outside for five minutes without seeing a few of them. When I lived in San Francisco, it was a minimum of $20 to take a cab, whether you were going 100 yards or two miles. Here you would pay 100 rupees to go five miles in an auto-rickshaw. That's like a buck fifty."

In most of the major cities the cabs and auto-rickshaws have a meter, but you'll have to fight to get them to use it. Elsewhere you'll need to bargain like crazy up front. Ask a local first what a reasonable fare should be. There are usually enough drivers hanging around that you can end up at a reasonable price by haggling. Prepaid taxi and auto rickshaw booths are available at major railways stations and airports with government-approved fixed rates.

Only a foreigner with a death wish would try to own and drive a car here. India has one of the highest road accident rates in the world and five minutes on those roads will show you why. You can hire a driver ($30 - $60 per day) and agree ahead of time on what is included in the price. Then kick back and let him navigate around the sleeping cows and loaded-down auto rickshaws.

If you're living here and need a car regularly, there are car services that can have a regular driver on call or if you have to commute each weekday, you can get a monthly rate. "For a lot of people who have corporate jobs, a driver is the biggest expense. If you found someone direct you could trust, it could be as little as $300 a month for just the labor, before fuel costs. But if you go through a firm, which is the best way to keep from getting fleeced, it'll be more like $600 to $1,000 a month," says Janet.

If you do want to explore on your own and you're not in a huge city, a motorbike is cheaper and probably safer. You can dodge the potholes and cows more easily. This is the transport method of choice for most foreigners in Goa.

City infrastructure in India has typically lagged far behind growth, but Delhi has been getting its act together and pushing through major projects. There's a high-speed rail line to the nice new airport and the fast-expanding, air-conditioned subway already carries close to two million people a day. It's planned to grow to 440 kilometers by 2020.

Other Costs

How much things will cost you in India depends a great deal on your bargaining skills. Buying almost any product or service requires a game of negotiation. Without participating in it, you'll get robbed. "The first time I got a taxi in Chennai it cost me 400 rupees," Janet says. "It took 20 minutes, and it was from the airport, so I thought it was very reasonable. By the time I finished living there two years later, I was paying 40 rupees for the same ride. Every time I'd come out of the shopping mall the drivers would all shout '150 rupees for a taxi madam!' Eventually I would ride home for 30."

Liz says utility bills depend a lot of your set-up and how you deal with the frequent power outages. A lot of people have solar hot water heaters so they can shower without being dependent on the finicky electrical grid. "Plus you always need some kind of backup emergency power," she adds. "Internet is really solid in a place like Bangalore and it's blisteringly fast, but you need an uninterrupted power source. Mobile internet is quite fast as well, but 4G isn't very widespread yet."

She stresses that in local currency terms, inflation is massive. "When I first got my apartment, the electricity bill was usually around 350 rupees per month. At the end it was 675 rupees, for the same consumption. Inflation is so fast that I would go home for Christmas, then come back from the break and prices were higher."

Most foreigners spending $800 or more a month here are living quite well because of all the domestic help that income can afford. "You *have* to have a maid," says Liz. "It's a social responsibility to have staff in India, as many as you can afford. If you don't, you're viewed as socially horrible in a way that doesn't really have a western equivalent. You have wealth, so you must spread it about. My maid's useless, but she's honest. Nearly everyone has a story of a maid who stole from them. You always have to get receipts from supermarkets. You have to be prepared to be fleeced a certain amount, but you must set a limit and don't let it go beyond that. (To see some great stories from Liz, including plenty about her maid, see her stories at MadamLetMeTellYouOneThing.com.)

Liz pays her maid the equivalent of $85 a month to work two days a week, which she says is very high by local standards. "Some expats are paying 12,000 a month ($207) for a cook or cleaner and they think it's grand," she says. "But really that's what a trained sous chef at the Marriott is getting."

Visas in India

Understand that India loves bureaucracy perhaps more than any country in the world and the civil service is a massive employer in the country. Picture an office with 50 people, desks stacked with papers in triplicate, those papers held down by paperweights since fans are blowing at full speed in the heat. Nobody is in a hurry, nobody is striving for efficiency, and rules are adhered to with glee at every level. Occasionally you can speed up the process with some *baksheesh* placed in the right hands, but otherwise you will need lots of time and even more patience than usual. You must apply in advance and be approved even for a basic tourist visa.

Because of this and the total lack of any easy permanent option, India is a hard place to move to full-time unless you are Indian to start with (or can demonstrate recent heritage). There is no such thing as a retirement visa here for people with no Indian blood. In theory Americans can get a 5-year or even 10-year multiple entry visa because of a bilateral agreement in place, but you can only stay 180 days at a time before needing to leave for at least two months before returning. Many go to Nepal, Sri Lanka, or Thailand on vacation to start the stretch over again, which isn't necessarily a bad thing, but just understand you need to pick up and get moving on a six month/two month cycle to infinity.

Australians can get a multi-year tourist visa, UK citizens up to five years (but only 180 days in a stretch), Canadians generally get up to 180 days. The clock starts ticking when the visa is issued, not when you arrive.

Making this even more complicated is that you can't buy property unless you are in the country 182 days in a fiscal year. As you may have noticed from the above, that's impossible to legally do in one stretch, so it takes two entries to accomplish in a specific calendar time period. You might want to just rent, especially since Indian laws aren't always known for having a strong base in logic and it's not hard to imagine the rules changing again for the worse after you've already invested in property.

There are myriad other visa types you can apply for, but understand that for a business or employment visa you generally need to be sponsored by a local company. These visas are typically issued for one year, but in some cases for longer. Some retirees have managed to get a part time local job to obtain a business visa, with the pay they're getting not really being the point: they're doing it to avoid leaving the country every six months.

Trying to come set up a business is possible, but it requires extensive paperwork, an attorney, and a pledge to only hire local workers unless you specifically need foreigners for work that can't be done by a local person. It gets much easier if you have an Indian spouse who can be the official owner on paper. Naturally if you marry an Indian person, everything gets much easier for a long-term stay as well.

Spend some time on your local embassy site and follow the instructions to the letter when applying for a visa. There is usually a private agency in place that handles the paperwork and they will have more information on their site. Take listed turnaround times with a grain of salt and double them to be safe.

Downsides

Some have written entire entertaining books about the downsides of spending time in India. There's probably no country in the world where the touts, the scammers, and the schemers work so tirelessly to extract a few extra rupees in every possible situation. Even the most patient people can end up snapping at some point.

The expats in this country all agree that it's a given you're going to get cheated and ripped off on a regular basis. "You will get fleeced by everyone, all the time, and have to accept that," says Liz. "If you get angry every time you're getting ripped off, it will drive you crazy. You need to have a limit you'll accept and stand your ground on that."

The infrastructure in this country is seriously overtaxed, with blackouts being common even in the tech center of Bangalore and broadband penetration being the lowest of almost anywhere outside Africa. With a population this huge, the more the government builds, the more it falls behind.

This is a very difficult and trying place to be an entrepreneur. Sure, you see people set up on sidewalks everywhere cutting hair or pulling teeth, but the World Bank ranks India near the bottom of their list worldwide for ease of starting a real, legal business.

India's weather is greatly impacted by the annual monsoon, so there are really no places where you get some kind of "eternal spring" climate like you have in certain highland towns of other countries. It's certainly much cooler and nicer much of the year in the Himalayas, but winter can turn downright brutal. Kerala during the monsoon can be a soggy mess for months. Delhi or Mumbai in the hottest time of the year will make you sweat a liter of water just walking out the door. So if you're not on a work permit in a real job, the six-month time limit is not necessarily a bad thing. You just take off when the weather is at its worst, coming back when that part is over.

For More Information

Retire in Asia - India (retireinasia.com/category/india)
IndiaMike.com (indiamike.com)
Transitions Abroad Living in India section
Madam Let Me Tell You One Thing (madamletmetellyouonething.com)
Expat Blog directory – India (expat-blog.com/en/directory/asia/india)
ExpatsBlog.com – India (expatsblog.com/blogs/india)
Hippie in Heels – Goa (hippie-inheels.com)

Chapter 25: Bulgaria

Pros: cheapest housing in Europe, fast internet in urban areas, stable currency, fresh food, good beer, cheap alcohol, well-preserved nature, skiing, outdoor activities, relatively easy residency.
Cons: government corruption, oligarch power, low birth rate with high emigration, very few jobs, poor shopping, inconsistent health care.

"I know who made the yogurt you are eating and who made the cheese. I've been to the farm where we got the eggs and know the guy who raised the pigs for the pork you ate last night. The rose petals in that jam are from our own farm."

In much of the world, this declaration I got from the owner of Tsousova Guest House in Bulgaria would seem boastful, the product of serious effort to establish credibility amongst the organic food police crowd. If true, it would require years of relationship building with the right farmers who could ensure a steady supply.

In Bulgaria, this kind of boast is followed with a shrug. "We buy from our neighbors because it's good for the village. And we like to know where our food is coming from."

I didn't expect to eat and drink so well in Bulgaria and I start salivating again when I think back on my meals there. When you get your bill at the end though, it's always a pleasant surprise. There's plenty to lament about the current state of Bulgaria: government corruption, a net population loss because of job seekers heading elsewhere, and not nearly enough jobs to go around for those who are left. Don't come here expecting to land a local job unless you can connect with a multinational in Sofia or get hired as an ESL teacher.

The country has managed to do three things quite well though: preserve its heritage, preserve its green space, and produce great food. Some 30 percent of the country is protected forest land. This is the kind of figure you expect to hear for some eco-poster-child country like Costa Rica or New Zealand, not for a former Iron Curtain nation in Europe.

As I hiked all three mountain ranges there, I was continually surprised by the rolling waves of green on mountains that show no sign of deforestation. I was also surprised by the purity of the springs, the lack of garbage, and the clear connection between the people and the land. With fewer than eight million people in a country that stretches from Serbia across the tops of Greece and Turkey to the Black Sea, there's plenty of wide-open space.

Cruising the highways now, despite the grape trellises and garden plots gracing almost every house, the Soviet era is still a dominant feature of the landscape.

Ladas, smoke-belching motorcycles, and even an occasional Trabant are parked in the towns. Abandoned factories with busted windows are a regular roadside fixture. It was three days into my trip before I saw a smokestack that actually smoked. In the old days, things were different. "We grew a lot of things here and could produce a lot," said my driver Marin, who once kept the export books at a steel factory. "The Russians weren't very picky, so they bought it all. Whatever we could make and package, we had a market for it. So you can imagine why some people think those were the good old days."

Marin told me this as we ate at the only dining spot in town, the Central Cooperative Restaurant that's survived since the fall of Communism. We paid 10 euros for three after feasting on our multi-course meals and beers. After I expressed what a bargain this was, I found out that the minimum wage in Bulgaria is around 120 euros a month. The average salary is less than €340/$500. So if you move here with a monthly pension or income of $1,000 a month, you'll be living an upper middle-class life along with elite computer programmers and VP-level executives.

Joanna Newman lived in multiple locations in England before moving to a small village in the gorgeous Veliko Turnovo region of Bulgaria. She lives in a house she and her husband bought outright for less than what most people spend on a new compact car. "When in the UK we would spend a £1500 per month on rent, food, and bills," she says. "But here I live on less than £200 per month." In US dollars, she cut her expenses from $2,500 to $335. And she's still in Europe.

She had plenty of time to give it a trial run and prepare for what to expect before moving. "My husband had a heart attack and this led us to move out here for a quieter life," she explains, "but we had to wait for redundancy in his job, which we knew was coming at some point and we did not want to lose out on the money which would enable us to get settled. This took three years, so in the meantime we came out a couple of times a year to soak up the atmosphere and do a bit of renovation on the house we chose to live in."

She's not alone. An article on the BBC website about Brits moving abroad to inexpensive countries pegged the number of them in Bulgaria at 18,000. There are at least 60,000 foreigners here overall.

This is primarily a rural country with small towns and villages. The second-largest city after Sofia has fewer than half a million people and it drops off fast after that. You'll find the most expatriates in the capital of Sofia as it's the largest city, the business hub, and the place you're most likely to find people who can speak English. Others settle on the Black Sea coast though, where a steady stream of tourists means a higher English (and German) proficiency. If I were moving there though I'd probably head to Veliko Turnovo up north. It's the kind of place that, in a more popular country, would be jammed with tour buses and hundreds of bored waitresses would know how to say, "Anything else?" If a luxury hotel opened, *Travel + Leisure* would soon be calling it the next "hot destination." That's because it's a beautiful town with lots of historic character and houses clinging to a hillside overlooking a river and a stone fort. There's a university to ensure lots of life and culture, and there's plenty to see and do in the countryside. It was the seat of power during Bulgaria's heyday in the 1300s, when the king's territory extended to three seas.

What you spend in Bulgaria largely depends on how frugal you're willing to be and how much you want to venture outside the country. "I was making about $32,000 a year teaching at the American College of Sofia," says American Carolyn Emigh. On that salary she lived well and spent vacations touring around other parts of Europe. "I did spend my first year in Sofia on a Fulbright where I made only

$1,000 a month and had to pay rent from this," she adds. "This was significantly more difficult to do given how much travel I wanted to do but if you were willing to stay in country most of the year and live simply one could pretty easily get by in Sofia on this amount of money—most Bulgarians do—but you wouldn't have a lot of Western comforts."

Outside the capital, you can live very well on that amount. You'd be spending more than twice the average local wage and probably more than almost any local in your town besides successful business owners and bank chiefs.

Bulgaria has done a major about-face from the Soviet era in one respect: it's quite open to foreign investment and business formation. Because of this, many find that coming here with a bit of money and some patience presents a lot of opportunities for entrepreneurs. Taxes are some of the lowest in the EU and there are relatively few bureaucratic hassles compared to many other countries on the continent.

While this country is part of the European Union, it has not met the requirements to use the euro as its currency. Instead you'll be withdrawing Bulgaria lev, plural leva, which generally trades at a rate of 1.4 or 1.5 to the dollar, a shade below parity with the euro.

Housing Costs

Joanna Newman wasn't even considering a move to Bulgaria until she saw a house for sale online that was too crazy cheap to believe. "I had a shop on eBay and while I was working one day a house for sale in Bulgaria popped up, it was a silly price and it piqued my interest. I showed my husband and we watched it to see what would happen," she explained.

"After this we checked out other eBay sales then looked elsewhere on the internet and did a lot of research. We decided to take a trip out to see the country, meet the people, and look at houses." After falling in love with the place, they ended up buying three properties for investment. "We found our dream home after looking at many houses over a couple of days. It was the third house we said we wanted. Had we seen it first we would only have bought this one. As soon as the gate was opened it was just love at first sight and I still love it as much as I did then."

What did she spend on this nice country home in Vinograd, northern Bulgaria? A whopping 8,000 pounds sterling, which is around $13,500. "In the UK it would cost hundreds of thousands of pounds!"

If you've got money to invest, real estate prices here are among the best values I've seen anywhere in the world. I frequently saw houses for sale for under 20,000 euros throughout the country when I was there. In the top ski destination of Bansko, there are multiple one-bedroom condos for sale for less than 20,000 euros, larger ones with a view going for what works out to $60 a square foot. That's $48,000/€35,000 for a 2BR newly constructed condo of 800 square feet. Really nice places in prime areas in Sofia seldom top 100,000 euros in the real estate office windows. This is one of the few places in Europe where you can get a condo with a sea view (on the Black Sea coast) for less than $80,000.

Technically foreigners can't own land, but there's an easy way around this by setting up a local corporation and buying through that. No local has to have a partnership or ownership stake. You can buy a condo as an individual very easily.

Rental prices are a good value in the capital, a screaming bargain in smaller towns. In some of the villages it seems like every second or third house is empty because the owners are off working in another European country with better job prospects. So it's a renter's market and if you have feet on the ground you should be able to find a furnished rental house for one-fifth or less what you would pay where you live now. If you ask how much a place is, they might ask, "Well, what can you pay?" If you spend 250 euros a month in Sofia, your neighbors will be firmly in the upper middle class.

Health Care

Joanna says she has had excellent health care and the cost is unbelievable. "My doctor is great and only charges 2 leva a visit and sometimes won't charge at all. I have been referred to a neurologist and was seen the next day. I was diagnosed, given treatment, and had a follow up appointment all for 14 leva & a big apology!"

Residents from the UK love the local system because there is almost never a wait. While they may have had to schedule appointments weeks or months ahead in their home country, here you can just show up and see a doctor most of the time, or at most you may have to wait until the next business day. A doctor's appointment seldom costs more than $25, even with x-rays or lab tests.

Medicine is not as cheap as the doctor visits though, especially name brand ones that require a prescription. Also, since hospitals tend to specialize, it can mean long journeys to get to the right one for regular treatments if you're not in the capital.

Sofia is a popular place for Europeans to come for dental treatment because of good care at a drastically lower cost. Crowns and implants are commonly one-third what they cost in Western Europe. Fillings and check-ups are one-quarter or less.

Permanent residents can tap into the national health care system, though with costs so cheap to pay out of pocket, most just use it as an emergency backup. In general the doctors in Bulgaria are well trained and in the cities the hospitals are good. This is a country with limited resources and a national health care system though, so you may not find the breadth of new equipment you would in a developed country. There is also a shortage of nurses since many experienced ones find they can earn far more in other European countries, so they move.

Food & Drink

There's nothing wimpy about Bulgarian cuisine. Restaurant portions are so huge that most salads could easily serve two or three. Every time I ordered a glass of house wine, it was filled to the brim. A shot of *rakia* must be lifted carefully in order to avoid spilling any. If something on the menu says it's for two to share, assume those two will be bringing leftovers home unless they're really starving.

This is not filler food piled high and cheap, however. Plates are loaded up with fresh vegetables that are in season, all picked when they were ripe. The meat is from free-range animals because they can't imagine eating it if done another way. Of course the beef is grass-fed and of course the bacon is really smoked in a smokehouse, not flavored by some nasty chemicals. Often when you eat in Bulgarian villages, the distances from the source are measured in walking distance, not highway markers. I'm not buying the premise that dairy is bad for you after seeing the muscle-bound men and curvy women of Bulgaria: every salad is covered with shredded cheese, usually with chunks of cheese in it as well, and a meal without yogurt is like, well, breakfast without cheese. They don't do this just to fill up; they do it because it's locally made and yummy.

Situated between Greece, Turkey, the Balkans, and Romania, Bulgaria has had a lot of different influences in its cuisine. A lot of it will seem vaguely familiar, while in some ethnic Turkish areas you'll feel like you're back in Anatolia.

Nearly everyone makes their own wine. If you need to buy some, you can fill up a jug in the market for a couple dollars. A good bottle will frequently be $3 - 8 in a store. In restaurants, it's common to pay $4 - $8 for a typical table wine bottle, $8 – $15 for the best. The delicious beer here is one of the best values on the planet, flavorful and varied but bargain priced. It's usually cheaper than ordering soda. Figure on 50 – 80 cents a liter in stores, $1 – $2.50 in a bar/restaurant for a liter bottle depending on decor. Liquor in a bar is as little as 75 cents for a shot of *rakia* (firewater distilled from grapes or plums), but generally $1–$2. Local vodka is as little as $2 a bottle for something drinkable in cocktails, imports are $3 - $9.

Non-alcoholic drinks like herbal tea and mineral water are the cheapest at 40-80 cents, coffee is often $1 or so or $1.50 for a nice cappuccino.

You can get good street food in Sofia for 50 cents to $2 that will fill you up. Typical menu prices for locals' restaurants are as follows: soups/salads $1.50 – $3, mains $2 – $6, desserts 50 cents to $1.50. Fruit and vegetables are abundant and bargain priced in season, though in winter most families switch to what's been preserved and pickled: not much is imported from warmer climates like it is in wealthier countries. You'll generally pay $1.40 a kilo or less for peppers, cabbage, potatoes, greens, grapes, plums, peaches, and turnips. Some items, like strawberries and fancy mushrooms, will be a dollar or two more. Dairy products are consumed with gusto here and are a great deal. Yogurt is around $1 a liter, milk $1.50, cheese is $4 - $6 a kilo fresh, $8 - $10 aged.

Transportation Costs

Once you figure out how to get to where you're going here, transportation is very cheap. With the local wages being quite low, many public transportation options are subsidized to keep them affordable to locals. Local buses, metro lines, and streetcars are around 75 cents in the capital and can be less in smaller towns. Taxi fares range from 40 to 70 cents per kilometer.

The longest train route is the Sofia/Varna trip, which is $25 round trip in 2nd class. Sofia to Plovdiv is under $10 one way. First class is around 40 percent more on all routes. You can easily reach Romania or Turkey by train.

Inter-city buses are priced roughly the same as the train, at $3 to $15 one-way, but they are faster on some routes.

Bike rentals in Sofia are $1.50–$4 an hour, or you can work out a daily rate. If you're going to stay a while though, you can pick up a new or used one at a good price and in the warmer months you'll have plenty of company on two wheels.

Cars and fuel are both priced at typical European levels here, which make them expensive by local standards. It can be worth it to have a vehicle here though if you're not in one of the cities. You can easily do without, but having a car gives you the freedom to explore and you can drive to other EU countries easily.

Other Costs

Rising fuel costs were enough to bring down a whole government in 2013, with the public blaming cozy relationships with energy monopolies for increasing bills. You can bet any future government is going to do its best to keep these prices from rising too quickly.

To give you a rough idea on utilities, here's what Joanna spends in her house. "My electric is 50 leva per month ($33), water 5 leva ($3.30). Home Phone with plenty of free minutes to call England is 16 leva per month ($11), internet 25 leva a month ($17), the mobile phone runs from10 to 15 leva a month ($6.70-$10)."

It won't cost you much to go sightseeing here. Only the Rila Monastery gets busloads of foreign tourists and that's free (like all churches and monasteries here) unless you want to visit the museum or tower. I visited stunning caverns, amazing citadels, and a great ethnographic village, all for 4 lev each, (less than $3).

Most museums and attractions are in the $1.50–$4 range for adults, half that for kids and students. The national park hiking trails are free and there are inexpensive mountain huts and hostels to stay in along the way. Skiing prices will make you think you took a time machine back to the 1980s. The most expensive walk-up one-day lift ticket in the country is under $40 and that's for a place where you can catch a gondola right in the center of town that takes you to the summit. Some slopes are half that amount. Full rental equipment packages are most commonly 10 euros a day ($13.50).

Visas

As in the other Schengen countries, you can visit Bulgaria for 90 days, but then you must leave the whole region for that long before starting the clock ticking again. So if you want to stick around longer, you need to apply for a long-term visa at a Bulgarian consulate or embassy in your own country, come in on that, and then apply for a long-term residence permit after arrival in Bulgaria. You'll have 90 days to work that out and get approved.

You can apply as an employee, freelance professional, or pensioner. Since employment is hard to find in this country, a work permit is mainly limited to English teachers, ski instructors, specialized tour guides, and those working for international corporations where English proficiency is essential. For the other two, proof of sufficient income to support yourself is the main criteria. If you have a clean record and can demonstrate you'll be bringing money into the local economy, you should get approval.

After five years as a long-term resident, you can apply for permanent residency. After five years of that and fluency in Bulgarian, you can apply to be a citizen.

If you've got half a million dollars lying around, you can also buy your way to permanent residency by investing it in

Bulgaria.

Downsides

Bulgaria is cheap for a reason: it's one of the poorest countries in Europe when you look at per capita GDP, average wages, or middle class wealth. The bloated communist system employed everyone, but now that everyone is on their own, the country is still struggling to attract enough industry to keep its population occupied and the entrepreneurial spirit has been slow to catch on with locals. There's an upside there for foreigners with good business skills, but of course you'll have to prepare plenty of paperwork in a foreign language, which will require a local attorney and some patience.

Much of the infrastructure in Bulgaria dates back to the Soviet era and hasn't had much attention since, with the exception of surprisingly fast internet for those who have it. (Broadband is widespread in the larger cities.) The admission into the EU in 2007 has had some positive impact, but it has also resulted in a lot of fake improvements just for show. There are recycling bins all over the place, for example, but all the locals say the separated items just get dumped in with the regular garbage. Internet penetration here remains stubbornly low in the countryside.

There is frequent petty crime in the larger cities, including pickpockets, plus there is a significant organized crime element that you don't want to get on the wrong side of. The police force isn't known for being highly effective.

The Bulgarian language is an especially tough one to crack and they don't use a Roman alphabet. It's Cyrillic, like Russian. But it's not quite the same as Russian, so you'll need a good phrase book and some language lessons just to navigate the road signs or bus schedules.

"Learning Bulgarian is really hard, especially when you are older," says Joanna. "Mine is rubbish. I can say basic Bulgarian and talk pidgin fashion, but I have friends who took lessons and are coming along great. It is a really difficult language for me and many others to grasp that many words means the same thing and the way you say it is very important. She gets by with the basics and pantomime and has both Bulgarian and Russian friends, "but I do wish I could speak better and have better conversations with them."

Shopping for clothes and durable goods leaves a lot to be desired. "Bring all the electrics, tools, and furniture you can with you as the quality here is really bad and costs a lot," says Joanna.

Also don't expect all Bulgarians to welcome you with open arms. T.W. Anderson, author of *The Expat Guidebook*, lived in Sofia for several years before moving to Mexico. "In Bulgaria the older people flat out hate Americans. We were the enemy in the communist days and some of them haven't forgotten it."

For More Information:

Expat Blog Directory – Bulgaria at Expat-Blog.com
Expat Blogs in Bulgaria at ExpatsBlog.com
Just Landed – Bulgaria (JustLanded.com)
Quest BG (QuestBG.com)
Melody Does Bulgaria (MelodyDoesBulgaria.wordpress.com)
Travellling Buzz (TravellingBuzz.com)

Chapter 26: Portugal

Pros: Sunny weather, mild winters, low crime, low pollution, classic European feel, good wine, inexpensive food, geographic variety, abundant local produce/meat/cheese, foreigner-friendly.
Cons: High unemployment, high import item costs, expensive toll roads, tough language, limited English outside cities & Algarve, limited restaurant diversity, difficult visa for non-EU citizens.

When Susan Korthase and her husband were looking to move abroad from Milwaukee, Wisconsin, they had already lived abroad and moved 17 times. They started diving into the options and considered all the touted suspects like Panama, Uruguay, Ecuador, and Belize. "We looked at a lot of spots highlighted by *International Living* and books on living outside the U.S.," she says." Portugal only came up once; it wasn't really discussed." They decided to go traveling around and check out different options, but they started in Europe, with plans to begin in Portugal and make their way east.

"The first place we started with was Portugal, but we went to the Algarve and really disliked it quite a bit. We went to Lisbon, and that was better, but at the very end of our two-week trip we got on a train and went to Cascais and said, "Wow, this is it!" We had planned to move on and check out other places, but we never did. We just stayed. We rented out our condo back home and eventually took a trip back to get new visas, but we have been here since January of 2011."

Let's face it—the dream of living in most of Western Europe can be hard for the average person to attain. High taxes, high labor costs, high fuel costs, expensive real estate...it all adds up to make nearly everything cost more than it does in the United States or Canada. So unless you're loaded, it's hard to imagine moving there unless you're working for a big company that's posting you there on a job transfer.

Portugal is the odd man out though. Even before the

recent economic debt crisis, it was a country that was drastically less expensive to travel in than its other euro-using counterparts. Since the crisis started, prices have flatlined for anything not imported. I visited Lisbon and then did a week long bike trip through the rural Alentejo region of Portugal and found the prices on many things comparable to what you would find in Eastern Europe. But you get those cheap prices in a warmer climate that borders the ocean. And if you learn the language here, you can at least use it later in huge Brazil.

With the economic crisis in Europe still hitting Portugal hard, it's a buyer's market for real estate and a renter's market for apartments—at least outside the university towns. With unemployment high, there's little opportunity for living expenses to rise for those renting and buying groceries either. For those who do have a job, the minimum wage is only €566 per month and many Portuguese people will tell you that €750/$1,000 is a pretty common amount for locals to live on. Sure, several family members will generally pool resources in one home, but still, if you move here as a couple that can bring in $3,000 a month, you're going to be considered very well-off by local standards.

Julie Dawn Fox had been teaching English as a second language for 12 years, mostly for the British Council. After living in Spain, Tanzania, and Venezuela, she was getting tired of the transient lifestyle and wanted to settle down somewhere in Europe. "I missed the boat on buying a house in the UK; had an opportunity when I was younger but passed on it to go traveling instead," she says. "While I was gone, prices skyrocketed and there was no way I could afford it. I looked at Portugal and the prices were much more affordable. I knew I could buy a house there on my own. I got a job teaching, but then I met my Portuguese husband there. He had already bought a house in the countryside. We looked into buying a city place closer to where we worked, but it can take a long time to sell a house, so we didn't want to depend on that if we bought another one. So we stayed put and we only pay a couple hundred euros a month for his place. The drawback of that is we need two cars. We're about 35 kilometers from Coimbra city where we work. We spend €200-250 a month on petrol. It's usually more than our mortgage"

Julie and her husband regularly put €1,200 a month (around $1,620) from their teachers' salaries into a joint account and that covers all their expenses. "If you aren't extravagant, you can live well on a decent wage. Occasionally there's enough left over for eating out and a bit of travel. We could probably could do it on €1,000 a month if we had to." They are living in a spacious three-bedroom house, but the low mortgage cost definitely helps. "This house would probably be 700 - 800 pounds a month in the UK," she estimates. "We wouldn't be able to afford it."

The great wine here is a terrific bargain and there's a tremendous amount of inherent beauty. The big drawback for Americans is this is a full member of the EU, with the same residency difficulties you will face anywhere else in Western Europe. It's much, *much* easier to move here if you're from the EU than it is from Canada, the U.S., or Australia.

There's not the huge gulf in prices between the capital Lisbon and the countryside like you find in some countries. It's harder to find cheap eats like street food in the countryside and in smaller villages the locals don't really seem to eat out that much. They may hang out at a cafe all day nursing an espresso or a tiny beer (25 CL), but restaurant choices get pretty slim sometimes.

Gail Aguiar has plenty of places to compare with her new home in northern Portugal. She was born in the Philippines but moved as a toddler with her family to Canada. "I grew up in several regions of Canada, where she spent time in Saskatchewan, Winnipeg, Vancouver, Toronto, and Banff. In between there was time in Australia, the UK, and the semi-rural northeastern U.S. This is it, though," she says. "I have no plans to move anywhere else unless my Portuguese husband suddenly decides he wants to try expat life for himself, in which case I would join him."

Hers is a fairytale story of falling in love, first with the man and then the place. "I was first in Portugal in mid-2011, on a birthday trip. It's a tradition of mine to visit a new country on my birthday, and I traveled solo using Couchsurfing to stay with locals. I had three hosts in Portugal, and I stayed in contact with them all after the trip, but especially my host in Porto, where I stayed for one week. We were in regular contact mostly by phone. More than a year later (2012) he visited me, we were a couple by the end of the trip, got married the following year, and a few months after that I landed in Portugal. There was, of course, a lot of paperwork, arrangements, planning, and coordinating in-between but that's the basic timeline."

Author Alicia Sunday grew up in the Leicestershire countryside in England, moved to London for fifteen years, then to Cambridgeshire for twelve years. "We were attracted to the warmer weather and being able to lose the mortgage and buy something with the equity from the house yet have more space and land," she says. "We had to move anyway as we needed more space, so when we sold the house thought we would give a foreign adventure a go. We had a similar experience in Spain a few years ago but rented. The friends we made in Spain had moved to Portugal and recommended it.

With Portugal we also liked the fact we could still afford to be less than an hour away from a fabulous capital city. Since coming here we have also discovered that expats are being encouraged here by lower taxes via the non-habitual residency scheme. The health care is good. Foreign investment is going into the area. School fees are reasonable. People are generally friendly and helpful. The scenery is stunning and there is so much beautiful coastline it's easy to live near the sea and have spectacular views. To know that within half an hour of where we live is the opportunity to go surfing, swimming, sailing, etc. Is just wonderful."

Portugal has a lot going for it. The country appeals to two broad kinds of expatriates: those who want to live a "civilized" European lifestyle without paying anything close to what it costs in France or Italy, and those who want to stop thinking about how much they're spending and just enjoy life to the fullest. Susan and her husband fall into the latter category. They were pulling in half a million dollars a year on their two salaries before, so they weren't moving abroad to scrimp and save. They've drastically lowered their expenses though by relocating. "Rent and utilities cost us about $1,700 a month, for a two-bedroom, two-bath home right in the historical center of Cascais. We do not inhibit ourselves on eating out and groceries, and we drink good wine. We probably spend another $2,000 to $3,000 a month more on everything else, including trips to Spain and elsewhere. For us all this seems very cheap, but of course it depends on where you're coming from and what your income was before. We've moved up to the 10-euro bottles of wine now, but to get that same level of quality where we came from would cost three times as much. The same goes for fine dining or nice hotels in this country."

This being Western Europe, infrastructure is good as well. "You can usually get broadband or Wi-Fi anywhere so if you can work on the internet then Portugal is a great place to be," says Alicia. "You can realistically 'live the dream' here, be working on your laptop under a palm tree and then a quick dip in the pool in a property that can cost a lot less than 100,000 euros."

You can drink the water, crime is low, and infrastructure is very good. The World Economic Forum ranks countries by how developed its infrastructure is and Portugal comes in at a very high #14, easing out Japan at #15 and just behind Canada at #13. (The UK, USA, and Australia aren't in the top-20.)

There's another place where Portugal is at the top of the list: liberal drug laws. Holland may get all the attention, but Portugal quietly dropped penalties for purchase and possession of any drug and has stuck with it. Despite the conservatives' fears, crime hasn't gone up and cities haven't turned squalid. What's defined as enough for "personal use?" That would be a 10-day supply. If you want to cut your costs while living in a liberal country with real democracy and no harsh winters, here's your spot.

This is a good country for families, with a safe climate and good schooling options, at least in the cities. "The main reason why we decided I would move to Portugal was because we want to raise children here," says Gail. "Portugal is much more child-friendly than Canada."

Housing in Portugal

Rents in this country aren't as dirt cheap as in Eastern Europe, but you get warmer weather, lots of sunshine, and plenty of historic architecture. You also have a lot of inventory to choose from these days. With the economic crises grinding on and unemployment still high, fewer young people are able to strike out on their own and many families have consolidated from two homes to one.

Gail lives about 10 miles from the center of Porto and while her husband already owned a place, she says rental for a two-bedroom apartment like she's in starts at around 400 euros per month ($540). In the center of Porto prices would be similar, but the apartment might be older and smaller.

Prices are similar in Lisbon, where a one-bedroom flat in a prime area can be found for under $600 a month and if you're willing to expand your zone of possibilities, you could get more space or a lower price.

Buying a place is very reasonable by European standards throughout the country. "In Coimbra, for a reasonable apartment you would pay 150,000 to 200,000 euros for a nice two- or three-bedroom place. In rural areas, it's easy to find a place that size for 100,000 euros or less," says Julie. "There are lots of repossessions and bank sales going on right now. Banks sometimes offer 100 percent mortgages on these so you don't need a big down payment, but restrictions are rather strict. When I was looking into it, they wanted an additional guarantor for the mortgage. They also wanted us to buy life insurance that would cover the amount in case something happened to us."

Alicia and her husband paid cash for their home from a sale in England and had enough left over for a fixer-upper project on top. They live near the Silver Coast in Central Portugal, half an hour from the ocean and an hour from Lisbon and the airport. "We have a pool and an olive grove, and gorgeous views. We also bought an incredibly cheap village house in Castelo Branco which is a stunning area," she says. "We get to experience real village life and the neighbors are very friendly. We are renovating the house and its slow going as we don't live there now but we plan to rent it out for holidays.

Property prices are incredibly low," she adds. "For the price of a tiny terrace or flat in, for example, The Midlands area of the UK you can get a lovely three-bedroom house with a garden near the coast or a two-bedroom flat a stop or two away from the center of Lisbon. We viewed a three-bedroom flat with a view of the sea for €35,000 just a ten-minute drive away from the city of Lisbon and only a 5 minute walk to the metro.

They don't have rent or a mortgage since they own the house outright, but Alicia says, "You can get something decent from about €350 a month in Central Portugal and on the Silver Coast." For their five-bedroom house near Lisbon they pay €890 per annum in property taxes. For the two-bedroom house in the countryside it's only €100.

Foreigners can own real estate outright in Portugal, but closing costs can be high: figure on 7-8 percent.

Food & Drink

Do you get excited about drinking good wine? Do you get even more excited when it doesn't cost you much? Portugal is much like France, Italy, and Spain in the sense that a glass of wine with lunch or dinner is considered a God-given right. So if you get a meal of the day at a lunch cafe, it will often come with a carafe of house wine that's surprisingly large. If you want to order a bottle with dinner, it will likely cost the same or less than most of the food items on the menu. Plus it'll likely be quite good. "For two euros in a store, you can be confident it's going to be a drinkable bottle of red wine," says Julie. It could take you a lifetime to figure out which labels from which region are the best as production here is very high, but most wines are blends and don't depend on a specific grape from a specific place having an especially good year.

Portuguese restaurants are much cheaper than the rest of Western Europe. Lunch is usually less expensive than dinner, especially if you get the *prato do dia*. "That's usually six or seven euros in the rural areas, more like eight to ten euros in cities," says Julie. "That gets you a starter, soup, main dish, and then maybe dessert or coffee. There's always wine of course."

Typical main dishes for dinner at a basic restaurant are €2.50 – 10, in a really nice restaurant, €5 – 18. "Coffee and cake in a cafe are also reasonable," says Alicia. "A round of lovely pastries and drinks for four can still only add up to €5.

We go to cafes far more than we would in England."

Here are some other typical prices:

Coffee: €0.50 – 1.50
House wine: €1 – 2.50 per glass
Better wine: €2 – 5 per glass, €5 – 15 per bottle in a restaurant
Wine in a store: €1 (really!) – 12 for most, "Reserve" brands €12 and up
Beer: €0.50-0.75 each in store, €0 .75 – 2 in restaurants (liter draft €3-4)
200 grams of cheese: €0.79 – €3
200 grams of dry sausage/pepperoni: €0.89 – 3.50
Baguettes: €0.30 – 0.60
Can of tuna or pate: €0.59 – 1.50
Seasonal fruit and vegetables: €1 – 2 per kilo for most, €3 for berries
Oranges in season: €0.50 – 0.80 per kilo

At a local market in Estremoz we bought a wheel of aged cheese (enough for two to share) for €2 and a bottle of olive oil for €3 – both from local farmers.

One oddity here is that nothing placed on your table is complimentary. If you don't want to be charged for bread, butter, soft cheese, or olives, you have to ask the waiter to take them back or push them over to the side so you won't get charged.

Transportation

The cost of getting around in Portugal has a lot to do with whether you're driving a car on the highways or not.

Gail says in Porto a monthly public transit pass for their (outer) zone is €36, with individual trips as needed into the city being €1.50 each. One subway, bus, or tram ride in Lisbon ranges from €1.40 to €2.85, but an all-day unlimited pass is €6 and a whole month is the same as in Porto: €36.

A taxi in Lisbon for two people is officially €2.25 to start, then €1.60 per km. This can vary a lot across the country though. When I was in Evora it was €3.25 to go two blocks, but only €0.80 per km after that.

Bus routes in rural zones are not very frequent, but between the larger towns and cities it's a different story. The 1.5 hour bus ride from Lisbon to Evora is €12.50 one-way. A 2.5 hour bus ride (Lisbon-Western Algarve towns for example) will run around €20 one-way, while the three-hour one between Lisbon and Porto is €24 to €42 depending on how luxurious it is.

Gail just relies on this reasonable public transportation most of the time, renting a car to go exploring further now and then. Renting a car for a week ranges between 150 and 260 euros. Besides the hefty fuel costs Julie and her husband pay—about double U.S. prices—they also pay a few hundred euros per year to insure each of their not-so-new cars.

What can really kill your budget in a hurry here though are the tolls on the expressways. "The highway tolls can really have a big impact on the cost of your trip," says Julie. "Below Lisbon to Algarve, there's a short stretch of road that's 20 euros, for example. But it saves loads of time, so people pay it if they can afford it. The good thing is, the motorways are pretty empty when you're on them because of the high cost."

"Motorway tolls are a definite minus," agrees Alicia. "They are far too expensive and thus not well used."

You need to check the routes you don't know in advance because you don't stop at a booth and pay: you get charged automatically via a sticker on your windshield. You could return from a jaunt around the country to find a hefty bill on your account.

Health Care

The World Health Organization ranks the effectiveness of care in Portugal at number 12 in the world, well ahead of the United States, England, and Canada. Portugal also has the 10th-highest life expectancy for women in the world, at 84. Pregnant women get 120 days of paid leave at full salary and you won't get stuck with a hefty bill if an ambulance picks you up at the scene of an accident.

Julie and her husband both have health care through her employer, but says if you're on the national health scheme, you pay €5 to see the doctor and €10 for emergency care. You pay out of pocket for lab tests and x-rays, but then you can charge them back to insurance and get reimbursed 60 to 80percent. "The health programs are all pushing more generics on patients because the name brand drugs are rather pricey. It seems to me that the doctors all over-prescribe medicines."

In general terms, you will be treated like a local in terms of the health care system. Some costs are free, while others require a token payment. Dental costs are mostly covered by taxes, plus children, pregnant women and pensioners have the right to receive dental care for free.

To choose your own doctor or hospital outside the national health care system, various insurance schemes are available at a reasonable cost. Is Lisbon the care is excellent and if you ask around you'll easily be able to find an English-speaking doctor. This also applies to tourist zones like the Algarve and larger cities such as Porto. In smaller towns you may just have a local clinic, which is fine for basic problems, but then you'll likely want to travel to a larger city for surgery or serious tests.

Other Costs

For utilities, Julie says the two of them average €60 for electricity, €16 or €17 for water, and almost €50 for ADSL internet that's not all that fast. "You can get better broadband for a better price in the cities," she says. A propane gas bottle is €100 and that's good for around six months of hot water and cooking on the stove top for them.

Alicia says gas is their biggest utility bill in the winter, running them about €100 a month as sometimes both of them are working at home all day. "That heats our large living room, cooker, and supplies the hot water. Summer is about half that amount." They spend around €100 for a package that includes phone, internet and a premium batch of TV channels. Their electric bill averages €60 a month and "It is cheaper per unit than the UK." Their water bill is estimated at €12.50 a month.

Gail works at home, but her electricity bill doesn't rise above €50 for two until the winter hits and they need some heat from their electric system. Their water bill is around €20 and the gas bill averages €10-30 per month. Their bundled cable package of internet/phone/TV is only €36.

Services such as shoe repair, hairdressers, auto mechanics, and such have lower labor rates compared to the rest of the EU," says Gail. "Portugal is also known for textiles, so clothes and especially shoes are cheaper. Camping is cheap (even private campsites), so is all other lodging around the country when you go exploring."

Going to the movies is also affordable at around €5 an adult ticket and entrance fees to galleries and events are much more affordable than in most of Western Europe.

The expatriates I spoke to agreed that cars are more expensive than in many other parts of Europe, while gasoline (petrol), non-domestic food products, and clothing costs were about the same.

Visas in Portugal

"I married a Portuguese citizen in the Azores (which is under Portuguese law), and to enter as a spouse it couldn't have been easier," says Gail. "We made an appointment for the residency permit before I arrived for the nearest date available (5 days after I arrived), and two weeks after that interview I had a letter confirming my 5-year residency permit, which I picked up right away." She says this was the fourth expat visa she has applied for in her life and this one was by far the most straightforward. "The fees were also very low, especially compared someone pays in the USA."

"For EU residents, the visa situation quite straightforward," says Julie. "The most important thing is to be able to prove income, to show that you can support yourself. You need to have ample documentation to show them. Assuming that's in order, you go to the foreigners service desk and soon you'll have a residency permit for five years, which you can then renew."

For those without a local spouse or EU citizenship, it can be much tougher. "Almost all the articles you read about moving to Portugal talk about Brits or other Europeans," says Susan Korthase. Her and her husband spent around $400 in fees to get their residency visa, then another $3,600 for attorney fees. Each time they renew, they have to do it all again, though this last time they got two years instead of one. "There's a set of steps, with very explicit requirements," she says. "Then you have to overcome the language barrier, which is where the attorney comes in. You quickly forget how painful it was when it's done, but it was. Start to finish first time was about six months. If we had tried to do it without an attorney it would have taken longer and they treat you differently. You have to accept that bureaucracy will be a lot more complicated than you're probably used to and people in the offices will be asking for things they don't really need." Next year they'll be at the five-year mark though and can then apply for a five-year residency permit. At that point the big renewal bill they face each year from the attorney will go away.

For new arrivals, it turns out the prevailing assumption that you can only get a three-month visa is not true. Susan and her husband applied for six months at the embassy in Washington, D.C. before they left and after showing the means to support themselves, it was granted easily. In theory anyway, you could return to the USA for a bit and then do it again if you still didn't have residency sorted out.

Susan writes about living in Portugal for ExpatExchange.com and also does consulting for people considering a move to her adopted country. "I've been able to help a few dozen people who are considering Portugal but can't find a path through the confusing, capacious, and contradictory information about the process, costs, resources, and difficulties. Some of them cross Portugal off the list, opting for a Costa Rica or Belize. But for those of us who seek a first-world, high-culture experience, Portugal is among the most accessible."

Downsides

Bring a phrase book or good language app! English is not widespread outside of the cities and resort areas on the coast. If you speak Spanish it helps when reading a menu and some people can speak Spanish. While many words are the same, however, the pronunciation of Portuguese is completely different.

"Although most Portuguese speak a little English, not all do," says Alicia. "I worry particularly when I have to make a phone call to deal with utility services. It's quite a difficult language to get to grips with but there is usually someone around to help."

The economy in Portugal has been in rough shape for years, so don't expect to earn much money providing services for locals. "Anything imported, like cars, electronics, technology items, and fuel are expensive," says Gail. "Portugal doesn't have enough consumers for a big used market like what I've had with Craigslist in other countries."

The shopping choices are quite limited as well. "We always stock up when we go shopping," says Julie. "If you see something you like, you'd better buy it then as it might not be available next time. There is absolutely nothing in the village where I live. There's actually a bread van, a fish van, and a mobile supermarket and if you catch it at the right time you can buy from one of those. Otherwise, there's a small town 15 minutes away that has small supermarkets. We really need to do most of our shopping in the city where we work, 35 kilometers away."

You may not have the same constant temperature level in your home that you've gotten used to elsewhere. "Portugal is warmer than England, but it can still get nippy in winter and the older houses are built to keep heat out," says Alicia. "So realistically you need central heating in winter to be comfortable, but most houses don't have it."

For More Information

Julie Dawn Fox in Portugal (JulieDawnFox.com)
Living in Portugal (LivinginPortugal.com)
Anglo Info Portugal (Portugal.Angloinfo.com)
Moving to Portugal (MovingtoPortugal.org)
ExpatFocus.com Portugal
ExpatForum.com Portugal
Portugal Expat Blogs on ExpatsBlog.com

Chapter 27: Malaysia

Pros: good infrastructure, fast internet, wide variety of cuisines, inexpensive rentals, straightforward residency visa, drinkable water, good air connections.
Cons: repressive government, limited press freedom, higher costs than some neighbors, unstable economy, limited sightseeing or culture options.

Charles Vasels has lived in Malaysia for 15 years, first in Kuala Lumpur and then in Penang. He travels to the USA on business now and then, but can't imagine moving back there and enduring the high costs. "Even if all you have to live on is your social security payment, that's enough. For $1,100 or $1,200 a month you can live pretty well here. In the USA there's no way to live on that unless you bought a house 35 years ago that is paid off. Even then it's tough with property taxes and insurance."

A secretary or a clerk may make the equivalent of $400 a month in Malaysia. A pretty average wage for a good white-collar job in Malaysia is the equivalent of $700 to $850, so if you're pulling in $1,500—a very minimal income in the western world—you're earning double what a typical office worker does here and you'll be well off.

Peninsular Malaysia is a strip of land between slightly cheaper Thailand and far more expensive Singapore, and is very different than both. You have three distinct cultures and three distinct cuisines: Malay, Indian and Chinese.

Henning Nassler moved to the country in 1998, first working for a company from Austria where he's from, then a local one two years later. "When I came here, Malaysia was shaken from the Asian financial crisis but fighting its way back. There was a lot of opportunity and 'let's do this' spirit which sadly since has disappeared. Still, I like the climate here and the cost of living with kids is substantially lower than Europe. On a personal note, as an Austrian I always wanted an ocean nearby and I like it warm. Plus, in general I think the people in Malaysia are warmer and more open and...oh my god...work starts at 10am!"

Prices aren't rock bottom for any aspect of travel or

living, but food, lodging, and transportation all seem reasonable for what you get—and can be lower than some resort areas in Thailand. Peninsular Malaysia is quite westernized on the western half and while it feels exotic, you can be relatively sure you'll have a clean place to eat and a western toilet in your room no matter where you stay. Transportation is easy and comfortable, a lot of people speak English, and you can even drink the water in most locations. On the other hand, free speech is only occasionally tolerated and the local media is toothless.

The main attractions on the peninsula are the jungle interior and the beautiful beaches. The capital, Kuala Lumpur, attracts some expatriates, but mainly those who are still hustling and doing business. Georgetown (on Penang) has a nice atmosphere, with lots of interesting Chinese temples, and is well set up for expatriates. Many have also settled in the old, Portuguese port of Malacca, which provides an interesting mixed bag of colonial and Chinese architecture.

Housing Costs

If you look around and are patient, you should be able to rent a comfortable and spacious apartment in Malaysia for $500 a month or less, even in good areas of the capital. Step it up a bit from there and you can really find something grand. If you're willing to live on the outskirts, you can pay $250 a month and get something decent.

Charles lives in a rowhouse on the mainland side of Penang that he rents for $220 a month, with 2,000 square feet. "If I lived in a condo, I could pay less or pay more. On Penang Island it would definitely be more. To buy something there, prices have gone up 300 or 400 percent in the past decade."

Henning Nassler says, "I bought an apartment for 400K (around $120,000) which gets me 1,800 square feet in a medium class apartment complex with mostly international residents. Rent would be about $660 to $700."

Foreigners can own property outright in Malaysia and while prices aren't as cheap as elsewhere in Southeast Asia, there's an added incentive to buy a home here: instant residency. If you are looking for a tropical retirement paradise, Malaysia is one of the few Asian countries actively trying to lure more foreigners. If you meet certain requirements on assets and pension income for the "My Second Home" program, there are plenty of incentives on offer.

There is a robust lending system in place to buy property, with low down payments. The negative side of this is that many people, especially ethnic Chinese business families, buy property and just sit on it as an investment, knowing they can flip it later for a better price without incurring much in the way of interest payments. So check the real occupancy level on any condo building you're considering and see if any lights are on at night.

Health Care

Keith Hockton lives in Penang and wrote about his health care expenses for *International Living*. He talked of paying $15 for a dental check-up and cleaning, $22 for a check-up and filling, and $12 for a doctor's visit with x-ray and drugs after a mountain biking accident. After a fireworks accident at a local beach, however, his wife ended up with two blown eardrums, sparks in her eyes, and facial burns. That night they visited the emergency room at a good hospital in the wee hours and over the next month they got her a variety of appointments and treatments. They saw a local eye specialist, an ear doctor, and a British plastic surgeon (the surgery wasn't needed), with six visits between them. Counting all the medications and tests, the grand total was $338.

This was not atypical. Seeing the doctor is usually somewhere between $5 and $16—even if it's a house call. In Penang alone there are six government hospitals and nine private ones, all employing English-speaking doctors. They're well-staffed too: no four-hour waits to get treated here.

If you want to get private medical insurance that allows you to go to any doctor and hospital you'd like, you should be able to find a good policy for under $1,000 per year.

You won't need to put off your check-up at the dentist's' office. A cleaning is generally around $25-$30, a filling less than $20, and a porcelain crown $300 or so. For major procedures, the economics are equally enticing. This is a major medical tourism destination, with people flying from more expensive countries to cut their surgery bills by three-quarters or more.

Food & Drink

Meals are seldom dull in Malaysia because you usually have three cuisines to choose from: Malay, Chinese, and Indian. The latter two are cooked by descendants of Chinese and Indian nationals who were brought in by the British when the country was still a colony. Street stall or food market meals are $1 to $3 with sodas, even in the cities. Local or backpacker sit-down restaurants are only a little bit more. You can go from stall to stall in Penang and have a world-class feast. Charles often starts his day with an Indian breakfast for $1.50. It's easy to stick to a healthy, well-balanced diet in this country.

Even the top-end restaurants are quite reasonable by western standards. Usually $10 to $20 will cover a three-course meal in a fine restaurant—until you order alcohol. Beer is expensive for the region: generally $3 and up for a 12-oz. bottle due to high taxes. You can pay more than you would at home in a nice place. Local commercial whiskey or Arak (a local rice whiskey) is less money if you can stomach it. Many foreigners buy from a contact who somehow gets liquor across the border from cheaper countries in the region.

There's plenty of fresh, tropical fruit juice for cheap wherever you go, and you can safely drink the water in most of the towns and cities. Coffee is usually a letdown though outside the large cities.

When you buy groceries, some food prices are subsidized, such as rice, cooking oil, and sugar. Local fruit and vegetables are very cheap and items produced locally like fish and chicken are reasonably priced. Few expats spend more than $100 a week on groceries unless they have a large family or are buying a lot of alcohol. Henning says he spends a bit more, but "We don't try to save on food and we don't have to look for special offers, we are able to buy quality stuff."

Transportation

Malaysia has some of the best roads in the world, so buses are faster and more convenient, plus often they are the only option. All are air-conditioned to the point of being traveling meat lockers and they travel at speeds you don't really want to know about—sit away from the front or close your eyes! Tickets run from a few dollars to more than $20 for a long trip. A ride from Kuala Lumpur to Georgetown is a bargain $10 for a first-class bus, from KL to Malacca just $4. A bus from there to Singapore is less than $30. Almost all of the upper-end ones offer free Wi-Fi.

The train line in Malaysia is not too convenient—it only runs through the interior – but it's good for getting to Thailand from Kota Bahru (on the east side) or Georgetown/Penang (on the west). Prices start at about $15 for a cross-country trip or $18 for an excursion to Bangkok, just a few dollars for a short haul.

Big Mercedes share-taxis are a quick way to go between towns. After bargaining, a 100-km trip will cost $5-$10 each.

Local buses are comfortable and reasonably priced in the cities: they start at 35 cents and max out at $1 for a four-zone trip across the capital. Taxis are easy to flag down or call for in the cities, rickshaws exist in some of the smaller towns, and bicycle rickshaws are still around in Sabah and Sarawak. Taxis are reasonable overall at and official rate of around $3 for 5 kilometers, although it's 50 percent more at night. You can get to most parts of KL from the international airport by taxi for $15 or less in a regular cab (or for as little as $3 on public transportation).

Cars are easily 50 percent more in Malaysia than the same model would be in the U.S. On top of that, there's a poor market for used vehicles as nobody believes in depreciation and won't sell for much of a discount. Because prices are so high, banks give out car loans running 10 years or more. If you really need a car, suck it up and pay, but you're better off using public transportation.

Visas

Malaysia has gotten a reputation for being much more welcoming to foreign retirees because of its My Second Home program. If you have some money to invest in buying property in Malaysia, it's quite straightforward for you to get legal residency and be welcomed with open arms. Once approved, you are a legal resident for 10 years and can come and go as you please. You can also import a car duty-free or buy one locally that's free of taxes. You can also import household goods duty-free.

If you're under 50, you need to invest around $94,000 in a Malaysian bank (300,000 ringgit) and then after a year you can draw that down to half that amount if you are spending money on education, a home, or medical care. You then have to leave at least that amount in the bank, though you do draw a bit of interest income. If you are 50 or older, you can work part-time or open a business. At any age you can purchase property with no restrictions under this program.

If you're over 50, you can deposit 150,000 ringgit (about $47,000) in a Malaysian bank or show monthly income from a pension or other source of at least $3.120 per month—no small sum. Find all the details here: mm2h.gov.my/index.php/en/

Otherwise, you get a three-month tourist visa upon arrival unless you're from a communist country (14 days maximum) or Israel (can't enter at all). A visa run only requires an overland train trip to Thailand or Singapore. There are myriad other ways to apply for long-term residency, many based on your occupation or skills, whether you're getting a work permit or not.

As usual, if you're married to a local it gets easier. "I have a spouse visa (a Long Term Social visit pass, valid for 5 years)," says Henning. "I don't need a work permit with that. For my older son I got a Malaysian citizenship (since he was born in Austria he had an Austrian citizenship and needed visas as well). The documentation required (both for visas and citizenship) was extensive, but the process itself was not uncommonly exhausting or difficult."

Other Costs

Utility costs are quite reasonable in Malaysia, with most people paying $50 to $100 per month on electricity even if running the air conditioning regularly. Cooking and shower gas will be $5 to $15 a month and fast broadband internet ranges from $25 to $35. Figure on $20 to $45 per month for cell phone calls depending on whether you need data. A

Sim card will be $4 or so.

If you've visited Cambodia, Laos, or Vietnam before coming here, you may feel downright ignored as you walk the streets of Malaysia. There's no real "walking wallet" view of foreigners by vendors here as many of them are foreigners themselves—by bloodline anyway. When you're quoted a price, it's generally the same price any local would pay.

Local school costs may be around $100 a month, but you have to factor in uniforms, supplies and other fees. If you want to enroll your child in an accredited international school, however, that can cost as much as $2,000 per month for the ones the children of tycoons and political leaders attend. Henning pays around $420 per month for his two kids to be in a good private school.

For basic clothing made in Asia, prices are the same or less than they would be in the U.S. The shopping in Malaysia is not great, especially for handicrafts, but on the plus side you can get Chinese-made electronics for very competitive prices: no need to wait for a trip home to replace your phone or laptop.

Downsides

There's a kind of voluntary apartheid in the country, with ethnic Malays running the government, the ethnic Chinese and Indians running business. Many jobs are only open to Malays and this is perfectly legal.

This is a schizophrenic country in many ways, divided between ethnic Malays, Indians, and Chinese. This is great when it's time to eat out, but traveling from one coast to the other can feel like going to a complete different country—a strict Muslim country without alcohol if it's the east coast. This is no Thailand when it comes to permissive attitudes toward sexuality and sexual orientation. It's also not a place you want to settle if you're a regular recreational drug user. You know that *Return to Paradise* movie where Joaquin Phoenix faces execution for some hash found at their beach hut? Well, it's based on real laws on the books.

There's very little press freedom here and the government has shown time and again that it's not afraid to throw around its weight to stay in power.

Inflation has been running at double digits for years, sometimes compounded by currency fluctuations. In some regions there are many indications of a real estate bubble, so take your time if you want to buy instead of rent.

Charles sees a collapse coming at some point in Malaysia. "The locals are all trying to borrow their way to prosperity. Everyone is living hand to mouth while craving a western lifestyle, borrowing to feed it. There's been a sharp rise in foreclosures and bankruptcy."

Henning agrees that trouble is on the way. "If the current economic situation persists, Malaysia will become less attractive. Prices have already risen substantially, debt is increasing rapidly, and there is probably a financial crash in the near future. Malaysia is becoming unattractive for foreign investment. The service quality is lower than for example Indonesia and even Vietnam, but cost is a lot higher than there."

For More Information

ExpatsBlog.com – Malaysia
BlogExpat.com – Malaysia
LivinginPenang (LivinginPenang.com)
ExpatArrivals.com – Malaysia
Wood Egg Malaysia book

Chapter 28: Nepal

Pros: gorgeous scenery, can get by in English, extendable tourist visa, some of the cheapest prices on the planet, lots of outdoor activities, plenty of other foreigners to mix with in the two largest cities.
Cons: poor infrastructure, no water or sewage treatment, pollution, high poverty rate (especially in rural areas), barely functioning government, limited air connections, few long-term visa options, unstable currency, spotty electricity and internet.

"We've lived in a lot of different places, but the two months we were in Nepal were probably the best value of any of them," says Lisa Niver, author of *Traveling in Sin* and editor of the We Said Go Travel blog. "In Pokhara we paid 700 rupees a night (less than $8) for where we stayed. It was a regular sized room, but we took one on the top with a huge rooftop balcony that nobody else used. Dinner for two for $4.50 was pretty common, at a nice restaurant with good food." A friend of theirs rented a house in the countryside an hour from the capital for the equivalent of $50 a month.

Plenty of countries have historic monuments, miles of beaches, or pretty scenery. But nobody has mountains quite like these. If you're into hiking, white-water rafting, or just stunning mountain scenery, Nepal is Shangri-La. Or at least it was, before the rebels and the monarchy spent a decade fighting and the political situation started limping along in eternal limbo. Overall the power-sharing agreement looks to be keeping the former violence at bay, but the government is so dysfunctional here it makes USA's congress look downright effective in comparison—not an easy task!

Nepal is best known as the trekking and mountaineering capital that's the home of Mount Everest. Barbara Weibel concentrates on the other aspects of the country though, writing about "Nepal for non-trekkers" and the culture of the region. She's been living there on and off for five years, ingrained enough in the community in Pokhara that she actually went in with a local family on a house lease, staying there each time she unpacked her bags.

"This family I was really close to, where the husband ran a yoga and massage center, had been kicked out of their home with just 30 days' notice. They were all sleeping into a 5X7 storage shed behind the massage center, the open kitchen was outside. I figured if I split the cost of a house with them and stayed there, it would be cheaper for me than staying in a nice guest house, even if I was only going to come three months a year. Once they found one that met my criteria — mainly having a western toilet—they got a new home and I got a place to stay. "

The Himalayas are home to 9 of the 10 highest peaks in the world and most of those peaks are in Nepal. The scenic effect is pure majesty. And with food and lodging costing about five percent of what they do in say, Switzerland, you feel almost guilty enjoying such a moving experience for so cheap.

And it's not just snow-capped, five-mile high mountains that stick in your memory. The inspiring Buddhist and Hindu temples of the Kathmandu Valley and the Newari architectural styles are magical. The people drift by awash in brilliant colors and jangly jewelry and you can get things hand crafted to your liking—from clothing to furniture—for unbelievable prices.

Like India, however, it's not for everyone. Nepal's people have one of the lowest per capita incomes in the world, so the poverty is very real. The per-capita income is less than $600 per *year*. So if you pull out a brand new iPhone and start taking selfies, you're probably flashing around something that costs more what a rural Nepali earns in 12 months of labor. Sanitation is deplorable, especially in the capital city, and smog is a serious issue there and in Pokhara. But when you get out of the capital and you're hiking or rafting through nature's splendor for a pittance, you realize that Nepal has a different kind of wealth and it's hard to miss home.

It's difficult to stay longer than five months at a time in Nepal unless you have a permanent job or have married a local. January and February are months to avoid anyway. The weather gets cold and few places have adequate heat. These are also the most polluted months in the cities, so you can go days without seeing the mountains.

This is a tough country to live in if you need always-on fast broadband connections for running your online business. "We averaged 16 hours a day of outages the first year I was there," says Barbara, "but everyone has a generator. In the most expensive place I stayed, we had Wi-Fi around the clock. There was a published schedule for outages; they had a solar generator so Wi-Fi was always available. Some places don't have the router hooked up to generator though, so when the power goes out, so does the connection. When I was staying elsewhere I had to go to reliable restaurants. Those who host westerners know they need good reliable internet. I knew the passwords at every hotel in town! If one would drop, I'd log into another. Eventually I learned to get a USB stick for a cell signal. I think it's around $30 a month and I used it everywhere."

So who ends up here? As an article in the VisitNepal.com site says, most fall into two camps. "Many of these expats are working for the giant organizations drawn to the country by the greatest contributor of Nepal's economy: foreign aid.

But, then there's another side to the expat community. Yes, the old hippies from bygone days and the spiritual seekers—definitely some overlap with these two groups."

If you're looking for the absolutely cheapest place to live for a while and shore up your finances, Nepal may be your best bet. An experienced government worker will likely make less than $100 a month, a maid or a gardener less than that. It requires a very skilled private sector job or a management job at a charity to earn more than $150 per month. So there are expatriates getting by for $200 per month here and not feeling all that poor. A couple spending $500 a month will be living an upper middle class lifestyle. Come in receiving a typical U.S. social security check of $1,250 per month into your bank account and you could go from destitute in the land of your birth to deliriously rich here. (Ironically, the fattest fat cats in Nepal, the ones dining the most at the fanciest hotels, are working for international aid organizations. Get one of those jobs and you'll be sitting pretty.)

Housing Costs

Finding a place to sleep while you look for something more

permanent is not going to cost you much in Nepal. Three dollars will cover a spacious room with shared bath in some parts. Most hotels have solar hot water heaters; so hot showers are standard in tourist areas even in the cheapest places. Spending $4 to $10 (the latter in high season) gets you a private bath and generally better conditions, possibly a restaurant or bar. A step up to $10 to $20 rooms will include maid service, a phone, room service, and satellite TV. Most hotels have a roof deck with a view.

"I've spent $22 to $25 per night at a really nice lodge in Pokhara," says Barbara. But I have stayed in another for $5 a night long-term. The average for a decent place is probably around $10. Now when I go back I stay with a family I'm close to, but since I know where to look I'd probably be paying between $7 and $10 a night to stay for a few months."

If you spend $10 a day at a hotel, that's $300 for the month, with no utility costs. Long-term rentals go down from there if you don't need a whole house to yourself.

Food & Drink

Everything may look and taste great in the tourist zones of Kathmandu and Pokhara, but be careful! Just because you can order salads, crepes with cream sauce, or ice cream desserts doesn't mean you should. A large percentage of visitors get sick in Nepal, usually because they play Russian roulette with their stomachs, lulled into a false sense of security by a pretty restaurant and an extensive menu.

If you avoid tap water, raw fruit and vegetables (unless you peel them), cold milk, and food that isn't hot, you'll eat like a king or queen for a few dollars a day and stay healthy in the process. There are plenty of good restaurants in the cities and prices are overwhelmingly reasonable. Even with a few drinks there are only a handful of places in the whole country where you can spend more than $20 a person on a meal. Most of those are in luxury hotels. After all, it's more than most people who live there earn in a week. A 13 percent VAT is usually included and a tip of 5 to 10 percent is expected in tourist restaurants.

The typical Nepali diet isn't so extensive though and doesn't have nearly the variety and complexity you find in

India. In the mountains, your food choices will be limited. You'll be eating a lot of dal (lentils), potatoes, flat bread, and yak cheese. It's not all that exciting, but it's filling and hearty. Eat like a local and your food bill will be a minimal part of your budget.

This is not a good place to drink for cheap though. The beers are mostly imported brands and as the local currency has declined and ingredient prices have risen, the cost of a beer has doubled to a range of $1.50 to $3. Granted, these are big bottles, but in local terms it's an extreme extravagance. With a bottle of beer costing the same as an ounce or two of marijuana or a finger of hash, guess which kind of buzz wins out? Marijuana grows like a weed on the mountains and is priced accordingly. You'll be offered it daily in the tourist district of Kathmandu whether you want it or not.

So, most people stick to soda, water, or tea with their meal. The varieties of tea are quite good (including mint and ginger), and generally cost less than 75 cents for a full pot.

Transportation

Most travelers fly into Kathmandu and if you're moving with more than one or two suitcases, that's your best bet. You can fan out from there to other areas, including the second-largest city Pokhara by plane ($80 - $100) or express bus ($12 including one meal).

Public buses in Nepal are much like public buses in the rest of the Indian subcontinent: super-crowded and uncomfortable. Even if you're on a budget, you will probably want to pay for the best private one available.

Throughout the country, rugged terrain, crummy roads that get washed out every year, and buses of less-than-optimum quality all contribute to journeys straight out of a harrowing "bad trip" travel essay. The scenery is nice along the way, but you probably don't want to be on a move too often between cities.

Taxis and auto-rickshaws generally cost less than a $2 for a trip of several miles and you can rent mountain bikes for $3 to $4 a day or buy a Chinese one for cheap. Hiring a car and driver for the day is a much better option than trying to drive anywhere yourself unless you're out in the countryside. You'll spend less anyway: from $20 to $60 a day depending on the condition of the car, whether it has A/C, and how good you are at bargaining. Many expatriates who settle here end up finding a driver they like and hiring him when they need a big shopping trip or excursion.

Health Care

India has great health care in the cities. Nepal is a different story. You can get the basics taken care of for next to nothing and simple accidents like a fractured bone or stomach illness can be dealt with locally just fine. If you have a serious condition that needs regular care, however, you'll probably have to work flights to Delhi or Bangkok into your budget. The doctors who are here have sometimes trained in the west, or at least in an international hospital in India, but there just aren't that many of them and most are in the capital.

On the other hand, if you like to treat problems through homeopathic methods, yoga, and meditation, you'll be in fine shape. If nothing else, you can walk into any pharmacy and self-prescribe almost any medicine you need when the natural methods don't cut it.

Visas in Nepal

"You can apply ahead and get a 90-day visa for Nepal, which you can legally renew easily for two more months within the country. It's then up to immigration whether you can stay for a sixth month or not. After that you need to leave and start over," says Lisa.

So really, you can get 150 days straight without a whole lot of trouble, but beyond that it's quite difficult. You'll have to stay away for a while too before you can return and start over to get another 150 days.

Trying to live here year-round is a tough prospect and becoming a permanent resident is even tougher. "Residents are generally working with NGOs or people who have married a Nepali," Barbara adds. "It is illegal for anyone to get citizenship. Indian people can cross at will as much as they want, but they and their children are not eligible for citizenship, even if the child was born in Nepal."

Much of this comes down to Nepal's precarious geographic position between China and India, with Tibet right on its border. This is a tiny country with a small population and insufficient funds to support a large military. They figure if they opened the floodgates to foreigners to move in and get voting rights, in a generation they'd be assimilated into a larger, more powerful country.

In theory there is a residential visa available for people who want to live here without working. The rather unclear rules give an option of investing $100,000 locally—essentially buying your way in—or spending enough that they deem you to be extra supportive of the economy. The amount they supposedly want to see for this is $20,000 per year, with proper documentation. It's actually quite hard to spend that much within the borders of Nepal each year unless you are fixing up a very nice house or eating in 5-star hotels all the time.

The other option is to get a business visa or work permit, which isn't all that hard to arrange if you can do something for an NGO. There are plenty of those to choose from, so you could teach English for peanuts or do computer programming for them—something that they can't easily find a local to do. Your best way to work this out if you can't find something online in advance is to come in on a tourist visa, make lots of local contacts, and then get a work permit before your tourist visa runs out. (You may have to make a trip to Thailand or India and return.) These can be granted for up to five years and of course you can work for a regular profit-making business as well. There just aren't a whole lot of them employing foreigners in this geographically isolated, poor country.

Downsides

The government of Nepal hasn't gotten anything done for years. The rebel Maoists got seats at the table in trade for laying down their arms in 2009, but they haven't been any more effective at creating change than the old guard. There was an interim parliament charged with writing a new constitution by 2010, but they missed the deadline and kept rolling the deadline over to another year. So then they passed a law that it would have to be finalized by the fourth year and they missed that deadline too. The whole group was disbanded and there's still no constitution—or a legitimate government to lead and regulate. As Barbara says, "Basically the whole government has been in limbo since 2009. Life still goes on, but a lot of critical things aren't getting done at the national level."

Frequent caste strikes hit the capital and if you've got a meeting to get to or a plane to catch, too bad. Nobody dares go on the roads when this happens and everything comes to a standstill.

Infrastructure is poor and until a functioning government is in place, isn't likely to get much better. The World Economic Forum puts Nepal's infrastructure near the bottom of their list, up there with Nigeria, Mongolia, and Angola. Roads are poor, you can't drink the water, waste treatment is rudimentary, and the electrical grid is aged and overtaxed. Nearly everyone depends on generators to have a steady supply of power, in combination with solar hot water heaters on the roofs.

There are lots of constraints on being a digital person," says Lisa. There are constant electricity and connection problems. Friends who were trying to run a virtual business in Nepal were constantly talking about how to deal with connection problems, generators, and batteries."

It's easy to point at corruption in any country, but Nepal takes it to a new level through the charity rackets. "There are somewhere between 40,000 and 60,000 Nepali NGOs in the country because there's no oversight," Barbara explains. "They get kids from poor areas, telling parents they'll give them a good education. They're used to solicit donations from westerners and, disappearing into the system and never seen again. The top people in these organizations are living in mansions, driving expensive SUVs. There's a saying here that these unregulated NGOs 'use kids like crops to harvest." If you intend to volunteer in the country, do your homework on who you're working for and how they're truly improving the lives of people at ground level.

Garbage is an epic problem, which Barbara blames in part on all the western multinationals bringing plastic packaging into a country that wasn't ready for it. "People are used to throwing everything on the ground because before a few decades ago, everything was organic. Now the ground is covered and the rivers are choked with garbage." She sees hope for the future though in the heavy fines in Kathmandu that look like they're being enforced.

For More Information

VisitNepal.com (visitnepal.com/expatriates)
The Longest Way Home – Nepal section
(thelongestwayhome.com/Countries/Nepal)
Hole in the Donut – Nepal section
holeinthedonut.com/tag/nepal
ExpatsBlog.com – Nepal (expatsblog.com/blogs/Nepal)

Chapter 29: Peru

Pros: Gorgeous Andean scenery, varied climates, interesting food, (especially in Lima), good medical care in the capital, good handicrafts and crafts workers.
Cons: Usually gray capital city, expensive internal flights, wide gulf in wealth, poor environmental protections.

"Peru has long lines, every task is far more complicated than it needs to be, and the men can be terribly rude. But I think, just maybe, the best relationships happen when you can love someone (or a country) deep enough to see past their faults. I know I love Peru because when I reflect on my past year, it's hard to remember what was difficult. All I can think about is what I've gained."

That was the opening quote from Danielle L. Krautman on her GoMadNomad.com blog after spending a year in Lima. Later they moved north to a town outside the mountainous city of Cajamarca and she started liking it much better.

Peru often pops up as the favorite of travelers who have spent a lot of time in South America. The scenery really is as spectacular as any glossy travel magazine spread and the prices are low enough to allow the average tourist to do and see everything. And "everything" is a lot here: desert canyons, mountain cities, the Amazon rain forest, Andean peaks, and of course those Inca ruins. Peru is the home of Machu Picchu, the continent's most popular tourist attraction, but still arguably one of the most magical sites on Earth.

The central hub for most travelers is Cusco (or Cuzco), a stunning city perched at over 11,000 feet/3,500 meters above sea level. From here, travelers can set out for Machu Picchu or many other Inca ruins in the Sacred Valley or just wile away the days in a beautiful, historic Andean city.

Nora Dunn, who runs The Professional Hobo blog, decided to unpack for a while in Pisac, in the Sacred Valley between Cusco and Machu Picchu. "My 'move' to Peru—for me—signifies a shift in my travel mentality of being "homeless." After over seven years of transient wandering,

I'm ready for a place that I can call mine (even if it's rented), that I can use as a base for other travels, and also as a retreat to simply do my own thing. And Peru (specifically Pisac) resonates with me very much as a place I feel comfortable enough to call home, and yet exotic enough that I feel like I'm still travelling every time I leave the house!

The colonial city of Arequipa is another highlight, with white-capped mountains in the background of the main plaza and a rambling monastery that is a photographer's delight. Travelers with more time can tour nearby Colca Canyon, see the mysterious Nazca desert drawings, take a boat trip on Lake Titicaca, or visit the "poor man's Galapagos" of Ballestas Islands near Paracas, and that's just the south. There's plenty more to see and do off this main tourist route in the rest of the country and more interesting ruins up north.

A lot of travelers come to Peru and spend a fortune. There are hotels, after all, going for more than $600 a night, and they fill up sometimes. That $600 is about the annual average monthly salary though, so unless you're living in the most posh part of Miraflores, Lima, you should easily be able to live a half-price life in this South American country without trying very hard. Some NGOs tell prospective volunteers that they can get by here from $400 at the most frugal end to $800 going out a fair bit and eating at nice restaurants now and then, so if you're coming in with monthly earnings of $1,200 or more you should be able to live an upper middle class lifestyle rather easily, not counting travel.

Walter Rhein came to Peru to study Spanish and ended up staying when he found there were plenty of jobs in Lima for English as a Second Language teachers. He rented a room from a local family, which kept his costs low. "I spent about $650 a month living in Miraflores. That budget included rent (and all renting expenses such as cable TV, heat, water, etc.), going out to eat once a day, going to the movies about three times a week, going to the US once a year, and going to other South American countries about 3 times a year. That was a few years ago though, so you may be looking at $750 or so now. "However, you can still get inexpensive health care down there," he says.

Peru is an oddity in the sense that the largest city is not

one that enchants and pulls in foreigners. The nightlife, art scene, and culinary scene all get high marks, but the weather sucks. I've been to Lima four times now and have never seen the sun more than an hour or two at a time. "You need to come in January" was one resident's reply when I told her this. There's a constant haze and cloud cover over the city most of the year and unless you like the color gray, it can get old fast. It's also a city where the historic center is small and not very attractive. So unless you're transferred there for a job or marry someone who lives there, you'll probably want to settle down somewhere else instead.

Housing Costs

There are several clear strata of housing prices in Peru, from dirt-cheap in the countryside to first-world expensive in the heart of Cusco or in the best neighborhoods of Miraflores or San Isidro in Lima. In general, you can find a two- or three-bedroom apartment or house in most parts of the country for $600 to $800 a month quite easily, less for smaller quarters. The smaller the city, the less it will probably be. Where things get out of whack are the most elite neighborhoods or the heart of the historic center. As always, if you get feet on the ground and look around you'll find a better deal than if you try to set it up in advance. Just get a cheap hotel or vacation rental apartment while you put out some feelers.

To give you an idea though, the site Numbeo.com has the average rent in Peru at 16 percent of the average rent in New York City. If you can read enough Spanish to figure out the local classified ads in Cusco, you can easily find a one-bedroom apartment for $300 or less and it's not a whole lot more to step up to a two-bedroom one. Even in Miraflores or Barranco in Lima you can find a deal if you're patient enough.

Foreigners cannot own land within 50 miles of the border, but that only really impacts Puno near Lake Titicaca, so it's not really an issue for many foreigners. Closing costs are reasonable though as in most developing countries, mortgage options are minimal, with rates at 10 percent or more. Expect to pay the full amount unless you arrange seller financing. There are terrific bargains in the countryside, but prices in the desirable parts of Lima are ones better suited to executives on a fat banking salary than those trying to cut costs.

Health Care

While not quite up there with Panama and Mexico, Peru is becoming a major medical tourism center and Lima has a variety of gleaming modern hospitals with English-speaking doctors. Costs will vary by procedure, but you can often expect to pay one-fifth to one-quarter the price of a similar treatment or operation in the United States if you go to the very best facility. You may pay all of $35 to see a specialist (who will take his time and not rush off to another patient) and $15 an hour at most for a physical therapist.

You can buy an insurance plan in Peru that's kind of hybrid between insurance and a discount card. You pay $300 to $400 per year and get at least 20 percent off and up to 100 percent reimbursement on some services, like an ambulance. With one of these plans a doctor's house call can be as low as $20.

Dental care in Lima is quite good and if you need some serious work done it'll cost a small fraction of what you're used to. I've seen prices posted online of $120 for a crown or root canal and a check-up/cleaning will probably cost you $40 or less—at the nicest office in town.

Service and English fluency declines quite a bit as the size of the city gets smaller. There will be at least one good, modern hospital in good-sized cities like Cusco, Arequipa, and Trujillo, but in small towns you may be limited to a basic public clinic. These clinics may think things like rubber gloves, sterilization, and general hygiene are optional. Spending money to get to a big city (or buying evacuation insurance before moving) will be money well spent.

Food & Drink

Peruvian food has gone from completely unknown to "hot cuisine" in just over a decade and generally the hype is well placed if you're dining in a nice restaurant. Some local dishes are not for the squeamish, as in roasted guinea pig, bull penis soup, and another soup made with boiled cow hooves. Get away from the sensationalist TV show fare, however, and the food is quite impressive overall, especially at nice restaurants on the coast and in the capital.

More standard fare includes pastries stuffed with meat, a wide variety of potatoes, corn, rice, chicken, plenty of fruit, and lots of seafood, especially ceviche. The food varies widely from region to region, however, and you'll actually have an easier time finding pizza these days than you will finding a roasted guinea pig. For most travelers, the food ends up being a pleasant surprise. At the cheap places it's not amazing, but it's consistently good and filling, and a nice break from the beans/tortillas/rice diet of much of the Americas. Quinoa is actually the most popular grain in the Andes region and is used in a lot of dishes. You can eat healthily here without trying too hard.

The street food is cheap and filling, with kebabs, fried potatoes and sausage, and empanadas being the most common. You can always get a cheap meal at local markets, or stock up for a hike or picnic. Mild cheeses and sausages that can be sliced like salami are easy to find. In the cities, there are plenty of cheap set meal places and local fast food options outside the tourist areas. Spit-roasted chicken restaurants are also numerous.

In the mountains, expect plenty of vegetables and rice, with a bit of meat thrown in for flavor. In the jungle, bananas, plantains, yucca, rice, and river fish are the staples. Along the coast, you'll find plenty of ocean fish and scallops, though the preference is often ceviche preparation (not cooked, but cured in citrus juice).

You can generally find a set meal in a locals' restaurant for $2 to $4, or $3.50 to $9 in a tourist restaurant. This will include a soup, main dish, bread, and tea or coffee. The dining scene is so competitive in Cusco that even the smallest tourist restaurant will usually throw in a free glass of wine or pisco sour to get you in the door. Chinese food is available in most towns and there are ample vegetarian choices in the cities and tourist areas.

Going up a notch, spending $8 to $14 per person on a meal will enable you to eat almost anywhere, with pretty surroundings, maybe a fireplace, and cloth napkins. There are only a handful of restaurants outside Lima where a couple would spend over $70 on dinner, almost none outside of the five-star hotels. You'll be expected to leave some change for a tip if a service charge isn't included. If there's a music performance, you'll find an additional charge tacked on and fancier places also levy a hefty tax.

Fruit juices, bottled water, and sodas (including "Inca Cola") are everywhere. Peruvian wine is a hit and miss affair, but it's seldom more than $10 a bottle in the stores and $3 a glass at a restaurant. Better stuff from Argentina and Chile isn't much more. Most beers are similar regional lagers that are good enough, but you can also find a malty black beer here and there. They run from $1.25 a bottle at happy hour to $1.50 or $3 other times, sometimes for a large bottle that's actually double sized. Peru is proud of its pisco and this clear grape brandy is sipped straight or mixed in cocktails. It'll sneak up on you, especially at high altitudes.

Coca tea is not only legal, but encouraged. It provides stamina on your treks and helps with altitude adjustment, without giving you any real buzz: think coffee without the shakes or the comedown afterwards.

When shopping for your own food, if you buy what's local the prices are very good. Seasonal fruit and vegetables average 75 cents a kilo and staples like rice, potatoes, and beans are about the same.

Transportation

In general terms, getting around within a city or town in Peru is very cheap. Bus travel prices are affordable, but the trips can be quite long. Where you'll really get socked though is when you buy a domestic flight.

A local bus in Peru will generally cost you 25 cents to a dollar—the latter being from a far-flung suburb to the center of town. When you take a taxi in Lima, Cusco, or Arequipa, a three-kilometer ride will usually be under $4 if you're getting the right price. This makes the trip from the Cusco airport to the center one of the cheapest in the world, at around $7. You have to haggle sometimes though, especially in Lima, where the driver may be quote you $20 just to see if you're gullible enough to pay it.

Long-distance buses come in a variety of classes and companies, with the one from Lima to Cusco running anywhere from $29 to $80 depending on how luxurious it is.

The ones running up and down the coast are significantly less as they don't have to cross the Andes. Many people just suck it up and buy a flight to cross the mountains, but there's a two-tied pricing system in effect, meaning you'll probably pay twice as much as you should for a domestic flight. It can often top $200 for a very quick jaunt that's barely long enough for drink service.

In many towns and cities you can easily get by with public transportation, but if you're an expatriate living in the outskirts of Arequipa or in the Sacred Valley, you might want to keep a car to get around in. You'll pay more than you would in the USA for one, but maintenance will be much cheaper.

Visas

Peru makes it very easy to stay for six months, but a good bit tougher to stay on a permanent basis. When you land in the country, you can get a visa for 30 days or in various increments up to 183. For the latter, you just have to ask (assuming you're from a country on the right list, like the USA, UK, Australia, or Canada). Immigration can ask for proof you have sufficient funds to support yourself. You can't extend this beyond that six months though and in theory it's only good for six months within a year. In reality, as soon as you leave the country and then come back again, you can request another 183 days. Some people go on like this for years, traveling to other parts of the Americas or going further during rainy season to sunnier climates abroad. If you overstay your visa by a few days it'll generate a frown, but not a big penalty: $1 a day.

Nora plans to coast for a while on tourist visas and then figure out the next step later. "Tourist visas are normally six months long, depending on who you get at customs/immigration. I can renew those by leaving the country and returning —an easy task given that I will still want to travel and explore South America while basing in Peru. Eventually, should I decide in the long run that I want to stay, I'll either buy land, or get sponsored for a permanent visa by being employed by a local company, (which is possible since I have friends here who run companies and could put me on the payroll). But this is all too much forward planning at the moment; for now, I just want to try my hand at living here and see where it goes!"

You can upgrade a tourist visa to a work or resident one without leaving the country by just paying up and showing the proper documents. There is a freelancer visa available here for those who can easily demonstrate income from elsewhere and document their "professional standing." You can get an investor visa for sinking just $25,000 into the local economy.

A *rentista* visa or retirement visa for foreigners only has an income requirement of $1,000 a month plus $500 for each dependent, but the money needs to be flowing through a Peruvian banking institution or you'll need an onerous amount of extra forms and signatures. With all of these, you then need to get a local residency card, which is renewed annually. After two years you can apply for citizenship if you speak Spanish well and know plenty of Peruvian history for an exam.

Most of the expatriates I've run across who are living in Peru have a work visa or are married to a Peruvian. You don't see nearly as many foreign-owned businesses here as you do in many other Latin American countries, which is probably a testament to the difficulty of doing it. You can't just roll into town with some cash and have a coffee shop or B&B running a few weeks later as you can in Colombia or Panama.

Getting a work visa is relatively straightforward if you have a job. You'll just need to show the right paperwork and you'll get a visa that lasts as long as what's on your employment contract. As long as you have the job, it'll keep getting renewed with no hurdles. There are probably tens of thousands of foreigners working in Peru right now, in industries ranging from mining to hospitality to oil to agriculture to charity. (Yes, that is a very large industry too.) If you do a little legwork ahead of time, you'll find plenty of networking opportunities, though be advised these are mostly centered in Lima.

Other Costs

In theory at least, you owe taxes on income as a resident, even if that income is from outside the country. If you're

American that's no big deal if documented correctly because unless you earn six figures that will shield you from owning U.S. taxes if you're permanently away. For some other nations though, or big earners, this could mean double taxation.

If you want to pop into an internet cafe here while you're out and about, some spare change in your pocket will be enough: it's often about 40 cents an hour.

If you're in Lima, you can find a good bilingual school for your child for $350 a month or less unless it's part of a major international network. In other cities there will be private schools for the same price, but they may be Spanish only.

Downsides

This is still a poor, developing nation overall and there's a lot of very real poverty in the shantytowns and the very rural areas. A lot of export wealth is generated in Peru from mining, agriculture, and oil, but very little of that is trickling down to the people at the bottom and there are constant protests against extraction companies taking over indigenous lands. Sustainability and environmental protection are seldom near the top of the list when planning business ventures or how to run tourism programs.

There is a good bit of petty crime throughout the country and more than a few cases of muggings and assaults in Lima and Cusco. You also get the typical Latin American annoyances like machismo, widespread graffiti, public urination, litter, a lack of change for purchases, and stray dogs.

The political situation looks like a circus to many outsiders and there's plenty to complain about in terms of corruption, an unfair judiciary, and poor infrastructure.

For More Information:

Expat Peru (expatperu.com)
Peru This Week (Peruthisweek.com)
Streets of Lima (streetsoflima.com)
A Gringo's Life in Cusco
(agringoslifeincusco.wordpress.com)
Expat Blogs in Peru_ (expatsblog.com/blogs/peru)

Chapter 30: Other Places to Consider

The country breakdowns that preceded this section are not meant to be a comprehensive list. They were primarily chosen because of popularity, ease of residency, and value. There are certainly plenty of other countries where foreigners have settled down to live a better life for less money than they were spending before. If one of the following was on your short list before, by all means investigate further because it may be just the right place for you. If a hundred people e-mail me after this book comes out and tell me I was crazy to not have a full chapter on the Philippines, the Czech Republic, or Bolivia, then I'll make some additions in the second edition down the road.

The Philippines

Few countries provoke such a love it/hate it reaction from travelers as this one. It's not as good a value or as attractive as many other countries in Southeast Asia and I've yet to hear anyone rave about the food. The cities are downright ugly throughout.

It's also a tough place to gain residency unless you marry a local. For the gray-haired men with a paunch that easily find a hot Filipino wife, that's not considered an obstacle and this is the main group you hear championing the country as paradise on Earth. I'm not being judgmental since both parties get something they want out of that arrangement, but more than a few would-be expats find the prevalence of this a bit too creepy.

The others that love the place though are (mostly male) entrepreneurs who come here for the great business environment. It's easy to find English-speaking workers at bargain prices and you can live for cheap while you're ramping up your operations. Internet access is fast, flight connections are good, and a nice beach is always just a short hop away when it's time to recharge.

You can't buy property here as a foreigner and if you have a local spouse, the house will go in his/her name, even if you put up 100 percent of the money. On the plus side, it's very easy to find a condo for less than $50,000 and you can own that outright. If you form a corporation, you can't own more than 40 percent. For more information on starting and running a business here, check out the *Wood Egg Philippines* startup guide.

You can get a six-month tourist visa here if you apply in advance and can document income or savings to support yourself. Then you can extend it for 60 days by paying a heap of Philippine pesos. If you're not retired and you want to stay longer, unless you have a work permit you either need to marry a local or buy your way in, by investing at least $75,000. For retirees, the amount is lower, but you still have to put money into the local system, to the tune of $20,000. See pra.gov.ph for the latest requirements. There you'll find the options under such friendly names as "Smile," "Classic," "Human Touch," and "Courtesy."

One of the best ways to get around all this is to open a local business, like a call center or a place outsourcing virtual assistants. If you have 10 or more employees you can get a permanent residency visa. One of the guys running the Tropical MBA podcast lives in the Philippines much of the year and he and his partner run several successful businesses from there, including some local employees. See TropicalMBA.com. British expatriate Chris Ducker operates two companies in Cebu, including the Virtual Staff Finder company.

Ron Meyers is one of those happy guys who married a lovely local woman and settled down on the island of Cebu. "You can still buy land for cheap here, like beachfront under coconut and mango trees for under $43 per square meter. Building a nice new house will cost around $580 per square meter. He admits though that, "If it were not for the younger wife, I would not be here for the living experience. I have a five-year-old now. I had no children before and now I'm living life in reverse of most guys; that part I really like."

One thing to keep in mind is that this country is quite hot and has a long history of being the victim of natural disasters. "Unless you like the jungle heat and humidity I think it's hard here for the average foreigner," says Ron. "Without A/C I would have already been dead. Also, I lived through the big typhoon last November. We were without power for 22 days. My friend who lives just outside of Tacloban was without power for seven months."

Indonesia

I'd love to live in Indonesia. I've spent months there on two different trips and it's a terrific country. It's basically a long string of islands with terrific beaches and snorkeling, it's quite cheap, and if you start getting tired of the heat you just go up into the mountains. I'm not alone: there are as many as 10,000 expats in Bali alone.

There's just one big problem: it's tough to get a visa to live here long-term unless you're working for a company that's giving you a work visa, you have an Indonesian spouse, or you're over 55 and have a decent income. You also can't own property and in much of the country the internet is far from fast if you want to run a business online.

The easiest way to live here is to be old and patient. There is special visa for retired people of 55 of older. You must show proof of income exceeding $1,500 per month, proof of health insurance, and proof that you're spending a sufficient sum on your housing: at least $500 per month in Bali, Jakarta or Bandung, at least $200 elsewhere. You also have to pledge that you'll employ at least one domestic worker on a full-time basis.

Some people manage to make it work though. David McKeegan and his wife run Greenback Tax Services, doing tax returns and advisement for expatriates. Their virtual business employs 22 accountants around the world. This is not their first time around the block: they've lived abroad as a couple and eventually a family in London, Brazil, Uruguay, Spain, and two cities in Argentina. They're now living a good life in Bali though on a fraction of what they spent in Europe. "We have a three-bedroom house with two-car garage that we turned into an office. We pay about $14,200 per year in rent. Housing tends to be more western pricing, so that's the biggest expense, but just try to find anything like that within 60 miles of New York City! Each bedroom has A/C and its own bathroom. We have a nice yard with a vegetable garden, a swimming pool, and a place for the two kids to run around."

They pay $4 an hour for their babysitter/nanny and "she used to work at the Hyatt." Their housekeeper comes six days a week for a salary of $70 per month, which is also the amount for the gardener and pool cleaner who comes three days a week. "We have two different internet set-ups to be safe, which runs us $90 a month. Electricity is $200-$250 a month because of the pool and air conditioning."

They go out to eat a lot in Bali and it's not a big expense. The night before we talked the family ate out at one of the nicest restaurants on the beach. "We had four main courses, two beers, and three juices for about $25. Sometimes we'll go eat at the night market and the total will be $3."

The big downside is the visa situation. "Every two months we fly to Singapore and back to renew our visas," David explains. "That's when we do our doctor and dentists appointments and do a little shopping." It's a hassle, he says, "but the flight prices are reasonable if you plan ahead."

Stuart McDonald, who runs the authoritative Travelfish.org site on Southeast Asia, says you can go for years though if you arrange a "social visa" with an agency and follow the renewal rules properly. He's been living in Bali for years with his family and only has to leave the country every six months to get a new visa in Singapore and go to immigration once every two months for a half hour or so in Indonesia.

What you find online for this visa looks much more daunting than the reality on the ground. "Yes you need a local sponsor. In practice an agent can arrange this—in our case one of the housekeepers does it," he says. "In theory you need to be living in the same district as the sponsor; in practice, it doesn't matter."

All this requires some patience and a willingness to pay an agent to eliminate much of the uncertainty, but a long-term stay is possible for the patient. "There are plenty of stories online of people having dramas and moaning but, that really hasn't been our experience," Stuarts says.

If you're in a popular expatriate spot like Bali, what you spend will depend a lot on how savvy you are. Stuart has this to say about the food options in his adopted home: "Where we currently live in Seminyak, I can get a simple noodle soup in the local *warung* for 5,000 rupiah (about 50 cents). In the 'tourist warung' 100 meters away it is 15,000 and in the tourist restaurant, 30,000 rupiah. Yes, six times the price for essentially the same meal (though the tourist restaurant dish will come with a carved tomato on the side)."

This is not a good place to live if you're a lush, Stuart advises. "If you're on a budget, don't drink alcohol! A small Bintang will cost anything from $1 to $2.50, a large one $2,50 to $4. While these costs may still seem affordable compared to grabbing a pint in your home country, they're disproportionally expensive compared to the cost of food and accommodation. Have a large Bintang with that *rendang* and you'll more than double the cost of dinner. Wine and imported spirits are extremely heavily taxed and, for those on a budget, best avoided. Expect a mixed drink or cocktail to cost $5 to $15 and a glass of imported wine slightly more. Local wine isn't all that good and the local spirit (arak) can be of very, very variable quality."

Belize

You can hardly pick up a copy of the moving abroad publications or visit their websites without hearing raves about Belize. And why not? The language is English, it's a short flight from the USA or Canada, and it's easy to get a residency permit. The perks are good and you only have to be 45 or older and be able to show an income of $2,000 per month to qualify as "retired." They're not big on rules or a strong government here, so it appeals to libertarian types who just want to be left alone and pay as little as they can in taxes. There's just one problem with all this: the coast is costly.

If you live in the interior, it can be quite reasonable in Belize. But that's not what people picture. They imagine living by the Caribbean Sea, walking off the beach and going snorkeling or scuba diving, chilling out with a plate of fish at lunch with a cold beer in their hand. Unfortunately, the oceanfront communities here will not allow you to live a half-price life. That quickly became apparent to me when I started talking to expats living in Placencia and Ambergris Caye. "We're here for the weather and lower stress, not the savings," was one typical reply.

In the interior, it's a different story. Mike Campbell estimates that he lives on around $1,000 a month in the small town of Banque in the Cayo district, not far from the

Guatemalan border. "I have a four-bedroom, four-bath house with fancy tile, mahogany furniture, A/C, wood cabinets, and a garage. My rent is $400 per month. For food, $50 a week would be stuffing myself. Despite having a big fridge, computers, and air conditioning my electric bill never tops $100."

It wasn't always this way though. "I have been in Belize for 30 years," he explains. "I lived in San Pedro on Ambergris Caye for 25 years, working as a building contractor. But living in San Pedro got to be too much. Prices have risen really fast and with all the new wealth, crime has gone up a lot too. You really have to have to have a good amount of money to retire in San Pedro or Placencia. Looking at it from where I was before, I didn't see how anyone could retire in Belize for a decent price, especially if buying real estate. Here in the interior they could actually afford it." He's also worried about the effects of climate change, which he has seen first-hand by the water. "Ambergris is a very vulnerable place. They are going to need sea walls eventually or half the island will disappear."

Instead of building, Mike now helps others find a place to live in the Cayo district. "I went to look at lots and houses when I decided to move here and there was no real estate agency in town. So I opened one. I have a list of five houses now selling for $50,000 or less, all with a yard. There is room for appreciation here, but meanwhile you can retire without being rich." He says medical care is actually better in this area too, with clinics and labs five minutes away. There's a big medical center and a district hospital across the border in Guatemala and one in the capital of Belmopan in Belize.

The low requirements and incentives in Belize outweigh some of the cost factors that make it more expensive than Guatemala, Nicaragua, or Honduras. Getting residency as a retiree at age 45 is not an easy thing to do elsewhere and if you keep $24,000 in a bank account at all times, that qualifies you for that $2,000 a month income you need to show. Under that program you'll pay no income tax, import tax, or capital gains tax. You can't work for a local company, but you can start a business or be a freelancer getting money from abroad. You're allowed to bring in all your household goods and either a car, boat, or airplane with no duty charges. You only have to be in Belize one month a year minimum, but the time you are there doesn't count toward permanent residency. If you do the whole process on your own it'll probably cost around $1,600 plus half again for each dependent. With an attorney, double it.

If you're planning on staying put, there's also a permanent residency program. You only have to be in the country one year before you can apply for it. After five years of that you can become a citizen.

To be a snowbird, you can come in on a one-month tourist visa and then extend it a month at a time for up to six months. When you leave the country and return, the process starts over again.

Bolivia

If they were more welcoming to foreigners, Bolivia would be an expat paradise. Prices are very low, labor is cheap, and in places like Sucre, both the climate and the aesthetics are quite pleasant. Supposedly, you only need to show $1,000 a month in income—not carefully checked--to become a resident. Bolivia has been Venezuela's closest ally besides Cuba for a long while though and the anti-Americanism has lived on past the death of Chavez.

Because of the political track record, this is not a place where you want to buy something of great value: it's not unthinkable that the leadership will freeze or take your property, as it has already done with many private companies. There are more than a few wealthy Bolivians in Panama City who are stashing their money in a country they feel is a much safer long-term bet.

Getting permission to live here for a year or two is technically not hard, but actually getting to the finish line of that takes superhuman patience. Check out this blow-by-blow blog post with each document needed to get an idea. But hey, you get 90 days on arrival while you're sorting it out. Or you can just come for three months and move on.

I'm planning on doing just that one of these days: coughing up $160 for a tourist visa, finding a three-month rental in Sucre, and doing some local adventure activities and excursions. I would imagine my wife and I could do it for $1,200 a month or less and have a grand time. Then we'll fly to Peru, or Argentina, or Ecuador for longer.

Uruguay

This is not the cheap destination it once was and the Punta de Este beach region probably has the highest concentration of millionaires in Latin America during peak vacation times. Think of the coast here as The Hamptons for Latin Americans. Still, Uruguay is reasonable compared to many parts of the U.S. and Canada if you go elsewhere in the country (or come to the beach outside of high season). The capital Montevideo is certainly a less expensive place to live than Santiago or Rio.

It benefits from being a very liberal country in the traditional (non-political) definition of the word. It's a "live and let live" place, with minimal regulations but strong privacy protections, low health care costs and enlightened drug laws. The government wants to keep everyone safe and healthy, but it's not interested in acting like your mother and infringing on your personal freedom.

When it comes to health care, this is one of the best values in the world. You get excellent care at reasonable prices, whether you're paying out of pocket or buying into one of the good-value insurance policies that covers most of your costs at private facilities. This is not a big country, so getting back to the capital for serious medical care is not an arduous task and provincial hospitals and clinics offer good care for routine issues.

The expatriates who live in Uruguay are generally not those trying to live on a shoestring budget, but rather those looking for a European kind of lifestyle at a much lower price than Europe. Think of this country as a more organized, better managed, and less melancholy version of Argentina. To make that step up, you'll need to spend maybe $3,000 a month as a couple instead of skating by for $2,000 across the water in Buenos Aires. If that's within your budget, getting residency here is not complicated.

Once you apply for residency, you can remain in the country that whole time everything is being processed if you'd like. You need to have a clean police record and the right vaccinations, but then as long as you meet the income requirements there's very little chance you'll be rejected—

there's no quota on the number of immigrants and few hassles from power-wielding bureaucrats. There's no expressly stated income requirement, but some say the floor is $1,500 per month for a single person. Once you're approved, you have all rights a local does, plus you can import household goods duty-free. Once you've been a resident for three to five years (depending on marital status), you can become a full citizen and get a second passport.

Romania

Oddly enough, Romania has one of the highest average internet download speeds in the world. According to Speedtest.net, it ranks #3 in the world. So if you're running an online business and want a cheap place to hang while you ramp up, head to Transylvania. I loved my time traveling through that region and Dustin Overbeck liked Brasov so much he decided to base his business and his family there.

He and his wife were planning to spend three months there because of a business connection, then check out other spots in Europe. "After we arrived though, my wife found out she was pregnant," he says. "Plus the first three weeks we were here we had such positive experiences with the people we met, the landlord, babysitters, and people in a co-worker facility I found, so we decided to stay.

A connection in the co-worker facility hooked me up with an immigration person to form a business. I met the attorney within an hour and within eight days had a business formed. I spent maybe 400 euros for the attorney and business formation. My wife and I are directors and hired ourselves. After that we filed all the paperwork and got residency permits, which was maybe another 1,000 euros total for both of us. It all took only two months from start to finish. Then the renewal is much easier and cheaper a year later."

Their first apartment was right in the historic center, for 633 euros a month, furnished with all utilities and a regular cleaning lady, for a place of around 1,100 square feet. Now they're in a bit smaller place, but still in the center, paying 500 euros a month including internet and TV. It's another 50-100 euros extra for utilities. Dustin spends another $100 a month for a co-working facility so he has people to collaborate with and doesn't have to have room for an office in his home. "We're probably spending a bit over $2,000 a month total," he says, "but that includes buying diapers, a stroller, and taking language classes. Outside the city center you could probably do it for less than half that, but we wanted to be central and it's far less than we'd be spending in Wisconsin!"

If you're young and single though, you might prefer Bucharest. Vice.com praised its nightlife options with this summary: "It's a place where you can smoke indoors, a bottle of vodka costs a quarter of what it does back home and where the closing time is whenever the last person passes out."

African Countries: Morocco, Togo, & ...?

If you remove South Africa from the list, the vast majority of foreigners on the continent of Africa did not move there because of a lifestyle choice. They are there because they're working for a charity organization, an NGO, a religious organization, or the United Nations. The next largest group would be those who are getting paid well to relocate there (often reluctantly) for work: oil workers, engineers, hotel general managers, and those heading up local operations for international conglomerates such as Unilever or Deutsche Telekom.

Also, for a whole host of reasons, many countries in Africa aren't nearly as cheap as you would think they'd be. When you look at online cost of living estimators, the majority of countries on the continent that have sufficient data aren't any cheaper than small-town USA for a basket of living expenses. Sure, if you want to live and eat like a real sub-Saharan African you can do it for very little. After all, 20 of the 25 poorest countries in the world are here. If you want to have even a few comforts and conveniences of home, however, you'll pay a huge premium for a nice bathroom, a modern kitchen, and a real school for the kids.

It's futile trying to find a local job in most of them and broadband internet access is still hit and miss—when the power stays on. The jobless rates in some countries make the ones in Spain, Italy, and Greece look like the lands of opportunity. (Thus the boatloads of African immigrants that keep washing up on those shores.) When a job fair took place in Nigeria this year, 16 people got trampled to death when 65,000 desperate job seekers stampeded stadiums set up to test applicants for government job openings. Health care is far from ideal across the continent. This year, the World Health Organization said that "The risk of a child dying before their fifth birthday is eight times higher in the WHO African Region than a child in the WHO European Region." Of the 20 health care systems the WHO ranks at the bottom of their list, 18 of them are in Africa. (The others are Cambodia and Afghanistan.)

You also have some of the most corrupt and regressive governments in the world to deal with, especially if you're gay. Of the countries that still have enforceable laws on the books against homosexuals, 33 are in Africa. That means more of them there do than not. (Avoid Nigeria and Uganda at all costs; you could get thrown in jail just because of your sexual orientation.)

Former expat haven Egypt recently sentenced more than 1,100 protesters to death in a show trial, while also jailing journalists from Al-Jazeera, saying they were inciting violence. Kenya just legalized polygamy (for men, not for women of course.) Throw in slavery, constant civil wars, Boko Haram, and limb-chopping warlords, and urban Honduras starts looking like a walk in the park in comparison.

Writing off 50-some countries with one brush stroke is not fair though, of course, and there are some people who move to Africa just to move to Africa. If you're hell-bent on doing so, dig in, travel overland, and do some research. Here are two places to start where you can definitely live for less and still have some comforts.

Morocco

The best overall value in Africa and with some of the best infrastructure on the continent, this is the place to get exotic without paying a fortune. With some judicious house hunting and a limit on how much alcohol you drink, you could squeak under the half price mark here in the main tourism centers, or live more comfortably on that amount elsewhere. The per capita GDP is only around $5,000 per year, but prices are high in tourist areas just because...there are so many tourists driving up prices. Be advised that English is often third or fourth on the list of languages though, even in the tourism sector. Arabic, French, and Spanish (in the north) are more commonly understood and French is the language of government and diplomacy.

The country has some of the highest internet penetration in Africa and broadband is more prevalent than on most of the continent. Air connections are good, especially to Europe, and you can take a ferry to Spain. Medical care is decent in the cities, but poor elsewhere and you'll likely encounter a language barrier if you don't speak French. Petty crime and property theft is a nagging problem and the touts of Morocco win the international bronze medal for annoying schemers, just behind India and Egypt.

Foreigners are allowed to buy homes here and there is some financing available if you can pay 35 percent of the purchase price as a down payment and another six percent in various fees at closing.

You can stay up to 90 days on a tourist visa, but if you want to stay longer as a temporary resident you have to register within the first 15 days after arrival and apply for an alien registration card. If you can show sufficient means to support yourself, it should be granted. For a work permit, you need to show a signed contract from the employer and to live here as a freelancer you need to get a work authorization. Once you have that though, it's good for a decade.

Togo

Andy Graham the HoboTraveler has holed up in the long-time coastal expat enclave of Lome, Togo for a half year at a time on several occasions and says there are plenty of French expats and a few scattered others living there. In stark contrast to Uganda and Nigeria, gay couples are legal and accepted here. "The expats here are a weird bunch, with a 90 percent chance they are working for a save the world organization, and a few old French guys, a hangover from colonization."

It's certainly cheap enough. When the per capita GDP of a country is under $500, as it is here, you don't have to have a lot of cash coming in each month tobe richer than the locals. Andy easily coasts by on $500 a month, though the hotel bill is usually half of that. It has an easy visa policy: "Togo grants a seven day visa on arrival, and Americans can extend it for one year for $30 dollars. I have done this 4 times," he says.

Where Else?

There are some expats living in areas with lots of tourists in Tanzania, Kenya, and Botswana, mostly in the hotel or tour industries. If their expenses are covered, they can save a bit of money and have a wonderful experience. There are some independent foreigners living in Mozambique, Madagascar, Malawi, and Ethiopia because they like it there, as well as Tunisia up north when it's stable. If you've traveled to one of these and love it, or have a connection that can help you get a tourism job, try it out and tell me how it went!

Chapter 31: Safety in Perspective

When your number comes up, statistics say it'll most likely be from something mundane like cancer, heart disease, or old age. If it's an accidental death, you'll most likely die in a car crash. That's how 33,561 people died in the USA in 2012 and how 1.2 million died worldwide. And driving is much safer than it used to be. That 33.6K number is down from more than 50K a year when I was in college. But it's still the equivalent of having a 9/11 terrorist attack every six weeks, year after year.

I'm not saying don't ever get behind the wheel again, but understand that hanging around your suburb and driving to work is more likely to get you killed than changing your address to Mexico or Cambodia.

If you're a smoker, be advised that cigarettes cause an estimated 480,000 deaths a year in the U.S. alone. If you're obese and you light up regularly, your odds of dying early are already so high that on-the-ground safety shouldn't even be on your worry list. One of those things is probably going to kill you, not some random thug on the corner in a foreign land. Some 200 people a day die from hospital infections; that's more than all the foreign violence in the world added together, including attacks on military personnel.

One potential cause of death is almost sure to decrease if you move out of the USA: the chance of getting shot to death. No country has a higher rate of gun ownership than the United States and only a few dots on the map have a higher rate of gun deaths. Most of them are either war zones or drug gang zones — which themselves are their own kind of war zone.

The number of Americans killed each year by firearms is only slightly lower than those killed in auto accidents: around 32,000 annually. For those between the ages of 15 and 19, this is the second leading cause of death after auto accidents.

Here's another sobering stat to put things in perspective. According to an article in *The Guardian* in late 2013, the number of Americans killed in *all* the wars since 1775 is 1.17 million. The number of them killed by firearms just since 1968 is 1.38 million. The TSA seized 3,369 firearms in 2012 and 2013 at U.S. airports (842 of those in Texas alone). So living in a war zone could be safer than being in the wrong place at the wrong time where you are now.

When three people were shot dead on the tourist strip in Myrtle Beach, SC over Memorial Day weekend, it didn't even make the national news because there was a worse rampage in Santa Barbara, California that had a more interesting back-story. Similar shootings happened in movie theaters, restaurants, and churches across the USA as the year went on. There was probably a random shooting the week you're reading this, no matter which week of the year it is.

It's probably going to continue to get worse, in the red states at least. The state of Georgia even passed a law as I was finishing up this book that people could bring guns into bars, churches, schools, libraries, and some government buildings. (What could go wrong?)

The USA only has 5 percent of the world population, but it has 25 percent of the world's prison inmates. The truth is, your safety odds are better in most places you'll move to than they are in your current home town, especially if you're American. Let's start there and *then* let's look at the real dangers and how to stay safe.

You Do Need to Be Smart

I'm not saying it's going to be an idyllic Eden where you're going, a place nobody hurts or robs anyone. Even Sweden, Singapore, and Japan have policemen solving break-ins and murders as we speak. In early 2014 violent anarchists rampaged through a French city "burning cars, smashing car windows, and throwing rocks at riot police, who responded with water cannons and tear gas." Similar scenes have taken place in such diverse locations as England, Thailand, Turkey, Greece, Spain, Peru, and Brazil in the recent past.

Although I'll talk until I'm blue in the face about how the drug cartels in Mexico have never targeted tourists, I do know people where I live who have had their houses robbed while they were out. A friend was hit in the head with a beer bottle and would have had his wallet taken if he hadn't swerved out of the way and ran. I'm in a safe city overall, but shit happens, especially in the wee hours of the night.

Lord knows there was plenty of crime to fret about in my former homes of Hoboken, Nashville, and Tampa in the United States though. There were so many lawn mower thefts in my neighborhood of Nashville that the neighborhood association made joke t-shirts about it and sold them as fundraisers. My garage and car both got broken into. When I lived in Hoboken, New Jersey, my license plates were stolen off my car the first month after arrival and I ended up replacing four broken car windows in four years from break-ins. Heck, I had two bikes stolen where I went to college in small town Virginia. I know plenty of people who have suffered some kind of incident abroad too, though thankfully I haven't myself except for a camera stolen 20 years ago in India. Recently, my two years in Tampa were incident free, as have been my 2+ years in Mexico. Maybe my luck is turning. Or maybe I'm just getting better at keeping my valuables.

My point is only that crime happens everywhere. It's just the frequency and deadliness that varies. Often your perceptions of what is dangerous are very different than the stats would support if you really did your homework and looked at it logically. I've talked enough about my home country, but thuggery is rampant in England and Canada's crime stats would surely be higher if an estimated 50 percent of its property crimes didn't go unreported. The worst cities for pickpockets are in Italy, which is not exactly a country tourists avoid because of safety worries. Instead they avoid Mexico City, where your chances of getting pickpocketed are close to zero in the tourist zones.

To give you an idea of how low the assault or murder chances are around the world, Statistics Canada only lists eight countries where the five year average of Canadians assaulted or killed is higher than it is on home soil. Only one in this book makes the list (Mexico), and barely. The worldwide average is 0.5 incidents per 100,000 people, compared to 1.2 at home.

So living abroad is probably not going to be any more dangerous for you than staying home would be unless you're moving somewhere like Tijuana or Nairobi. Spend some time on research to make sure, of course. Understand that you need to zero in on towns and cities, not the whole country. The two largest cities in Honduras are teeming with drug gangs. The island of Roatan is not. Guatemala City is a place I wouldn't even want to spend one night in. But a town on Lake Atitlan? I wouldn't hesitate to move there.

There are some general trends to be aware of though. In general, murder rates are highest in Latin America and Africa is next. Asia and Europe fare much better, partly because of a better-trained and less corrupt police force. According to a UN study, the Americas have a vastly lower conviction rate for murder, at 24 percent, compared to 48 percent in Asia and 81 percent in Europe.

Usually the places foreigners have gravitated to—especially retirees—are not high-crime areas. That's true in the USA and Canada too. (Scottsdale, Victoria, and Boca Raton? Pretty safe. Detroit and St. Louis? Not so much.) So find the message board or online English newspaper for that place you're considering and you will probably get a pretty good feel of what's going on there, good and bad. Then spend some time there on a trial run and ask a lot of questions of locals about safety and crime if you're worried. Ask the old hands who have seen it all and ask a few newbies who just arrived this year.

If they all say, "This place is going to hell," then at the very least just rent instead of buying. Maybe go back to the drawing board and look elsewhere. If the answers are neutral or positive, you're probably better off than at home.

Don't do this in isolation, without looking at what goes on where you live now at the same time. What would be the impression of people thinking of moving to your home town if they watched your evening news every night? If they read your local paper? If they dug up the local homicide and robbery stats? What would you tell them to put it in perspective?

Apply the same sensibilities to where you'd be moving. Your town is probably just "the devil you know" and you're looking in fear at the one you don't know. Put the emotions aside and weigh them the same.

Petty Crime

If you live in a guard-protected gated community in the suburbs or you're in one of the safest areas of Canada or New Zealand, there's a good chance you'll be exposed to more petty crime where you're going. All the countries in this book have legitimate issues to worry about in their capital cities, though in the countrysides of the European countries you've probably got very little risk.

In some places there are pickpockets, in others there are house break-ins, in some spots you may hear about muggings or carjackings. The two best sources of news on this are going to be the local newspaper (sometimes in English, often not) and the local expatriate message board(s). Keep in mind both can make the problem look worse than it really is: newspapers everywhere seem to follow an "if it bleeds, it leads" policy and if two or three expats out of 1,000 have something happen to them, it's treated as a major trend and a cause for alarm. People forget that just as many incidents or more happened where they came from, but if it wasn't in their immediate neighborhood or happening to their friends they ignored it.

Knowing what the problems are and how to avoid them will make you safer though. If there are a lot of pickpockets where you're going, go out with less in your pockets and make sure those pockets are secured. If there are a lot of break-ins, get the right bars on your windows and invest in good locks or an alarm system. If there have been muggings at 2 am, don't make it a habit to stagger home drunk well after midnight.

Most expats will tell you they feel safer in their new country than they did in their old and often statistics bear this out. According to the European Institute for Crime Prevention and Control, you're more likely to get assaulted in the USA or Canada than in Mexico. New Zealand, Scotland, Italy, and Ireland have higher assault rates than Hungary, Slovakia, or Portugal. The burglary rate is higher in Australia, New Zealand, England, USA, and Canada than it is in most countries featured in this book. So be reasonably cautious and savvy, but don't use safety as an excuse to stay put and keep struggling financially.

Getting Sick

When you move to another country, your stomach is going to encounter all kinds of ingredients and bacteria it's not used to facing. It's inevitable that you'll have a little adjusting to do. Whether you're headed to Thailand, Togo, or even Turkey, you probably want to give it a few days before you starting diving into street food and market stall meals.

After that though, most expatriates don't suffer anything worse than they would at home as long as they take normal precautions. After all, it's not like you're immune to this risk where you live now. The Center for Disease Control website says, "The CDC estimates that each year roughly 1 in 6 Americans (or 48 million people) get sick, 128,000 are hospitalized, and 3,000 die of foodborne diseases." The percentages are even higher in some other developed countries where food safety laws aren't as strict or there's more risky food (like raw meat or raw fish) eaten regularly.

In developing countries, the biggest risk comes from untreated water and contaminated vegetables. So you have to drink bottled or filtered water and wash your vegetables in an iodine solution. This is not necessarily a big hassle. Where I live in Mexico guys deliver 5-gallon bottles of water to my door two times a week for less than $2.50 each and I can buy iodine drops in any little convenience store. Some expats install a whole-house filtration system for their water.

In a poor country like India or Nepal that has lousy sanitation standards, you may have to worry about the meat as well. You'll need to seek out a butcher with higher standards and you probably don't want to eat anything with meat in it from a cheap restaurant. The first time I visited India and Nepal, I stayed a vegetarian the whole time. The second time I ate more meat, but only when we splurged at nice places with a good reputation. As a result, I never got sick in either country, which is a minor miracle. My wife got laid low for days with food poisoning from a cream sauce that apparently had unpasteurized milk in it.

The flip side of this is, most people end up eating a more healthy diet when they go abroad. American fast food and packaged junk food has infiltrated nearly every corner of the globe now, but in most countries they don't eat as much of it as the source population. And it's not as cheap as eating what's been consumed locally for centuries already. I lost 10 pounds in a few months after moving back to Mexico and am now down 15 from where I was at the start. That's almost completely from eating less junk food and walking more. When fresh fruit and vegetables cost a fraction of what they do in your local Tesco, Safeway, or Kroger, you tend to eat a lot more of them.

Chapter 32: Working Abroad and Making a Living

In the first section of this book I wrote on the connection between how you'll support yourself and what kind of visa or residency permit that enables. I want to circle back to this subject though with some food for thought as you look to the future.

The very best way to move abroad and leverage your first-world currency is to either be living off retirement funds in your home currency or to be earning a living remotely in your home currency, or a strong one anyway. If you're getting paid in dollars, pounds, euros, yen, or Swiss francs, you're going to be in good shape almost anywhere.

It's far more desirable to take your portable job with you and get paid in dollars or euros than it is to try to support yourself locally in a country where typical wages are a quarter those of the place you left, at best. If you're trying to get a job locally, you've suddenly lost all your arbitrage benefits. You're not earning in a rich country and spending in a cheaper one. Instead you're doing what all the locals are doing: trying to scrape by on what are typical local wages.

There are ways around this of course, but most require specialized skills or enough capital to start a business. In the first case, for example, you could be a systems analyst or programmer working for a local company and because your skills and experience are on such a higher level than the local labor pool, you could get a higher salary or be made a team manager. Your salary may be lower than it would be in your home country, but it'll be high by local standards.

Or if you're a surgeon, architect, or experienced business consultant, again you may earn less than you could before, but since your expenses are so much lower, you could still be much better off in the end. Many executives get a posting abroad and then don't ever want to come back because their standard of living is so much higher. I once met an oil company expatriate living in Indonesia who got less than half his old salary but felt 10 times richer. He had a maid, cook, gardener, and nanny, plus a driver at his beck and call.

Running a business has long been an expatriate route that can be satisfying and downright lucrative. In many towns all over the world, there may be only a few hundred foreigners in town, but they often own the best coffee shop, the top restaurant, and the best boutique hotels. In many destinations it will only take you a few days to see huge service gaps in the local business landscape. When foreigners jump in and open a better hotel, a better bar, or a better bakery than what is offered already, they can do quite well in a hurry. The expatriates all flock there and then the trendy and wealthy locals follow. This requires some capital and navigating the local business rules (sometimes it's best to take on a local partner), but the payoff can be close to a sure thing if you've got enough capital and demand is sufficient.

Teaching English

If you don't have a portable skill, this is one you can pick up that's not a big stretch, assuming you're a native English speaker with a decent command of grammar. When I was a young backpacker making my way around the world two decades ago, I got a TEFL (teaching English as a Foreign language) certification from Cambridge by doing a four-week course that involved both classroom lessons and live teaching practice. I did the course in Bangkok, but this program is offered all around the world and is widely recognized. Besides helping me earn a higher pay grade later, it also fully prepared me for whatever came at me in the classroom and made me a great teacher, if I may say so myself.

Armed with my certification, my now-wife and I taught in a suburb of Istanbul, Turkey on one trip, and then taught for more than a year on a contract in a suburb of Seoul, South Korea. The Istanbul gig barely paid enough to cover our expenses. The Korea one made us feel downright rich.

In much of the world, teaching English as a second language is something you do to get by, while in others it can be quite lucrative. Some expats make it a long-term career and do quite well. In general though, the most desirable places to live are not the ones that are going to pay you handsomely. The highest wages are in the Middle East and the richest Asian countries. For the countries in this book with the lowest cost of living, the locals simply can't pay the kind of money for classes that students can in Tokyo, Seoul, Dubai, or Taipei. On the other hand, you won't need as much either. The problem though is that while East Asian and Middle Eastern countries often provide an apartment and cover your airfare over if you sign a contract, that's seldom the case in the rest of the world.

Your experience will vary, but in the destinations covered in this book, an hourly pay of $3 to $12 is the general range. That's a wide range, yes, but even at the high end you're not going to be living large, especially if they can't guarantee you enough hours to make it a full-time job. If you have lots of experience you can bump that up by teaching at a university or by teaching business English classes that get paid by the company. You could get up to a range of $2,000 or $3,000 a month and be doing well. Those jobs generally go to people with lots of experience though. You can increase your pay by lining up private lessons, but that takes some time to build.

Some of the people profiled in the country chapters started out as English teachers, while some did it for more than a decade and are still at it. It's a rewarding job and you end up with a large social circle right away, so it can be a lot of fun. Just understand that your pay will be limited by the locals' salaries, so it's not a way to live significantly better than a middle-class local.

If you're really short on funds, the best route may be to pack this book and go teach for a year or two in a rich country, socking away lots of cash for later or paying off your student loans. Then go live where you really want to live, having enough of a cushion to get you by while you figure out next steps for income. (If you want to keep teaching elsewhere, you'll now have experience and hopefully a recommendation letter.) To give you an idea of how this can work, my wife and I worked our butts off in Korea teaching a little more than a year and put more than $30,000 in the bank. It was the richest I ever felt in my life: we traveled a lot around Korea, ate out whenever we wanted, and still saved a small fortune.

In terms of resources, the *Teaching English Abroad* book by Susan Griffith is great and Dave's ESL Cafe is a great gut check online. Both have been around since before I started teaching in the late 1990s. You can also find info on local expatriate message boards, on the local Craigslist site, and country-specific sources. Really though, unless you're going to work for the JET Program in Japan or something else that has a well-established recruiting system in your home country, it's best to just show up and start looking around. Often what you see on paper or online bears no relationship to actual conditions on the ground. Your main concerns when taking a job with an English school are financial stability, number of hours you'll get weekly, and the pay rate—in that order. There's no point in taking a $30 an hour job in Korea if they school's going to stiff you out of your pay a month after you've started.

On the plus side, these are pretty easy jobs to get, especially if you have a college degree, and most governments will look the other way if you're teaching English while on a tourist visa. (Bangkok's ESL industry would collapse tomorrow if their teachers all required work visas.) From Buenos Aires to Guadalajara, Marrakesh to Yogyakarta, you can probably find a job teaching English if you are patient, persistent, and presentable. Just don't expect that to happen in India and Nepal—anyone educated already speaks your language.

Running a Business

When it comes to running an expat business, the story of Lucha Libro Books in Granada, Nicaragua is a typical one. Typical in the sense that a hobby kind of turned into a business over time instead of being some grand plan from the start.

Tony Fuss tried to sell some of his used books on the street but wasn't doing very well, so he put a shelf in a local donut shop and every day or two the owner would give him some money. He brought in more books, and in a town with a fair number of English speakers but no other bookstores around, business kept growing. Eventually the books were selling more than the donuts, so he and the owner of that shop turned it into a bookstore and eventually moved into a larger space. Now it's a thriving operation that sells new titles and a constantly churning collection of used books from up north. Tony makes enough to live on and is a fixture in the community.

Speaking of tasty treats with a hold in the middle, when Charles Vasels landed in Malaysia and was trying to figure out how to turn his interests into a job, he noticed there weren't any donut shops in Kuala Lumpur. It seemed to him that if you were the first one, you could do pretty well. He called up a donut machine manufacturer when he was back in the USA and found out it was $5,000 to buy one. "I had them send it to Malaysia, my Chinese girlfriend and I rented some space, and the next thing we knew we had a successful donut shop. I asked myself, 'Can it really be this easy? Can you just step off a plane and start a new life with a new business?'"

His background was in product design though, so he kept looking for opportunities in that area and in film production, where he worked before, but wasn't able to make it happen. "So instead I took advantage of the blank slate, the ability to be a pioneer." Eventually he gave up the donut shop and started other companies, one doing product design and another producing forms used in courts in California, made in Malaysia. He has 20 local employees.

Charles and many like him have followed a simple path to success: meet a demand that isn't being filled, but start off small enough that you aren't betting everything you have. Follow the *Lean Startup* model in testing the market to see if your hunches are correct. If they are, you can expand into a larger space, a second location, or a larger regional area. Just keep in mind you will probably spend as much on lawyers and business license fees as you will on the first few months of rent. And in some countries with very strong labor laws, it's next to impossible to get rid of a lousy employee just because they're lazy. Take your time hiring good people instead of snatching up warm bodies. Get lots of local advice from other expat business owners before taking the plunge and you'll have a lot fewer headaches later.

Your Own Virtual Business

As I've said several times in this book, the ideal situation when moving from a rich country to a poorer one is to keep earning money from a rich country. Money in your bank account has no borders. If you can pull it out in a place where you don't need so much of it, that's the true "half price life" dream.

This is also the path for those who want the minimum amount of bureaucracy. Many digital nomads simply bop around the world on tourist visas, never even bothering to get permanent residency anywhere. Since they're adding to the local economy instead of subtracting from it, nobody in government is going to bat an eye unless these people start running afoul of local laws.

If you do apply for residency, in most countries you'll be welcome to come stay a while as long as you can show proof of sufficient income. That "sufficient" number is always much higher than what the average local lives on and it varies from as little as $600 a month to as much as $3,000.

There are as many different virtual business opportunities as there are people reading this book. If you go to Flippa.com or EmpireFlippers.com you'll see all kinds of them for sale. If you have a little capital (sometimes less than $1,000) and some basic tech skills, you can skip a lot of building time by buying something already up and running that is generating cash flow. Many people do quite well being solopreneurs, farming out their skills in web development, coding, technical writing, or translation—nearly any job that can be done remotely is a candidate for that. Some get to a point where they have more work than they can handle and they need to scale. The next thing they know, they have three or four virtual employees or additional freelancers.

The world is full of opportunities for those who can meet a market need. Assess your skills, be observant, and be attuned to where what you can do intersects with what people are willing to pay for.

Chapter 33: Taking Care of Details

As Charles Vassels, an American living in Malaysia says, "Many people dream of this kind of life, but they don't have the guts to really do it. They don't take that step to get on a plane and get off in another country where they don't know anyone."

The big leap to actually getting on that plane and moving abroad seems the scariest, but unfortunately there are seemingly a million things you need to do before that point.

Many books on moving to a specific country will give you some kind of checklist for what you should be taking care of one year ahead of time, six months ahead of time, three months out, and the week before you leave. Since I'm covering so many places that appeal to so many different kinds of people, I'm not going to try to repeat that here. I do link to some examples in the Resources section though where you can find these checklists. You need to have some kind of to-do list and it's going to be a long one. Consider the list you would have for moving to another state or province in your own country, then double it. If you're a couple and one of you is more organized than the other, designate that person as the checklist maker and paper gatherer. Otherwise you may never get on that plane.

Here are the broad categories of steps you'll need to take to prepare.

Mail

You'll need to move everything you can online, like paying credit card bills, getting back statements, and paying quarterly taxes if you're a self-employed American. You'll probably still need to maintain an address in your own country though, both to have a place for lingering mail to go (like with those remaining utility bills that aren't online) and to avoid hassles from your financial institutions. You can have a mail address that forwards to you overseas, but a more practical approach is to use a relative's address so they can alert you when something fishy or urgent comes in.

There are also services that will receive your mail for you

and some will scan it so you can see what you got online. You can then have them trash or forward the physical copies. My friends Ryan and Ang of JetsLikeTaxis have set up residency in South Dakota, for example, using a service there specifically meant for people roaming the USA in a recreational vehicle or roaming the world without a fixed address. In Mexico I use a service where I have a United States mailing address in Laredo, Texas and a guy actually drives up there each week to bring everyone's mail down to San Miguel de Allende. When I go to San Miguel for visa issues or shopping, I pick up my mail.

Don't forget to alert everyone you get mail from of the new address as your forwarding order will only last 6-12 months depending on the items. This is especially essential for tax documents since those are still mostly sent by mail.

Finances

There are things you need that you probably haven't even thought about when it comes to financial instruments. Do you have a credit card with a chip instead of just a magnetic stripe? You might need that where you're going. Do you have a credit card that doesn't charge a foreign transaction fee? You'll pay a lot more if you don't. Do you have a bank account that will allow you to withdraw your money without getting dinged for $4-$5 every time? Over a year, this can make a huge difference. (In general, credit unions and the cash accounts of brokerage companies are the best bet for this.) Don't forget bank alliances that can save you money: your current bank may be connected to another one in your destination country that will allow you to withdraw money at no cost.

You want backup plans in all these cases too. If one debit card gets eaten by a machine or lost, you will be glad you had a second one, preferably to a different account. If one credit card gets denied, which happens all the time for no good reason, you want to be able to pull out a second one. In some places Visa is not common but MasterCard is, so you want both.

Ideally you want to have several bank accounts (easier if you're with a spouse) and you want to be able to transfer money between them. Unless you have six figures sitting around in cash accounts, you're probably going to need to move money around now and then.

Naturally you want to be able to access your account online and pay bills with it. I highly recommend having a Paypal account as well if you'll be doing any kind of regular transactions with people in other countries. You can connect this to a bank account to transfer in and out.

Keeping in Touch

The expatriate life is far easier than it used to be. By paying a few bucks to Skype, MagicJack, Vonage, or Google Voice, you can talk for hours with your relatives if you want. You can set up a phone number in your own country that will ring to your laptop or smart phone. You can do video conferences for free via Skype or Google Hangouts. You can transfer files by Dropbox and share photos on social media.

None of these services costs much or is difficult. But it's one more thing to put on your to-do list.

If you want to stream video or audio, you might want to set up a proxy service as well. This allows you to tap into an ISP in your home country so it still looks like you're there. None of them are perfect, but the Hotspot Shield one I've been using the past year gets a bit less buggy the longer I use it.

Really though, all this detail stuff is pretty easy. It's just time consuming. What you really have to worry about is the emotional part...

Chapter 34: The Resistance You Will Face

"If you limit your actions in life to things that nobody can possibly find fault with, you will not do much"
- Lewis Carroll

In 1902 a man named Owen Wister published a novel called *The Virginian*. It is widely credited as the first true "western" and had a huge influence on a whole class of books, movies, and TV shows that followed. Although this launched Wister's writing career and he spent the rest of his life publishing other books and living a life of celebrity, he never wrote another western. This fact is glossed over without any explanation in most biographies, but apparently it was a scolding from his mother that was the reason. She reportedly thought it was beneath his talents to write that kind of trashy story and she reprimanded him for the frequent violence in the book. With that one rebuke, Wister stopped doing what had broken new ground and return to doing "normal" writing again. He went on to write four more novels, 11 non-fiction books, and a large body of short stories.

It is that one revolutionary book that Wister is still known for today though. None of the others came close to selling the 200,000 copies *The Virginian* did its first year. Five movies and a TV series have used it as the basis of their story and it has never been out of print.

When you do something that seems different or radical to others, you can expect lots of resistance. Perhaps even contempt. A whole mix of emotions erupts when someone else freely embraces a drastic change. So when you excitedly announce your plans to move abroad, your mother may not approve. Don't expect your friends and relatives to be universally excited for you. Some will get downright hostile. To your face or behind your back, you may be called a deserter, a runaway, a slacker, a coward, a communist, a kook, or worse.

If the TV news channel you watch all day keeps telling you that you live in the greatest country in the world and everyone wants to be like us, sooner or later you start believing it. In an article I read right before this book came out about the ten most popular countries for Americans moving abroad, the nasty comments underneath it included gems like this.

"I ALREADY LIVE IN THE BEST COUNTRY IN THE WORLD WHY WOULD I WANT TO GO ANYWHERE ELSE!! EVEN AT OUR WORST WE ARE WE ARE BETTER THAN THE REST!!!" (Typos corrected, screaming capitals left.)

"Well now anyone who is on the run from the Law knows where they can ESCAPE to, as you put it. Bye, maybe we can empty the prisons and send them to these places."

Read any article online about moving to Mexico and you'll find a large number of comments that are hateful, paranoid, ignorant, and just dead wrong. Most of the people writing them haven't traveled out of the country or if they did, it was on a safe and predictable cruise ship. They ignore the troubles in their own town as if they don't exist, but proclaim to be experts on all the troubles you are bound to encounter if you go live in Mexico. Hey, they saw it on TV.

While the rah-rah USA types are the worst, you'll also get strong resistance from people you are close to if you're moving from Manchester to Porto or from Toronto to Trujillo. Some cultures are more open to moving abroad than others, especially if you're only doing it six months a year, but that doesn't mean your blood relatives and close friends are going to be thrilled that you're abandoning them and will be eight hours away by plane.

The Emotions Behind Resistance

If you understand why people are not happy about your grand plans to move abroad, it gets easier to deal with the criticism (or wall of silence). Then you can just say, "Excuse me, there's someone over there I need to talk to" when someone starts criticizing your plans instead of getting red in the face and telling them off.

1) They haven't traveled much.

Most people who don't understand why you would take off

around the world for a year or move to another country haven't spent much time outside their own country. (In many cases, that's a good thing for the rest of the world.) If they have traveled, it has been on a secluded ship, in a secluded resort, or a very tightly organized tour. They don't know much about real costs and they probably don't believe things are as cheap where you're going as you are telling them. Or they think if your rent is $250 a month, then you must be moving to a cave with dirt floors and no indoor plumbing.

2) They're envious because their own boring life is all mapped out.

"Going on an adventure" is a depressingly rare event for nearly all the adult population of my home country. Vacations are strictly planned, and time off is a too-rare commodity that can't be spent spontaneously. The race for more stuff and more money to pay bloated health care and university systems saps the life out of most people who have managed to land a good job and keep it. Ask them how their life will be different in five or ten years and they may not be able to think of anything. Or they'll just say something weak about a hoped-for promotion, retirement, or their kids going to college.

For a majority, the closest they'll get to an adventure is having an illicit affair with a co-worker or staying up all night "getting crazy" at the next convention in Vegas. They are slaves to routines, commutes, the kids' activity schedules, and the big-screen TV. They'll say, "I wish I could do what you're doing" and will have plenty of the usual excuses as to why they can't. It's all mapped out, pre-ordained, set in stone. They have responsibilities. There are two car loans to pay off, a big mortgage to keep paying, promises to keep, ladders to climb, plus they just got that new riding mower for the lawn... They're in a jail of their own making but they don't realize they have built it themselves.

You represent a threat because you're showing them it doesn't have to be that way. And that's as scary as the revelation in *The Matrix*. Every time you tell them about your adventures abroad, it's going to be a reminder of what's on the other side. The life they may have dreamed of before than put on so many shackles and chains. They won't tell you all this. They might not even be able to see it and verbalize it. But you may be making them feel some negative emotions without you even knowing it.

3) If you're leaving, that means this place is not perfect

If you're in some kind of membership club and people start dropping out, that makes you wonder what's wrong. If the star performers in your company start taking jobs elsewhere, you're going to think that's a bad sign. You may feel like a sucker for still being there.

If someone tells you they're moving away from where you live and that they think this whole lifestyle they've been living in your town is not the best they can do, how's that going to make you feel? If they moved away to Silicon Valley because of a great job offer, that's perfectly logical, but to move just because there's a better life somewhere else? That's..well..."different."

Some will just think you're nuts and they'll feel okay because you're obviously off your rocker. Some will feel envious and maybe a bit bitter (see #2). Others will start wondering if this club they thought was perfect may not be so great after all. This life they've been told to pursue, the one that's supposed to represent fulfillment, is not feeling so fulfilling and now you come along saying there's a way out and you're hopping on a plane to take it.

Maybe they had a nagging feeling that this land of opportunity they're in is not so full of opportunity anymore, that getting ahead financially is getting tougher every year. Now you're regaling them with tales of half-price living in a place with better weather and less stress. They might be happy for you, but you're not making *them* happy. Because they're stuck in this place that's looking a lot less perfect now.

Empathy and Strength

You don't want to hear your mother say, "You're an idiot for doing this and you should feel guilty for leaving me."

But then again, hearing "We're so happy for you" while seeing a dark cloud pass over your friend's face is not so great either.

Understand that your radical decision (in their eyes) can

spur heavy emotions and soul-searching, no matter how much that person knows you're going to have an amazing time. You'll be told you're an idiot, people will say, "See you back here in six months!" with a laugh and a pat on your back. Just smile, keep making your arrangements, and then post lots of photos seven months later.

Understand why you may meet resistance and don't let it get you down. Understand their position, but be extra resolute about yours. This is your life and doing what other people tell you is "normal" is probably going to put you on a treadmill that's not going anywhere. It's your decision to make and it's a good one, so lock the storage shed door and go!

One good solution to all this if you're not getting much support on the home front is to find new people to talk with. Join up with groups of like-minded people who are thinking of moving abroad or are already doing it. My Cheap Living Abroad groups are a good solution of course, but you can also find destination-specific listservs and message boards to drill down further and make new friends where you're going.

Chapter 35: Family Considerations

Wherever you end up moving to, there will be foreign families living in that country. Sure, there may be more empty nest retirees and young English teachers, but plenty of families move abroad for job transfers, proximity to relatives, a slower pace of life, or cost savings. A family can live anywhere other expats can live: children are everywhere of course. There's one major factor though that can limit your choices: schooling.

If you're the kind of patient, educated, meticulous parents who can pull off home schooling, you'll have it easier. You can get all your lessons and meet your home state or province's requirements online, just as if you were home schooling back in that location. This takes lots of up-front preparation before leaving and your child has to be the type that can thrive outside a classroom environment. You'll also miss out on some of the language immersion benefit that comes from mixing all day with local children. When you factor in the ability to live anywhere and make your own schedule though, the parents that go this route are usually happy with it.

For everyone else, the local school situation is going to be a big factor in where you can and cannot live. Sure, there will be local schools almost anywhere you would choose to live. You can't assume they're going to be good schools though, and they will likely be in a foreign language if they're not private international ones. The public schools may not be anywhere close to the standards you're used to and the classrooms may be overcrowded.

Within a country or even within the same state in that country, the number of foreigners or wealthy business people can make a huge difference in the choices. Where I live in Mexico, for instance, my daughter has gone to two different private schools, which after initial fees have cost a very reasonable $300 or so per month. Classes have been in Spanish only though, and there is no English language option. We wanted this for her and she has adjusted, so it hasn't been an issue, but some children really struggle if they don't have a good language base already.

Just an hour and a half away in San Miguel de Allende, however, there are several schools with bilingual classes and one accredited international school in English. If we lived in the industrial "shoe capital of Mexico" an hour in the other direction, we'd have even more options. In Guadalajara or Mexico City, we could choose from many elite international schools affiliated with the International Baccalaureate program.

Keep this dynamic in mind when considering family locations if you are not going to home school the little ones. In general, capital cities and industrial cities will have plenty of options. Smaller towns and cities though—which are often more desirable places to live—may not have more than one or two options. The best ways to find out are to seek out other parents already living there to get info, as well as visiting prospective locations in person to pound the pavement and see the possibilities for yourself. Also check into tutoring options. For a fraction of what you would spend at home, you can probably get a private tutor to help your child in subjects he or she is having trouble with, at a slower individual pace.

Don't automatically assume your child will quickly pick up a new language and make new friends immediately. The common assumption is that children are sponges when it comes to languages, but that's often an oversimplification. Sure, they pick it up faster than adults, but it still takes months to get to a halfway reasonable level of fluency. The older they are, the tougher the classroom vocabulary: imagine taking history, science, civics, and math in a language you barely comprehend, at a high school level! Do everything you can to get them past the basic level before they step into the classroom and face a sea of unfamiliarity. It's tough enough moving to a new country with a different culture. Add in language difficulties and different customs and it can be emotionally trying to say the least.

Once they get through it though, the payoff for the rest of their life can be substantial. No matter what field they go into, having a second language is a big plus (especially if it's a commonly used one) and that experience of adapting to new challenges is great preparation for the demands of the modern workplace or business building.

English or Not for School

At the risk of generalizing, the more useless a country's language is outside that country, the more likely it is that the elite private schools will be run in English. In Thailand, for example, Chiang Mai alone has six international schools and several more with bilingual programs. The choices are even greater in Bangkok, though naturally they decrease in resort areas where there is not as much of a business reason for them. With Thai being such a limited language internationally, a lot of business is conducted in English and most education administrators you deal with will speak English well.

In a country like India, Nepal, or Malaysia, English is already the language of politics and business, so it will be very easy to find a school with classes in English.

In other countries, especially Spanish or French-speaking ones, get ready for immersion unless you want to shell out very high rates for an elite private school.

We were parents that actually wanted that. We felt we were giving our daughter a huge leg up in the world by giving her the means to become truly bilingual. But some kids really struggle with this, so evaluate your situation closely. Just as your home neighborhood where you are now may be influenced by the school options, the case may be the same when you decide where to move abroad.

Domestic Help

I mentioned earlier that it's generally quite inexpensive to get a private tutor, something that's especially true in university towns. In many of the countries profiled in this book, there's a long history of quality domestic help, so parents can get assistance in the form of a nanny, housekeeper, a tutor, and even a daily driver for very reasonable rates.

Diversions

"This is a rapidly modernizing country with all the things kids love: shopping malls, great movie theaters, amusement parks, and big swimming pools." That's what one moving abroad publication said about Thailand, but it could also apply to Malaysia, Panama, Mexico, and others. Unless you're moving to a very rural area, there will plenty for your kids to do. If they're in school, they'll probably get invited to all kinds of local social events with other kids. You probably won't have a problem finding a playground or a pizza shop. In other words, whether your child or children will be able to stay entertained is probably the least of your worries.

Books

You'll want your child to keep reading, but there probably won't be the big selection of English books you're used to. There are some anomalies like San Miguel de Allende or Oaxaca in Mexico where there's a big English library. Some bookstores in India have a great selection of new English books and some resort towns have a lot of used ones. In general though, you should get a Kindle, Nook, or Kobo for your child so you can download books over Wi-Fi wherever you happen to be. Or if they're at picture book age, an iPad is a better choice because of the graphics.

Diet

If there's a vegetarian in the family, you'll have a much easier time in the Asian countries featured in this book than the others. Residents of developed countries are spoiled for choice and they forget (or don't know) that this wasn't always the case. Being a vegetarian in the 1950s in the USA or Canada was no picnic and that's how it still is in much of the world. If you are a local and don't eat meat, it's usually not by choice: it means you're too poor to afford it.

In India, however, it's a religious choice for a large portion of the population, so especially in the south, it's easier to be one than not. (And lessens your odds of getting sick.) Because there are so many ethnic Indians in Malaysia, it's the same story there, in the western half of the country anyway. In Nepal, Thailand, and Vietnam it's relatively easy to eat vegetarian, especially if you have a phrase book or translation app for situations where nobody speaks English.

In other places, if you're not too strict about it, you'll have choices, but if you are a strict vegan, you'll be doing a lot of your own cooking. Even in Vietnam, they use fish sauce for flavoring. In Latin America, your refried beans, empanadas, and tamales may contain lard. The beautiful salads you order in Bulgaria will be covered with grated cheese and everything comes with yogurt. In any of these places though, after you've lived there a while you'll find your favorite spots that can accommodate your special requests.

If you have an intolerance to lactose, gluten, or nuts, don't be surprised if nobody knows what you're talking about in your new home. In the U.S. especially, these issues are either over-diagnosed or caught more often—depending on which medical study you read—and in the rest of the world they're treated more like "my kid has digestion problems."

Otherwise, anywhere you go you're going to have the normal picky kid issues where your little one doesn't want to touch all those strange things on the plate and it's a battle to get them to expand the culinary horizons. Many expats find the best approach is to take it gradually, mixing in the new with the familiar. Often you can find something that's semi-familiar, like chicken satay, breaded chicken breast, or corn dogs that will do in a pinch. Some families force their kids to try new things in restaurants, then cook what's more familiar at home. It's pretty easy to approximate what they're used to in most of the world these days, though you may find certain spices tough to find and certain ingredients to be more expensive. Those are the things you ask friends and family to bring when they're visiting or you buy when traveling elsewhere.

Chapter 36: Caveats and Legalese

You've reached the end of *A Better Life for Half the Price* and I hope you've found it useful. If you've joined one of the Cheap Living Abroad groups, we'll keep exploring the advice and topics in here. I'll always emphasize, however, that I'm just one person and that you should recheck what I tell you before making a life-changing decision.

I'm not a lawyer, CPA, tax advisor, financial advisor, or doctor. I'm just a guy with a bachelor's degree from university, a blog, and a few books with my name on the spine. So consult with a professional who has letters after his or her name before making any major decisions. The information presented in this book is a collection of advice and opinions from a person who has lived abroad and talked to many others doing the same, but none of it is guaranteed or insured to be without fault. Nothing in this book should be construed as legal, financial, or medical advice that should be taken without secondary verification.

Also be advised that prices, tax laws, visa requirements, and exchange rates are in a constant state of flux. Anything written in these pages is subject to change, so always verify key items before basing a decision on them, especially something so important as where you are going to live. All attempts have been made to ensure visa/residency information was correct at the time of writing, but it's especially important to verify this information with your local consulate or embassy—or the people living where you want to live—before proceeding.

As I have stressed many times, some people are not cut out for a move away from the land of their birth. The best way to ascertain this for yourself is to travel widely and do a trial run in your potential target(s). Reading 100 books and message boards is no substitute for having feet on the ground for an extended period and living like a local instead of a tourist. Please invest the time and resources to see if what looks good on paper is really a good match for your wants and needs.

Happy trails!

Chapter 37: Resources for Living Abroad

This is by no means an exhaustive list of resources and you'll probably want to check the CheapLivingAbroad.com website to get the most current version and just click on links. Here's plenty to keep you busy though as you research your plans to live a better life for less money.

EXPAT/LIVING ABROAD WEBSITES

International Living (internationalliving.com)

Live and Invest Overseas (liveandinvestoverseas.com)

Escapeartist.com (escapeartist.com)

Transitions Abroad (transitionsabroad.com)

Expatfocus.com (expatfocus.com/moving-guide)

Retire In Asia (retireinasia.com)

Expats Moving and Relocation Guide (http://www.expats-moving-and-relocation-guide.com)

South American Living (southamericaliving.com)

UK Government Living Abroad Guides

Viva Tropical (vivatropical.com)

EXPAT FORUMS AND BLOGS

Expatexchange.com

Expatforum.com

Expatfocus.com

Alloexpat.com

Expatsblog.com

Marginal Boundaries (marginalboundaries.com)

Jet Set Citizen (jetsetcitizen.com)

The Professional Hobo (theprofessionalhobo.com)

Almost Fearless (almostfearless.com)

Lonely Planet Thorn Tree forums (lonelyplanet.com/thorntree)

EDUCATION

Waldorf Schools Directory (whywaldorfworks.org/06_Global)

International Baccalaureate Schools Directory (ibo.org/general/who.cfm)

HEALTH CARE AND HEALTH INSURANCE

CDC-Centers for Disease Control (cdc.gov)

LAMAT English-speaking doctor database (lamat.org)

World Health Organization country statistics (who.int/gho/countries/en/)

World Nomads Travel Insurance(worldnomads.com)

Seven Corners Insurance (sevencorners.com)

Healthcare International (HCI)(healthcareinternational.com)

Aetna International (aetnainternational.com)

Cigna Global Health (cignaglobal.com)

Bupa International Health Insurance (bupa-intl.com)

GeoBlue(geo-blue.com)

HTH Worldwide Insurance (hthworldwide.net)

AXA International Health Insurance (axa.co.uk/healthcare/international)

Allianz Worldwide Care(allianzworldwidecare.com)

MAIL
Mailboxforwarding.com

TheUPSstore.com

MOVING SERVICES
Search for movers in the US, Canada or Europe

Compare International and Overseas movers – get quotes

Register for free moving quotes with trusted movers

WORKING ABROAD
Overseas job listings (overseasjobs.com)

Overseas jobs – About (jobsearch.about.com)

US State Department Resources for International Jobs (state.gov)

Teach Overseas info (teachoverseas.info)

Dave's ESL Café job board (eslcafe.com/joblist)

Expat Teaching Job Listings (expatteaching.com)

US State Department Careers (careers.state.gov)

USAID Careers (usaid.state.gov)

French Foreign Legion recruiting (legion-recrute.com)

Peace Corps(peacecorps.gov)

US Federal Government Jobs and Military Base Jobs(militarybases.com)

ContractJobs.com(ContractJobs.com)

eLance(Elance.com) and ODesk (ODesk.com)

Monster.com International_

STUDYING ABROAD

Transitions Abroad resources for studying abroad (transitionsabroad.com)

VISA INFORMATION

State Department – US Passports and Int'l travel_ (travel.state.gov)

A Briggs Passport & Visa Expeditors (abriggs.com)

Travel Visa Pro (travelvisapro.com)

Visa HQ (travelvisapro.com)

CIBT Visas (cibtvisas.com)

EmbassyWorld.com (embassyworld.com)

PRICING INFO

Numbeo (Numbeo.com)

Priceoftravel.com_

COUNTDOWN LISTS

Medical Checklist and International Relocation Lists (expatexchange.com)

US State Department moving abroad checklist (state.gov)

Moving Abroad checklist 6 weeks out (clockworkremovals.co.uk)

International Moving Checklist (moving.about.com)

Moving Overseas Checklist (expats-moving-and-relocation-guide.com)

International Moving Countdown (hansenbros.com)

RESOURCE BOOKS

The Family Sabbatical Handbook by Elisa Bernick

Getting Out: Your Guide to Leaving America by Mark Ehrman

The International Living Guide to Retiring Overseas by Susan Haskins

How to Retire Overseas: Everything You Need to Know to Live Well (for Less) Abroad by Kathleen Peddicord

The Expert Expat: Your Guide to Successful Relocation Abroad by Melissa Hess and Patricia Linderman

Retirement Without Borders: How to Retire Abroad by Barry Golson

The Tax Book for US Expats by Dan Gordon

Culture Shock! Book series; various counties/titles about living abroad

Moon Travel Guides Living Abroad series

The Expat Guidebook by T.W. Anderson

Work Your Way Around the World: The Globetrotter's Bible by Susan Griffith

Teaching English Abroad: Your Expert Guide to Teaching English Around the World by Susan Griffith

The Grown-Up's Guide to Running Away from Home: Making a New Life Abroad by Roseanne Knorr

TAXES AND DOING BUSINESS

Top individual tax rates by country (KPMG.org)

DoingBusiness.org (World Bank)

World Economic Forum (weforum.org)

CIA World Factbook

Wood Egg series of books on business in Asia (woodegg.com)

THE SKY IS FALLING AND THE GOVERNMENT WANTS ALL YOUR MONEY

Sovereign Man (sovereignman.com)

Flag Theory (flagtheory.com)

Nomad Capitalist (nomadcapitalist.com)

PETS

Letsgopets.com

ipata.org

aphis.usda.gov/regulations/vs/iregs/animals/

HOUSE SITTING (FOR A TRIAL RUN)

TrustedHouseSitters.com

MindMyHouse.com

HouseCarers.com

MISC.

Global Property Guide (globalpropertyguide.com)

Freedom House (human rights and state oppression rankings)

ConvertIt (currency, measurement, time zones, & more)

ExpatFinder.com

Tropical MBA Podcast and Blog (tropicalmba.com)

Suitcase Entrepreneur Podcast and Blog_
(suitcaseentrepreneur.com)

Click Millionaires Forum (clickmillionaires.com/forum)

Besides joining up with like-minded people on the Cheap Living Abroad insiders group, you can also see my regular posts on the Cheapest Destinations Blog (CheapestDestinationsBlog.com) and sign up for the RSS feed, be alerted by e-mail when a post goes up, or get on the free Cheap Living Abroad newsletter list.

Here's where to find me:

tim@timleffel.com

@timleffel on Twitter

TimLeffel on Google+

Facebook.com/cheapestdestinations

63020835R00182

Made in the USA
Lexington, KY
24 April 2017